D1146142

Stockport Libraries

C2000003259007

The Lion House

BY THE SAME AUTHOR

The Struggle for Iran

In the Rose Garden of the Martyrs:
A Memoir of Iran

Rebel Land:
Among Turkey's Forgotten Peoples

Patriot of Persia:
Muhammad Mossadegh and a Very British Coup

The Islamic Enlightenment:
The Modern Struggle Between Faith and Reason

CHRISTOPHER de BELLAIGUE

The Lion House

The Coming of a King

THE BODLEY HEAD
LONDON

3 5 7 9 10 8 6 4 2

The Bodley Head, an imprint of Vintage, is part of
the Penguin Random House group of companies whose
addresses can be found at global.penguinrandomhouse.com.

Penguin
Random House
UK

Copyright © Christopher de Bellaigue 2022

Christopher de Bellaigue has asserted his right to be identified as the author of
this Work in accordance with the Copyright, Designs and Patents Act 1988

First published by The Bodley Head in 2022

Maps drawn by Michael Hill at Maps Illustrated

Endpapers showing Suleyman I the Magnificent taken from the
Suleymanname by Arifi (ms H.1517), 1558, Topkapi Sarayi, Istanbul.
Photo: Luisa Ricciarini/Bridgeman Images.

www.vintage-books.co.uk

A CIP catalogue record for this book is available from the British Library

Hardback ISBN 9781847922397
Trade paperback ISBN 9781847922403

Typeset in 11.5/15pt Sabon LT Std by Jouve (UK), Milton Keynes
Printed and bound in Great Britain by Clays Ltd, Elcograf S.p.A.

The authorised representative in the EEA is Penguin Random House Ireland,
Morrison Chambers, 32 Nassau Street, Dublin D02 YH68

Penguin Random House is committed to a sustainable future
for our business, our readers and our planet. This book is made
from Forest Stewardship Council® certified paper.

MIX
Paper from
responsible sources
FSC
www.fsc.org   FSC® C018179

For Bita

Contents

Maps

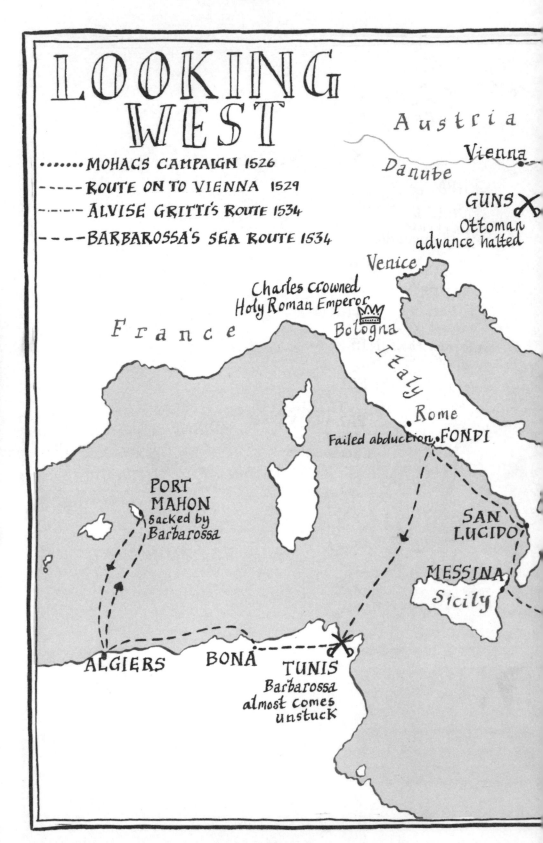

LOOKING WEST

- ...... MOHACS CAMPAIGN 1526
- ----- ROUTE ON TO VIENNA 1529
- -·-·- ALVISE GRITTI'S ROUTE 1534
- - - - BARBAROSSA'S SEA ROUTE 1534

Austria

Vienna

Danube

GUNS ✗
Ottoman
advance halted

Venice

Charles crowned
Holy Roman Emperor

France

Bologna

Italy

Rome

Failed abduction •FONDI

PORT
MAHON
Sacked by
Barbarossa

SAN
LUCIDO

MESSINA
Sicily

ALGIERS   BONA   TUNIS
Barbarossa
almost comes
unstuck

Carpathians

BUDA   Hungary

MOHACS
King Louis
dead in puddle

Siege MEDIAS

BRASOV

Transylvania

BELGRADE
Serbia

Wallachia

Danube

Black
Sea

Suleyman shows
off his Crown   NIS

Clissa

Bosnia

Alvise gives out
exemplary punishment

SOFIA

TATAR
PAZARJIK
Ibrahim's
Caravansaray

EDIRNE

ISTANBUL
CONSTANTINOPLE

Albania

Parga
Birthplace of
the Frank

Anatolia

The
Morea

Rhodes

White Sea
Mediterranean

LOOKING EAST

- -- HURREM'S ROUTE TO THE HAREM
- -·- IBRAHIM'S IRAN CAMPAIGN 1534-5
- ··· SULTAN SULEYMAN ADVANCES TO JOIN IBRAHIM 1534

Georgia

Caspian

Sea

Ibrahim's letter reaches The Sultan
ERZURUM

ERCIS

Lake Van

KHOY

TABRIZ

VAN

DIYARBAKIR

Kurdistan

Tigris

SOLTANIYEH Snowstorm

Zagros Mountains

Ibrahim takes revenge

Euphrates

BAGHDAD

Iran

Mesopotamia

Arabia

Persons of the drama

Suleyman I, tenth Sultan of the Ottomans

Hurrem, Ruthenian consort of the Sultan, known widely but erroneously as the Russian

Ibrahim of Parga, the Sultan's friend and Grand Vizier, known as the Frank

Alvise Gritti, known as the Beyoglu, a plutocrat

Hizir, known variously as Hayreddin, Barbarossa and the King of Algiers, a pirate

Mehmet
Selim   sons of Suleyman and Hurrem
Cihangir
Bayezit

Mahidevran, also a consort of the Sultan

Mustafa, son of Mahidevran and Suleyman

Mehmet II, Suleyman's great-grandfather, Conqueror of Istanbul

Selim I, Suleyman's father, ninth Ottoman Sultan

Hafsa, Suleyman's mother

Iskender Celebi, Ottoman Treasurer and Quartermaster

Figani, a poet

Charles V, King of Spain and Holy Roman Emperor

Ferdinand, Archduke of Austria, who will become King of the Romans, Charles' brother.

Francis I, King of France, known as the Most Christian King
Janos, King of Hungary
Tahmasp, Shah of Iran
Ismail, his father and predecessor as Shah of Iran

Andrea Gritti, Doge of Venice

Janos Doczy
Orban Batthyany   Alvise Gritti's supporters,
Tranquillus Andronicus   the Grittiani
Francesco Della Valle

Jerome Laski, Polish diplomat
Pietro Zen, Venetian diplomat
Marco Minio, Duke of Candia, Venetian diplomat
Cornelius de Schepper, Flemish diplomat
Marino Sanuto, diarist and failed politician

The Lion House

Act One: The Favourite

I

A spring morning. The Collegio meets daily in the Ducal Palace, under the Doge, Antonio Grimani. He and his cabinet of six councillors and sixteen other men of quality decide which items of business will come before the Senate. They also hear the most sensitive intelligence. Twenty-three men in robes of scarlet and blue, beneath mouldings which gleam and twist like ropes of gold. Prudence and Harmony observe from the walls. Through the open window a saltwater tang, the slap of waves. Venice.

The men shifting their posteriors on the benches of the Collegio are patricians. Their families have held power for centuries, the same names surfacing with a monotony that is at once reassuring and faintly unsavory. Venice's oligarchy revolves gently, protecting it from dynastic struggles and allowing it to get on with what it does best, which is to ship things from A to B and make B pay through the nose.

A republic on a lagoon, a front without a store, Venice can only look out. On Ascension Day the Doge's barge pushes off from the Lido amid a flotilla of lesser craft, their passengers straining to see His Serenity cast a ring overboard in symbolic marriage with the sea. St Mark himself was the gift of these waves, his bones smuggled out of Alexandria almost seven centuries ago and installed in the supersized chapel here that carries his name. In Venice a man's wealth is measured not in vines or acres but in bales, bolts and barrels aboard ship. Venice's patricians avoid land warfare if they can help it. Admiralship brings honour, generalship merely a wage.

A sea captain weighing anchor at the Molo, the broad stone pier at the sea entrance to the Piazza, doesn't lack for secure anchorage after Venice is lost to view. Garrisoned colonies and protectorates, scattered down the Adriatic, around the Morea and further afield, offer him fresh water, fitting yards and refuge. When one takes into account Venice's standing fleet, large, well-equipped and dogged in pursuit of pirates, and the Senate's efficiency as a board of trade, determining which convoys should take what merchandise where, and with what escort, the Most Serene Republic of Venice – the Serenissima – gives every impression of being divinely fit for purpose.

It's all there in Jacopo de Barbari's recent engraving of the metropolis, not so much a bird's eye view as God's view of each tower, each wharf, each retaining wall, beyond which may be distinguished the islands of Murano, Torcello and so on, while from eight different directions cherubs fill the sails of galleys with their cargoes of cotton, indigo, gold, nutmeg, saltpetre, silver, gems, silk, pepper and grain. And there in the middle, the tiny repetitious esplanade of St Mark's, and next to that, the Ducal Palace to which we now swoop, like one of Jacopo's small sea-fowl, and where on this day, the eighth of April 1522, there is to be a briefing on the Turk.

~

After visiting his mother and washing the salt from his clothes, the returning Venetian diplomat repairs to the Collegio to deliver his report. Venice has few comparative advantages over her rivals – city states and empires, for the most part, with big territories and solid alliances. The quality of the intelligence she collects is perhaps the most important.

Accuracy has made Venice the world's information gatherer. Accuracy and speed. After King Charles of France died at Amboise on the eve of Palm Sunday, 1498, the news reached

Venice before the bells of St Mark's chimed for Eastertide, thirteen horses having been ridden to death in the bringing of it.

And then there's Venice's pragmatism. If Martin Luther is reviling the Pope from a pub in Wittenberg, Venice receives the news without indignation, cheerfully resolved to turn it to her advantage.

What's said in the Collegio doesn't necessarily stay in the Collegio. Transcriptions are pirated or extracts slip between the cracks and into the canals, lanes and bridges of the city, where the foreign traders, diplomats and brokers collect them and send them home, and where Marino Sanuto, the city's gadfly diarist, scoops them up for his journal. England has copies of all the Venetian reports its agents can get hold of. So does France. So does Spain.

Two recent envoys to Constantinople died shortly after coming ashore at the Molo, before having a chance to deliver their reports. Marco Minio is bucking an unfortunate trend. In mercifully good health after concluding his recent mission to the Ottoman capital, he sailed directly to the Venetian colony of Candia, which he is now administering in the name of His Serenity, and rather than let his analysis moulder, he has sent it home with his secretary. It's Minio's report – the Duke of Candia's report, to use his new title – that the Collegio has convened to hear.

It begins with a welcome pledge not to detain His Serenity with a long writing. No one wants a repeat of the epic, four-hour harangue which Andrea Gritti subjected the Senate to after he guided Venice to a disobliging draw in the War of Cambrai. Not that Doge Grimani is in a fit state to take in much of what is said. His election last year, at the age of 87, made him oldest man ever to become Doge, and he spends much of his working day asleep.

After his preamble, Minio lays out his understanding of the Turkish question. It's a rational account, as you would expect from an influential figure at the University of Padua – that citadel of reason-based humanism – and admiring in its way, but none the less sobering for that.

'The Sultan is rich in revenue, men and obedience.'

From this we are to understand that the Grand Turk has all the elements he needs to wage total war.

'His revenue is understood to be three million in gold. The tax on Christians and Jews brings him 1,200,000 ducats, and wherever the Pasha holds an audience there are numerous leather sacks full of money, and the coins they collect are weighed, always an enormous sum. The other major tax is from sheep, so much per animal, and this revenue exceeds 800,000 ducats. He draws 800,000 ducats from the mines, the same from salt production, and the remaining sum up to three million he derives from businesses.' Minio isn't counting the money the Sultan receives in tribute from ports and cities beyond the Empire's frontier.

For forty months Minio was Venice's ambassador to the late Pope Leo. His discreet investigations showed Leo to be sunk in debt, his income of 220,000 ducats barely sufficient to pay for the theatricals and hunting expeditions of which he was so fond. To keep pace with his own reckless spending, the pontiff pawned everything not bolted down: cardinals' hats, indulgences, furniture. The Pope's poverty naturally affected his ability to combat external enemies. The Crusade he planned against the Turks was to be sanctified by him, paid for by others.

As for Venice, the Republic buys soldiers as she does any other commodity. A military administrator like Andrea Gritti must get his results using hirelings who have never seen the lagoon and disappear at the first setback. He must plead for money from a Senate that demands thrilling victories but fusses if he spends a handful of ducats building a wall.

The Sultan's access to human capital, on the other hand, is the result of his immense territorial wealth. He needs only scrape a little fat off the land, and *presto*, a vast fighting machine materialises. His huge realm, Minio explains, 'is parcelled out among diverse people, who are like feudatories, and all these are obliged to bring a certain number of cavalry to campaign without the Sultan paying them anything. Bearing in mind the

8

vast lands he controls, it can be easily believed that he is capable of making armies composed of innumerable people.'

The Sultan is expanding his shipyards at Constantinople and Gallipoli. Soon they will be big enough to keep and maintain his whole fleet. They may even rival the arsenal at Venice. 'And whenever the Sultan wants to raise an armada, he can mobilise cheaply; for the whole country is obliged to give him one man out of every ten, paid quarterly, to be placed under that army; the ropes and other items of tackle are requisitioned.'

While he is in Constantinople Minio is admitted to the Sultan's presence, each elbow gripped by an expressionless chamberlain, and prostrates himself three times before kissing the royal hand. The Grand Turk is remote, his eyes deep-set – not that they are really visible, as his spherical turban, its muslin folds implanted with two heron feathers, gives him a hooded, secretive air. Because the Sultan stays seated throughout the ceremony, Minio cannot say how tall he is.

The Sultan is by nature melancholic, generous, proud and impulsive. He has a strong arm and can fire an arrow farther than anyone else at court. Either that or no one at court sees much advantage in firing an arrow farther than him.

What else do we know? After subduing a revolt by the Governor of Syria, Janbirdi al-Ghazali, in the early days of his reign, the Sultan wanted to send the rebel's head to the Doge as proof of his power. It took all the urging of more experienced gentlemen to dissuade him from doing so. Barbarous notion, but somehow affecting.

In the absence of any meaningful contact with the Sultan, Minio cultivates his inner circle. The long discussion he has with Mustafa Pasha, Second Vizier of the Empire, with the Governor of Rumelia also in attendance, is not unrevealing. The grandees ask Minio about the Pope, about the size of his revenues and armies, which Minio naturally exaggerates, but not so much as to arouse his listeners' scorn or indignation. They also ask him about Charles V, the Holy Roman Emperor, and Francis I, the King of France, who likes to refer to himself as the

Most Christian King. Charles and Francis are the only two European monarchs who have sufficient money and manpower to fight the Turks. As for Henry VIII of England, he is poor, absorbed with matters of the bedroom and – as Venice's ambassador reports – no more concerned with the Turk than if he threatened India.

The Holy Roman Empire isn't an empire at all, at least not in the sense that the ancient Roman Empire was, knit together by a common administration and currency. It is a collection of loosely interrelated territories that account for the most populous parts of central Europe. Its only connection to Rome is that the Pope sometimes crowns the Emperor.

Francis and Charles competed for the imperial throne when it came up for election on the death of the incumbent, Charles's father Maximilian, in 1519. Charles won the contest after he borrowed a vast sum from a banking house, the Fuggers of Augsburg, enabling him to bribe his way to victory. Charles and Francis challenge each other every so often to a duel, which, for one reason or another, doesn't materialise.

And how, the Pashas enquire innocently, are relations between Venice and the two illustrious princes?

Minio replies that the Doge is particularly cognisant of the majesty of Francis but that a good peace exists no less with the Emperor.

This is an untruth. In the struggle between Francis and Charles for control of northern Italy, the Venetians lean towards the French. The Pashas know this. Minio knows that they know. But a fiction of Christian unity is better than no unity at all.

Next the two officials ask about the easiest route from Constantinople to Rome, and how long it would take; and if the Sultan were to attack Hungary would the Pope come to its aid?

Minio replies that he would.

Bearing in mind Leo's successor as Pope, the uncommanding Adrian, and the poor state of his finances, this, too, seems highly unlikely.

In sum, Minio's conversation with the Pashas isn't an easy

one, the diplomat trying by feints and wiles to divert them from a truth that is apparent if not openly acknowledged. Christendom is divided and prone. The Sultan's path to further conquests is wide open.

Millions of Christians are already the Sultan's subjects, a bitter reality that the Governor of Rumelia likes to rub in. 'We are established in many of your lands,' he says, 'and you in none of ours. Think how much damage we can do.'

While Minio is in Constantinople it pleases the Sultan to have one of his Pashas hanged. The Pasha in question is a person of means with many slaves. The Sultan sends a state messenger to his house, who tells him: the Sultan has decided that you will be hanged. And without any resistance, either on his part or that of his slaves, he is immediately taken away to his death. His household makes no resistance but accompanies him weeping.

How helpful is this anecdote in trying to understand Suleyman? Perhaps only moderately. If the Sultan receives instant and unquestioning obedience from his subjects, this may be due to his position and the reverence it inspires, more than his own character. So much of what is revealing of a person derives from that person's reaction to adversity. If the Sultan's orders were to be treated with contempt or scorn, if his authority were challenged by a rival or friend, what would he do then?

We must wait to learn more. The information will bear on the life chances of Venice. At present the Sultan has his hand on Christendom's entrails. His navy is strong enough to stop Venice's Levantine trade whenever he wants. The Serenissima must therefore cultivate the Sultan by secretly giving him intelligence and undermining Papal efforts to win support for a Crusade, all the while assuring Rome that there is nothing Venice wants more.

In the meantime her sailors must contend daily with Turkish whims, paying tribute, eyeballing corsairs, pleading for grain.

So states Marco Minio, Duke of Candia.

~

The Ottomans are the successors of the Byzantines. For the final century of its existence the Byzantine Empire was a lame foot inside a shoe, the shoe occupied but inert. This state of affairs lasted until 29 May 1453, when Sultan Mehmet yanked the shoe off the foot and tried it on himself. The Byzantine Empire perished. Constantinople, the Byzantines' seat, was reborn the capital of a Muslim empire. Its new name, Istanbul.

As the European power with the oldest and most extensive exposure to the Muslim states, Venice reacted calmly to the fall of Constantinople. The Doge of the day signed a treaty with the Conqueror and sent one of his best artists, Gentile Bellini, to paint sexy ladies on his bedroom wall. And Venice's patricians made an optimistic assessment of the trading opportunities that might come their way as a result of the change of ownership in Constantinople. Did the Turks not need to buy and sell, like anyone else?

Doge Antonio Grimani was nine years old at the time of the Conquest, an orphan in the care of his uncle, a trader in the Levant. For a while after the Conquest there was peaceful commerce in the Mediterranean; barely into adolescence Antonio was trading cargoes between Syria, Egypt and Tunis. Pepper was his speciality, husked and shipped from the atolls of the Banda Sea, and so keen was his eye for glut and dearth that when he sold his stock his compatriots took it as a signal to do the same, and when he bought up the excess they again followed his lead.

Approaching fifty, the age when the Venetians begin to take a man seriously, and with movable assets in excess of 100,000 ducats, Grimani naturally aspired to public office. Having married his sons and nephews strategically, he was spared the usual footling in subordinate posts and rose fast.

In the meantime, the shoe began to kick. Chalcis; Pylos; Euboea; these and other Venetian colonies fell to a reassertive Conqueror, as well as the independent states of the Morea, Albania, Serbia, Bosnia and Wallachia. By the time of Sultan

Mehmet's death, in 1481, a fat belt of Christendom where the pine tree grows was under Ottoman rule.

Meanwhile Grimani's sense of duty favourably impressed the pillars of the State; with the outbreak of war in 1499 against Sultan Bayezit, the Conqueror's son and successor, he was given charge of the fleet and told to defend Lepanto. Whoever controls Lepanto controls the Gulf of Corinth and trade in the Morea. But when the two fleets were on the point of engaging and it seemed that the Turks might be comprehensively defeated, the wind changed and the Venetian fleet was destroyed.

Not only Lepanto, but other colonies were lost, and the Senate ordered Grimani home in chains. Putting in at the Molo, he was met by his son, Cardinal Domenico Grimani, who held up the disgraced admiral's fetters to spare him their weight while he was led to jail.

Grimani's eloquence and the justice of his defence saved him from execution. Exiled to Dalmatia, he absconded to Rome. From a villa on the Quirinale he agitated for his own rehabilitation while lobbying loyally on behalf of the Republic. After seven years of receiving aid from a man they had spurned, the patricians of Venice were embarrassed into bringing him home with restored honours.

'In carrying him to success and then laying him low, Fortune has shown what stupefying jokes she is capable of.' This is how Paulo Giovio, ecclesiastic, historian and student of events, has summarised the actions of fate on Antonio Grimani. And Fortune's punchline came in 1521, when, after being awarded the procuratorship of St Mark's, Grimani was elected Doge.

His election took Venice's love of age to an absurd excess. The electors certainly thought so. Immediately regretting their decision, they offered him money to step down. But Grimani dug in, and now they have no choice but to wait for mortality to succeed where bribery failed.

~

Grimani is not the only patrician to have inherited connections with Constantinople. The depth and duration of the Gritti family's engagement there is exceptional.

In 1453 old Battista Gritti took part in the defence of the city against the Conqueror and was captured by the Turks. Ransoming himself, he went on to represent Venetian interests in the fallen city. It was Battista who escorted Gentile Bellini into the Conqueror's presence after the artist came ashore in 1479, and who, two years later, brought tidings of the Sultan's death to the Senate with the sonorous words, 'The great eagle is dead.'

In the summer of 1474, Battista's brother, Triadano, took six galleys to repel a Turkish attack on a strategically placed fortress on the eastern Adriatic coast. The fortress was saved but Triadano succumbed to malaria, Albanian mosquitoes succeeding where the Turks had failed.

By this time Triadano's grandson Andrea had made his entrance into world affairs. After completing his studies at Padua and accompanying his grandfather on diplomatic missions around Europe, Andrea lost his young wife Benedetta in childbirth. It was time for a change of scene.

Arriving in Constantinople in the late 1470s, young Andrea immediately loved the city for its position at the junction of three majestic bodies of water, the Bosporus, the Propontis and the Golden Horn, and for the fertility and beauty of the surrounding countryside. He set himself up in the Christian quarter, Pera, and became a player in grain, buying wheat from Black Sea ports and shipping it to Venice. Handsome, regal, he could also be hilarious and jocund. He was comfortable in seven languages, eight if you count bedroom Genoese. He loved God and St Mark. Show me the Venetian that doesn't. But as the son of a city built on water, he needed no convincing of the saliency of free will.

Sultan Bayezit preferred praying to fighting, and the forward policy of his father the Conqueror evolved into one of retrenchment. The Sultan spent much of his energy trying to get his hands on his rebellious brother Cem, who had thrown himself on Europe's mercy and was passed from court to court, something between a pretender, a captive and a set of antlers. All the while, the galleys, galleots and brigantines set sail with their cargos and the Venetian investors made fortunes.

In Bayezit, Andrea Gritti saw beyond the olive complexion, and the stature, tending to tall; beyond the peaceable nature and the abstention from wine. This is what everyone could see. He saw, too, beyond the formulas of Machiavelli, who prognosticated from his desk in Florence that if only the Ottomans produced one more Bayezit, Europe would no longer have need to fear the Turk.

Gritti saw the strangeness of the human temperament. Bayezit showed signs of thoughtfulness and humanity, and yet this same prince had one of his most effective ministers executed for being too proud. Such arbitrary justice would be hard to get away with in Venice, where the Doge is tied by councils and committees telling him what to do. And yet, if offered it, who would reject absolute and unquestioned power of this kind?

While he was living in Pera, Gritti intervened with the judicial authorities to prevent the execution of an Italian merchant whose wife he happened to be bedding, and, in the glow of popular acclaim, vowed to bed her no more. It was somehow typical of Andrea to emerge from a tale of adultery with his reputation for gallantry enhanced.

His powers of recall were remarkable. Europe's entrepôts remained as alive to him as the day he saw them with Grandpa Triadano, from whom he also learned the essence of transactions, the value of intelligence and the importance of gifts.

When tensions rose between Turkey and Venice, the Sultan imposed a ban on the export of grain, and, since the ban coincided with scarcity in Venice, the Venetians were driven almost to starvation. Gritti lobbied successfully to have the ban reversed. Then he rented ships and loaded them with 20,000 bushels of grain. In Venice, thanks to his convoy, the wholesale price of flour fell by eight soldi a bushel and that of grains by twenty soldi. By now the name Andrea Gritti meant something on the Rialto Bridge, the wooden counting house that humps the Grand Canal at its narrowest point. It meant something to the citizen breakfasting on her oven-warm *bovolo*.

In the 1490s relations worsened further. Turkish pirates ravaged the Dalmatian coast as far north as Venetian Istria and the mischief-making Milanese convinced Bayezit that Venice's new alliance with France was aimed at him. The Serenissima had no bailo, or resident ambassador, in Constantinople to resolve these problems; the last one was expelled for espionage. More important, and disregarding the absurdity of the sanction – is a bailo simply there to kiss the Sultan's hand? – Venice had no source of information about Turkey's preparations for war.

No one in Constantinople was better suited than Gritti for the role of informant, but as a private citizen he did not enjoy diplomatic immunity. Undeterred, he sent intelligence home in code. To any Turkish official who might intercept his letters, they were the correspondence of a merchant with his business partner. But when he wrote that a prisoner in the debtors' jail was to be released in June, he was really telling Venice that the Turkish fleet would sail then. A reference to the transfer of his own goods by ship and wagon was a warning to expect attacks by sea and land.

In the spring of 1499 he was placed under close surveillance but he still managed to tell the Doge how many ships were in the Turkish fleet and the names of their commanders. At the end of May he reported that the Turks would sail in fifteen days.

Then nothing.

At a river crossing in Macedonia, the courier carrying his most recent letters was pulled aside by a Turkish captain who was able to read them because they were not in cipher. And now Andrea's enterprising cock took another bow. The Turkish captain knew all about Andrea Gritti because Andrea Gritti was enjoying intimate relations with his wife. The captain referred the case to Ahmet Pasha – known as Hersekli, the Turkish word for Herzegovinan, to distinguish him from all the other Ahmet Pashas.

Hersekli Ahmet wasn't simply a former Grand Vizier. He was also Bayezit's son-in-law and a decorated military commander. He was born into Balkan nobility and retained a soft spot for the religion of his birth. And Gritti had already won his sympathy with a gift of 5,000 Egyptian gold pieces.

The Pasha could not bring himself to execute someone to whom he felt bound by friendship and honour. He stalled, the Sultan asked why, and the Pasha replied that the Empire was at war with Venice and Gritti was from a noble Venetian family, with important relations and friends, and that if, heaven forbid, some adversity should befall the Empire at the hands of these enemies, it might be useful to have such a man in reserve, as it were, captive but alive.

Gritti lived. His goods were seized and he was clapped in irons and incarcerated in the Seven Towers, the Conqueror's fortress which stands where the Byzantine land-wall runs down to the Propontis. The Italians of Pera were distraught at the suffering of their favourite, among them women who wept away the nights outside his bolted door.

All the while, in a succession of naval and military calamities, the Venetians were dismantled by the Turks on land and sea, losing more empire, more ships, more inviolability. For thirty-two months, Gritti sat in his tower, and once the fighting had run its course Hersekli Ahmet visited him to talk about suspending hostilities. With a loan from the Bank of St George, Genoa's version of the Fuggers, Gritti ransomed himself and took the fast ship up the Adriatic and home, where he was appointed to the Doge's Privy Council, the Signoria, before returning to Constantinople, this time an accredited diplomat, to negotiate a permanent peace. And when he came before the Senate on 2 December 1503, he was able to declare the successful conclusion of his mission, crowned by Venice's retention of the Ionian island of Cephalonia, which he achieved thanks to the intervention of his friend Hersekli Ahmet.

'This sir Andrea Gritti will be a worthy citizen,' Marino Sanuto wrote in his diary, 'because he has every good quality:

first he is handsome, generous, speaks well, etcetera, so that one might say, "Worth the more winning, when it appears in a comely person." He was elected in recognition of his merits, in that, to warn his native land, he wrote letters from Constantinople, warning our Signoria of the events and real preparations which the Turks made for a fleet; and his letters were found, so that he was in danger of having his head cut off.'

~

Venice isn't quite as free of cares as Barbari's engraving suggests. Maritime dependency brings vulnerability to rival navies and food blockades. To guard against this, the Serenissima has for some time been trying to expand into the northern Italian plain. Since Andrea Gritti's return from Constantinople, the Republic has been almost uninterruptedly at war in the peninsula. With the Pope over Rimini, Cervia and Faenza. With the Austrians over Verona and Vicenza. With France over Bergamo, Brescia, Crema and Cremona.

Venice's problem is the poor quality of her hired commanders. A nadir was reached on 15 May 1509, when disagreement between Venice's leading mercenaries, the Orsini cousins, led to a catastrophic defeat at the hands of the French at Agnadello. The news arrived in Venice that evening and the Senators heard it in stunned silence. Citizens hurried to the Ducal Palace to hear the rumours belied. They were not. The gains of the past century had been wiped out in a single day.

What Agnadello taught was the folly of supposing that Venice can replace its sea empire with a land one. Venice cannot be Austria or France. Her position, her ethos, her lack of a standing army, will not allow it. So rather than nurse fantasies of expansion the Republic had better guard her shrunken hinterland using planning and diplomacy.

This is the ethos of Andrea Gritti. After his successes in Constantinople, he was named to some of the top civilian and military positions on the mainland. His preference for tactical skirmishing over pitched battles encouraged comparisons with

Fabius Maximus, who was known as Cunctator, the Delayer, for his reliance on premeditated defence to frustrate Hannibal of Carthage. Gritti wasn't offering the Lion of St Mark fluttering over conquered bastions, but tactical retreats and double earthworks.

At the time of Agnadello, he reminded the Senate, the enemy had more artillery pieces in Verona than Venice did in its entire mainland empire, and he urged the Senators to invest in guns. Not that they should be used if at all possible. 'It is clearly best to fight with sword in sheath and with reputation,' he said.

In 1512 he was taken prisoner by the French but he used his detention at Blois to charm the Most Christian King and his powerful mother, Louise of Savoy, in the process smoothing the way to a new Franco-Venetian alliance. And when he was finally released and returned home, the palaces, stairs, courtyards and squares which he passed were full of people wanting to shake his hand.

Gritti Cunctator. An odd destiny for a man who survived being thrown from his horse under showers of arrows and was hauled over the walls of besieged Vicenza in a basket. His character suggests a return to the glory days, when Venetian galleys ruled the waves, but his tactics suggest the civilised management of decline. He is one of Venice's procurators, or government treasurers, from whose ranks the Doge is usually chosen.

~

It is May 7, 1523. Antonio Grimani has done the decent thing. His body is attended by patricians sweating in scarlet.

A few days ago he was fit enough to celebrate the Ascension, going out and dropping his ring into the murk. The Piazza still contains the stalls that were put out for the festivities. After a meandering decline Grimani's end came suddenly. Even now it cannot be said that the city wears an aspect of mourning and deliberation, the aspect of a city preparing to choose a Doge.

Many would prefer Antonio Tron, incorruptible man of the people, others Domenico Trevisan, a former Captain-General of the fleet, but Tron is a reluctant candidate while Trevisan has six sons, raising the possibility of a capture of the levers of power by a single clan. For all the traits of Trevisan and Tron, Andrea Gritti is the man to beat.

His connections are more than adequate. His mother was a Zane. His poor dead wife Benedetta was the niece of Andrea Vendramin, a former Doge. Such alliances seed secondary and tertiary alliances with other men who will have a role in deciding who will be Doge.

And yet, even after taking into account the services he has performed for the Republic, it must be allowed that Gritti is more respected than loved. Even the public's recognition of his patriotism and acumen is tinged with distrust for his arrogant manner, his long stare, his francophilia and his habit of impregnating nuns.

The mood in Venice is away from greatness and Gritti has greatness's vices. There's a general queasiness towards strong men. If he is elected he will surely try to gather more powers to himself than the *promissione*, the sheaf of legal restrictions that he will sign on the day of his investiture, allow. In theory he will be limited by the various bodies that surround the throne, but the Doge's appointment, unlike theirs, is for life. This distinction little availed Grimani, who was half-dead at the time of his election. But Gritti hasn't been ill a single day and he carries his sixty-eight years with the lightness of eternal youth. Outlive the pegs and the tent will fly.

~

You could think of a ducal election as a funnel. Democracy is its mouth, narrowed by divine intervention and pinched to a fine point by nepotism and bribery.

First the Great Council, all twenty-five hundred of them, must be brought down by lottery to thirty. The thirty then draw lots to reduce their number to nine, who elect forty. Another lottery sifts the forty to twelve who elect the next group of twenty-five, who are in turn reduced to nine. The nine elect forty-five who draw lots to determine the eleven who will elect the forty-one.

The forty-one elect the Doge.

On 17 May those members of the Great Council under thirty years of age are asked to leave the hall. That leaves 1,137 members, reduced by lot to thirty, four of whom are for Gritti and eight for Tron. At the next sortition Gritti catches up. Of the nine he and Tron have two backers apiece, and eight each from the forty, elected on May 19.

At the fourth hurdle Tron falls. The reduction of the forty to the twelve yields him not a single backer, to Gritti's four. Tron is out of the race but the patricians are determined to withhold from Gritti the resounding endorsement he seeks. Another contender, Lorenzo Loredan, reacts coldly to Gritti's suggestion of a marital alliance between the two families.

The Cunctator crawls on. Nine of the twenty-five declare for him; eighteen of the forty-five; six of the eleven. In Milan they put up an effigy of Gritti with a fish in one hand, representing Venice, and a frog in the other, symbolising France. The Milanese are not alone in fretting that Gritti will devote his Dogeship to pleasing his French friends.

There has been an outbreak of plague in Rome, from where Cardinal Domenico Grimani, son of the deceased, is hurrying home. Back in Venice mass is said and the sacrament administered in the Ducal Palace in conditions of unseasonable heat. The diarist Marino Sanuto records these and other developments with his usual punctiliousness.

Of the forty-one, the procurator receives three fewer votes than the twenty-five he requires. More negotiations, more promises. Anticipating that Gritti will shortly be able to make the traditional procession of triumph around the Piazza, the order is given for the Ascension shops to be dismantled as Venice will surely have a Doge by morning.

Not quite by morning, for the second vote of the forty-one is also inconclusive, but before vespers on 20 May the wait is over. The doors of the forty-one open and the bells of St Mark ring out. Rising from the Senate chamber, the Signoria enter the Golden Room, already hung with the Gritti arms, a shield divided into two bands, the upper one blue, the lower one silver, with a silver cross over the blue band. His Serenity is dressed in crimson satin with modified ducal sleeves and a new cap of crimson silk in the French style. He takes his seat and a rush of people come in to see him, patricians to take his hand. Having fought his way through the crowd, Marino Sanuto is rewarded with a pleasant greeting.

The next morning, a Thursday, the Piazza is full when Gritti emerges from the Palace and makes his way to St Mark's, where it falls to none other than Antonio Tron, as the oldest patrician in the forty-one, to announce the result of the election. No one present cries, 'Gritti!' Instead, looking at Tron, they shout, 'You! You!' Gritti receives the sacrament and the banner of St Mark but the traditional procession around the Piazza on the ducal litter is a muted affair, the children brandishing a doll that resembles the losing candidate and yelling, 'Tron! Tron!' Back on the Palace stairway, Gritti receives his crown, tosses coins and gives a short speech to the crowd, promising all the peace, justice, and prosperity in his power. Then he goes back into the Palace and the people go home.

Rarely has the election of a Doge gone off so flat. Even when he orders the price of flour to come down and has two thousand of his own bags sold at the new, lower price, the public response is chilly. On the night of Gritti's election, while sitting on one of the benches in the Ducal Palace, Alvise Priuli, another patrician, remarks that it won't do to have a Doge who has three bastard children in Turkey. Priuli's comment reaches the ears of the new Doge who seeks him out, and heated words pass between the two.

I I

His birth came under the auspicious conjunction of Saturn and Jupiter. There was no particular reason to believe that he would become Sultan, since his grandfather, Bayezit, had five sons, any of whom might rise to the throne, and his father, Selim ... well, no one was sure how many sons were born to Selim, only that just one, Suleyman, was allowed to survive.

He spent the first fifteen years of his life in Trabzon, a deprived Anatolian port city at the back end of the Black Sea, where Selim was Governor. There, learning arithmetic and Quranic Arabic and being taught to work gold by a Greek called Constantine, he heard, as every Turkish child heard, the story of Sari Saltik.

Sari Saltik was an orphan who slayed dragons and made good his escape, who converted priests and was rescued by djinns from a burning hayrick. His life was full of episodes in which the Christians were unrepentant and deserving of death, a fate which Sari Saltik, brandishing his sword like Mars holding his snake, happily administered.

Deep in Europe Sari Saltik came to a city with a vast church. On top of the dome was a globe in the form of an apple made of gold, which Sari Saltik ordered to be fetched down. His men were scrambling up the dome when the Prophet Khizr appeared and ordered them not to touch the apple. Number ten in a line of great Islamic rulers will seize the golden apple, the prophet said, and only number ten.

The number of fingers and toes, the number of Command-
ments in the Pentateuch, the number of the astronomical
heavens, the most perfect and pleasing of all numbers.

In Constantinople under the Byzantines, an equestrian statue
of the Emperor Justinian stood on a column in front of the
church of Hagia Sophia. In his hand the emperor held a golden
apple. As the Turks have pushed further and further into Europe, the apple has rolled and rolled and is now a long way
ahead. For some the golden apple is St Peter's in Rome, where
the Sultan will one day stable his horse; for others, Vienna. A
third theory identifies it with the apple which Alexander the
Great ordered to be cast from gold that was given by the wise
men to the infant Christ, since turned to dust and blown to
Germany.

The golden apple is beyond rivers and mountain ranges. It is
divinely ordained victory. It is riches that cannot be measured.

~

'If you are to be King,' Kaykavus of Tabaristan once counselled
his son, Gilanshah, advice that is preserved in his book of wise
words for princes, 'keep your eye and your hand away from the
possessions of the people. And before embarking on any course
of action, think of the after-effects of that action, and without
seeing to the end do not look to the beginning. And do not love
injustice, but view every thing and every word with the eye of
justice. A King whose eye of justice and wisdom is shut will be
unable to distinguish between the ways of God and those of
error.'

From the same source young Suleyman learned that by
rationing the number of pearls that drop from his lips, he could
foster the kingly aura, or charisma, that the ancient Persians
called *farr*. As the epistle put it, 'Speak little and smile less, lest
the rabble become insolent.'

Another text which his tutor put in front of him, the *Epistle
of Politics*, counselled the King to hear the complaints of his
subjects two days out of every seven, a practice that would

expose the misdeeds of the powerful and protect the weak. Its author, Nizam al-Mulk, was Grand Vizier of the Seljuk Sultans and also the founder of the Nizammiyah, in Baghdad, the first school built for educating doctors of the law. Ironically enough, the Nizam was undone by the very accessibility he recommended in an ideal ruler. One day he was being carried on his litter when a member of the Ismailis, a dissident sect, approached him in the guise of a dervish and, withdrawing a dagger from his robe, stabbed him to death.

Error was what young Suleyman's education was designed to protect him against. Error of the kind that had destroyed the Nizam and was festering once more in Iran, oozing into Anatolia.

The latest sedition started in Ardebil, beyond Anatolia's eastern marches, where the Iranian plateau meets the forests of beech and alder that grow along the Caspian Sea's western rampart. Here, beneath the glistening white cap of an extinct volcano, bathed by candlelight, the followers of a mystical order wept and sweated their love for the twelfth Shia Imam, whose name usurped that of God in their prayers.

Shah Ismail was the order's supreme guide. Ascending to the throne of Iran in 1501, he declared Shiism to be the country's sole faith and put Sunnis to the sword. His missionaries crawled over Anatolia and even converted members of the Ottoman royal family. It was feared that Istanbul contained thousands of the Shah's acolytes, and that they only awaited his signal to put on their red turbans, by which they honoured the blood that was shed by their martyrs, and fall on their Sunni neighbours.

The red-headed ones are to the Ottomans what the plague is to a healthy body.

Repeatedly young Suleyman watched Selim lead his army out of Trabzon, but no matter how many red-headed ones he crushed, they rose again like weeds fertilised from Iran, and he was obliged to go out again. And Selim was constantly being undermined by the half-measures of his father.

Sultan Bayezit's policy towards the sedition was one of

negligence. Rather than massacre the heretics, he exiled them nearer to Istanbul, doing the missionaries' job for them. In 1511 he was rewarded with a huge insurrection. The Shias burned down mosques and pulverised Qurans. A provincial governor was beheaded, impaled and roasted on a spit.

The Sultan was old and tired. Neither of the sons he was considering for the succession, Korkut and Ahmet, would deal firmly enough with the insurgents. The Empire was being lost. Islam was being lost.

That summer, Selim accompanied Suleyman, now seventeen years of age, to Caffa, slave and cotton mart on the southern shore of the Crimean peninsula, where the boy was to take up his first governorship. Selim was now in open defiance of his father and the Janissaries, the Empire's high-maintenance infantry, were demanding his elevation to the throne. On 24 April 1512, after marching on the capital, the prince and his supporters overran the Palace and deposed the Sultan.

On the day when Selim escorted his father to the Edirne Gate and sent him into exile, the Janissaries lined the road they expected their new Sultan to follow when he returned to the city, intending to smite their weapons against their shields as he passed and remind him of the power they had over him. But Selim did not like to be talked down to. Warned of the Janissaries' intentions, he changed his route and came along the sea wall with just a few retainers. Then, affecting ignorance of the Janissaries' insolence, he disarmed them with a present of fifty ducats a head. Mistaking the Sultan's generosity for weakness, a provincial governor came before him and demanded an increase in his salary. Selim drew his sword and cut off the man's head.

Within a few weeks Bayezit was dead, assumed to have been poisoned by his son, and Selim went on to deliver Korkut and Ahmet to the executioner's bowstring. He also did away with five nephews. After installing Suleyman as Governor of the Aegean province of Manisa, nursery of Sultans, he turned his attention to the heresy.

The doctors of the law obliged him with a fatwa authorising him to hunt down the red-headed ones using falcons, arrows and dogs. Over the next two years, making use of intelligence provided by his excellent network of spies, he killed some 40,000 Anatolian Shias, displacing, branding, and arresting thousands more. Most of the 40,000 were beheaded. Selim was good at logistics.

Then he went east.

Trudging through browning plains ringed by snake-infested hills, with no sign of an enemy or anywhere to loot, his men began to grumble and shots were fired at the Sultan's tent. Selim went unhesitatingly among them, this red man with short legs and long body, black brows and a soft bonnet engulfed in the folds of his shawl, and demanded, 'Is this how you claim to serve me? Let the cowards immediately detach themselves from those who wish to follow me.' After that there was no more talk of mutiny.

He had been sending his adversary letters, by turns irritable, grandiose and rude – one contained a set of women's clothes for Ismail's use. The Shah replied with the superior bemusement of a divine operating on a higher plane. Surely letters showing such extreme hostility could only have been written by addled secretaries – and to show his opinion of Selim's bureaucrats, he enclosed a gold box full of opium. Ismail went on to say that he had been hunting in the vicinity of Isfahan, in the middle of the country, but had now torn himself away from the leopards and lions and was on his way to teach the Sultan a lesson.

One late summer's evening, the Ottoman army appeared on the hills overlooking the plain of Chaldiran, on the north-western rim of the Iranian plateau. The following morning, the men came down into the plain, first the mounted Sipahis, each man an arsenal with his lance, sabre and musket, the latter tucked into his horse's girth, then the red-clothed light archery division, and finally the Janissaries in their conical white felt hats. The occasional glint of a golden saddle pommel indicated the arrival of a provincial governor with his levy. Through motes of dust trod the Sultan on his horse, Black Cloud, flanked by the oriflammes of the household cavalry.

Seeing the Turkish army, twice the size of their own, descend towards their camp, the Shah's commanders advised him to attack before the enemy had got into position. 'I am not a caravan thief,' Ismail replied contemptuously; 'whatever is decreed by God will occur.' The Ottomans lashed together two hundred cannons and a hundred mortars to form a fortress within which the Janissaries stood, each with an axe at his girdle and a mounted matchlock, or arquebus, in his hands, and only after the Ottomans were in position did Ismail order his horsemen to charge.

The Shah's warriors opposed the use of guns as an unworthy innovation. Their mounts had never been under fire. When Selim's men discharged their first rounds, the Iranian horses were maddened by fear and scattered uncontrollably over the plain. Ismail was unseated, his life only saved by a soldier who gallantly put himself in the way of a lance that had been hurled in his sovereign's direction. Then Ismail fled. After their victory the Turks continued to Tabriz, the Iranian capital, but winter was drawing in and the men were restless once more, so Selim gave the order to return to Istanbul.

After purging the army of Bayezit's favourites and replacing them with his own, Selim again marched east, this time towards the old and tottering Mamluk Sultanate, with its capital in Cairo and its fingers closed feebly around Islam's sacred sites. The Mamluk Sultan, Qansawh al-Ghawri, advanced to meet him and in August 1517 the two sides clashed in Syria. Again Ottoman firepower made the difference. Qansawh was put to flight and, by the spring of 1517, not only Cairo – after being comprehensively sacked – but also Mecca, Medina and Jerusalem were in Ottoman hands. As the owner of Islam's most sacred sites, Selim was now entitled to call himself Caliph, or leader of the world's Muslims, a title that had been previously held by the Abbasids of Baghdad. But pomposity was not among the Sultan's faults, and the Cairenes praised him when, attending Friday prayers after invading the city, he pulled back the rich carpet that was spread for his prostrations and touched his forehead to the bare floor.

In Rome the Imperial ambassador reported that Pope Leo had summoned 'the most excellent cardinals and all the foreign diplomats accredited to the Curia, to whom he explained that he had learned . . . of the victories and great good fortune of the terrible ruler of the Turks, the enemy of the Christian people, and of the manifold and grave dangers in which the whole of Christanity found itself, which, if not speedily removed by the Christian princes, would in a short time doubtless lead to the ruin of the whole of Christendom. Since the most ferocious Turk has brought Alexandria, Egypt, and almost the entire Eastern Roman Empire under his control and has fitted an imposing fleet . . . he no longer craves only Sicily or Italy but the empire of the entire earth.'

But the Christian powers the Pope harangued were immobilised by disunity and indecision. They were more likely to fight each other than the Turks.

~

The new Caliph, leader of the world's Muslims, Master of the Celestial Conjunction, was not known to show the slightest doubt about anything. He killed his viziers for the crime of living too long. He loved war and was endowed with masterful insight, committing his atrocities as if informed ahead of time that they would one day be recognised as the foundation for political and religious developments of lasting importance.

From Istanbul he went to Edirne, where Prince Suleyman had been summoned from Manisa to meet him. The Sultan's 24-year-old son had, over the years, received many letters and gifts from his loving father, among them a robe that was dipped in poison and killed the attendant who tried it on. At Edirne Suleyman came before this man who had in the blink of an eye doubled the size of the Empire.

Can trust exist between a man who has killed his own royal

father and his still-living son? However delicate the formalities when Selim and Suleyman came face to face, however affectionate their greeting, regicide and patricide were in the air. The young prince presumably kept in mind the words of his mother, the capable, well-organised Hafsa, who stopped him putting on the poisoned robe – the dos and the don'ts that enabled him to come out of this room alive.

~

On a September day in 1520 an officer of the Sultan arrived at Manisa, prostrated himself and told Suleyman that the world was bereft. It was agreed that Piri Pasha, the Grand Vizier, would oversee the transfer of the corpse from Thrace, where the lord of the world had succumbed to the after-effects of a lanced bubo, using the cover of a remittance of imperial coin. It was also agreed that Piri would go on ahead disguised as a courier.

Suleyman's ride to the metropolis, though attended by a sense of destiny, not to say filial grief, was far from devoid of apprehension. It would be perfectly in character for his father to have been luring him to his death.

On 30 September, Suleyman came to Uskudar, a village on the Asian shore of the Bosporus, and was rowed across to the New Palace, where his fears were allayed somewhat by the deferential manner in which the chief of the Janissaries welcomed him. Only now was the news of the royal death made public and blessings and prayers offered for the health and longevity of the new Sultan.

In the line of Osman, the Empire's founder, he was number ten.

~

In the second courtyard of the Palace, a young man with a dark complexion, an aquiline nose, a long thin neck, a prominent forehead, smooth cheeks and a thin, swooping, swallow-wing moustache sits on a throne while an official grovels at his feet and others wait their turn, their hands clasped before them in gestures of subservience. The garden has been cleared of the ostriches, peacocks and gazelles that usually graze and peck there unconcernedly. In their place stand officials in their best caftans.

It would be wrong to call what is happening a coronation, for the young man neither removes his bulbous white turban nor receives a crown. Each prone official affirms his allegiance and with these utterances Sultan Suleyman is confirmed in his office and entitled to the unthinking obedience of his subjects.

After his investiture, dressed in black, he rides out with Piri and the other Pashas to receive Selim's body. The Pashas dismount to shoulder the bier and bury it on the fifth hill, where Suleyman orders the construction of a mausoleum in the precincts of the mosque that his father already ordered to be built there. In his elegy, the judge and poet Kemalpashazade says that the dead Sultan did a great many things in just eight years and that, like the setting sun, he cast in a brief period of time an immense shadow over the earth. Later that day letters are written announcing the succession to the officials and tributaries of the Empire, as well as to the kings and princes of other countries.

In its first days each reign is a defenceless and bloody baby. Astrologers and soothsayers divine its chances of surviving the shock of birth. Selim's appointments and regulations are in abeyance until his successor renews them. The world stops moving, suspended between kings.

His first act is to sedate his father's army. The army that deposed Selim's father, and might take against his son. Each Janissary receives three thousand aspers. Other potential troublemakers get expensive caftans. Opening his eye of justice, Suleyman has five disorderly infantrymen and a sadistic admiral executed. He releases hostages who were captured during the Egyptian campaign and compensates merchants who were punished by his father for laying in heretic Iranian silk. This is one way of saying: I am not him. But of course this negation is not the same as being able to say: this is who I am.

By killing all potential rivals Selim spared his son the ordeal of fighting for the throne. In default of a credible competitor Suleyman enjoys the support of Piri and the rest. And the Empire itself is in rude health, never bigger, never richer, its enemies rarely less united.

Whoever he is, young Suleyman already has a precious quality, that of luck.

~

It's the first time he's been separated from Hafsa. She ran the household in Caffa and accompanied him when Selim appointed him to Manisa, endowing pious institutions and keeping tabs on the court-in-miniature while also pursuing bandits who had grown forward during his father's bloody and fratricidal campaign for power. Aside from restraining him when he was about to put on the poisoned robe , she also approved the concubines who have since given him three sons, Mahmud, now eight years of age, five-year-old Mustafa, and the infant Murat.

She is on six thousand aspers a month. A widow in early middle age, as handsome as she was on the day she was purchased, she will live in the Old Palace in a state of honoured manumission. With the mothers of the Sultan's children. With the children themselves.

After the Conquest of Constantinople, Sultan Mehmet gave orders for an area in the centre of the city to be marked out and a palace built there. But no sooner was it ready than he had a second survey conducted to determine the reliability of the water supply on a promontory two miles further west. The results of the survey being satisfactory, the Conqueror gave orders for the razing of the Byzantine buildings standing on the promontory and the construction of a second, larger complex in their place. His affections transferred, the palace in the centre of town ceased to be his primary Istanbul residence, becoming a place of claustration for his women.

The Old Palace and the New Palace are linked by the concluding stage of the Via Egnatia, the transcontinental highway that was built by the Roman Governor Gnaeus Egnatius in the second century BC and enters the city at the Seven Towers. This section of the Via Egnatia is called the Council Road because officials pass along it on their way to meetings of the Imperial Council. Travelling on horseback or in a litter, they pass Bayezit's mosque, behind which he lies in a modest limestone tomb. They also pass the remains of Constantine's column, the cross on top long toppled and the column itself reduced to the status of a useful landmark.

The Hippodrome is at the far end of the Council Road. It features a corkscrew column with three snake-heads, originally from Delphi, a smashed architrave that is home to heron chicks and an oleander, and two Nile obelisks, one of them made of a single stone with hieroglyphs, the other of different stones connected together and resting on a heavily sculpted marble base. All around, Byzantium's detritus is being looted, rivets, clasps and downspouts gouged from cracked fragments, blocks of stone lifted whole onto carts for use elsewhere. The emperor's lodge on its twenty-four massive pillars is especially perishable. Each winter flushes away a little more pagan–Christian tilth. A more recent addition to the Hippodrome is an arrangement of gibbets to encourage people to behave.

At the entrance to the Hippodrome stands the former church of St John. Its congregation is made up of wildcats, wolves, badgers, lions, porcupines, wild donkeys, leopards, bears, boars, an ox resembling the domesticated one, but with a lofty, slender neck, and a deal more skittish, and other beasts, possibly of Egyptian origin. The animals in the Lion House mate and eat and shit and die here. Whenever the Moorish keepers approach with the ox heads and horse steaks that they are given to eat, the creatures heave at their chains and raise dreadful howls that can be heard across the neighbourhood. Sometimes they are put into the wild so the young Sultan can hunt and kill them. Or they are shown off on festive occasions or brought to the Old Palace to amuse the women and eunuchs. It is said that a wild man is also kept in the Lion House.

The Sultan's two elephants also live here, one small and one big, and they are so well trained that when the attendants throw a ball at them they beat it back with their trunks, bearing out Pliny's dictum that the elephant is the most biddable of beasts. Whenever the Sultan returns from a campaign, the elephants have the honour of being driven twenty miles outside the city to welcome him. They enter in front of the Sultan, performing tricks, which takes the edge off his fatigue and reminds him that life is to be enjoyed. Coming along the Council Road, through the city's layers, he raises his eyes and knows he is home.

~

The pink mountain at the end of the Council Road was put up by Constantine the Great on the site of the ancient Greek acropolis. It was rebuilt, burned down and was again rebuilt on its current, Himalayan scale.

This, the Church of Hagia Sophia, or Holy Wisdom, heard its last Christian liturgy at the lighting of the lamps on 28 May 1453. Apart from the guards who remained on duty on the battlements, almost every woman, man and child in the city came to bathe in God's love. The last Emperor of Byzantium, Constantine XI, arrived before midnight and received absolution before returning to his post and dying in a charge against the invaders. Shortly after dawn came the news that the city walls had been breached.

That afternoon, the Conqueror dismounted at the door to the church. Walking towards the altar, he was displeased to see one of his soldiers hacking at the famous marble pavement, white with rippling bands of grey, like the waves of the sea, and ordered him to stop. On the Conqueror's word, an imam mounted the pulpit and read out the Muslim attestation of faith, a single Arabic phrase killing a church and giving birth to a mosque.

Even now, three quarters of a century after its conversion, Aya Sofya, as the Turks call it, remains a work in progress. Whenever one of the walls cracks they simply put another buttress up against it. Two massive minarets are being built to

34

remind it that it is a mosque. One can make out their heavy fluting through the wooden scaffolding. Inside the building, in the conch of what used to be the apse, workmen are slapping fresh plaster over a mosaic of the Virgin and Child that needs to stay hidden as it contravenes God's law against idols.

~

Next to Aya Sofya is a gateway crowned by two witch-hat towers which leads into the Court of Processions. From this vast squashed rectangle, wisps of conversation spiral into the sky along with wood smoke from the kitchens. Going along the cobbled path, cold-shouldered by the mosque's northern wall, the visitor passes the former church of St Irene, petite by comparison, an armoury now. And still after a quarter of a mile of shoe metal the visitor has yet to penetrate the palace itself.

The New Palace is an ambush of chimneys, towers, passages, courtyards, cloisters and belvederes, menacing the Straits, oppressing the Horn, haranguing the Propontis. It was built for seclusion but it is the semaphore tower of empire and it can be seen for miles from both land and water. The other name that people use for it, the Gate of Felicity, or, as the Venetian ambassadors prefer, the Sublime Porte, refers to the slab of Meccan stone that Abbasid Caliphs fitted at the threshold of their palace in Baghdad, over which no one might pass but on their knees. As faceless as the Mongol tent cities from which it derives inspiration, this expanse of stone and wood has no front, no back, but sheer walls giving onto steep hillsides, carpeted with poppies and asphodel in the spring, falling in terraces to the sea below.

At the far end of the Court of Processions one arrives finally at the Gate of Salutation. This is where foreign ambassadors dismount. Walking through the gate and into a second courtyard, almost as immense as the first, but regular in plan, they are met by a human wall.

Even in a ceremonial setting, the Janissaries present an unsettling spectacle. Each is wearing his white cone hat from the back of which hangs a strip of cloth that covers his neck and rests on his shoulders, similar to the hanging necklet worn by a French gentlewoman. When the Janissaries bow, it is like a field of corn moving gently and in unison. Then they are still as if made of stone.

The requirement of silence intensifies the closer one approaches the shadow of God on earth. In the third courtyard the silence is so deep one might be forgiven for thinking that something significant is about to happen.

After capturing Constantinople, the Conqueror took the pick of young boys from the vanquished population to be his body-guard and constantly near him, or, according to their merits, to be his pages. Subsequent sultans have continued his practice, levying slaves from the territories they capture. They wear long tresses hanging from both sides of their caps, like the prophet Joseph when he was Pharaoh's slave, and glide noiselessly between their dormitory and the small mosque in the third courtyard.

The Conqueror would make himself available at the Imperial Council. He would appear before his courtiers during banquets and accept their acclaim. His great-grandson is remote by com-parison. Suleyman comes before his grandees but twice a year. Otherwise he is accessible only to those members of the Council who are invited into the Chamber of Petitions. None may sit. They must stand with their hands clasped before them. Even the highest-ranking of the chancery officials may go no further into the third courtyard. They may not enter the inner palace, the Sultan's own apartments.

None but one.

~

As his nickname suggests, the Frank was born Christian. He began life a subject of Venice, at Parga, in Albania, across the water from the Greek island of Corfu. He was called Piero then. Papa sold animal skins. One day pirates came ashore and when they went away they took little Piero with them. This was 1498

36

or thereabouts. He ended up in Anatolia, where he was acquired by a well-heeled widow who brought him on. Dress and deportment; music and languages. He was playing the violin very prettily when Suleyman, then a prince, came to visit, and, not having anything else worthy of her distinguished guest, the widow gave him her pet, called Ibrahim now.

He travelled with his lord that nervous September when the Prince became the Sultan, hurrying from the coast to the metropolis. And the Pashas, expecting one but getting two, unable to tear their disapproving eyes from this unlovely young man to whom their new lord looked for reassurance and companionship, asked . . . who exactly is this?

Since the Conqueror's time the Sultans have promoted slaves because they pose no threat. Their destiny is tied to that of the Sultan who has favoured them. They have no independent source of power and can be dashed down as soon as they show signs of becoming a threat.

They are surrogates. Because the Conqueror in his wisdom decreed that the Ottoman Sultan may lawfully put his brothers to death, the Sovereign of Sovereigns is fated to have no brothers and, logically, no uncles. What an absence! What a contrast with the male companionship that exists in every other family, high and low! Rather than come into leaf in a grove of relations, the Sultan has stumps for company. Alien varieties are brought in for shade and protection.

The Frank.

He is thin, his face is perhaps a little small for his head, he is pale, physically unimposing. His teeth are few and crooked. But he compensates for his ugliness with charm and eloquence. He loves life. He loves his fiddle, Piacenza cheese and muscatel. He knows Italian, Greek, French, Turkish, Arabic and Persian, though his Arabic script is that of a child and his Italian more than a little whimsical. He enjoys learning about the lords of the world, about places and things. He reads about Alexander the Great, Hannibal the Carthaginian, wars and histories. When reading about Alexander it is possible that the Frank sees himself in the role of the great general's companion Hephaestion. Who knows? He has a musician from Iran in his suite, with whom he composes. He shares his pleasure in these things with his lord.

The Sultan is lonely. It is only natural.

~

The title 'Pasha' signifies a man of command. It is used to refer to the top officials of the Porte, like the high governors, the provincial governors and the high admiral, known as the Captain Pasha. On ceremonial occasions a Pasha is preceded by a man holding a standard on a high pole, from which also hang horsetails, and the number of these signifies the seniority of the Pasha. For this reason each Pasha is known as a Pasha of one horsetail, or two tails, and so on, depending on the number there are on his pole. The Grand Vizier is a Pasha of five horsetails. The Sultan has seven.

The tradition goes back to one of the Sultan's ancestors. When his army's banner was seized by the enemy and his men lost heart, this Mongolian khan used his sword to cut the tail from a horse, and tying it to a lance, shouted, 'Here is my banner! Follow it, all who wish me well!' His men were inspired by his improvisation and the battle was won.

The Pashas whom Suleyman inherited from his father are teaching him how to govern. They are Piri, who saw service under Bayezit, the youngsters Ferhat and Ahmet, and Mustafa Pasha, who is somewhere in between.

Having shown loyalty to Selim at the most perilous moments of his rise to the throne, the Pashas feel cheated by his untimely death and nervous about what the son will bring. And they are suspicious of Suleyman's friend Ibrahim, who has passed no test, presided over no council and won no battle, yet leads his master with a ring through his nose.

In response to the disapproval of the grandees, Suleyman can do one of two things. He can either dump the Frank or cling to him the harder. In choosing the second of these alternatives he creates a consternation so profound, a precedent so disturbing, the court prefers to pass over it in silence.

Suleyman knows that to appoint Ibrahim to public office prematurely would have undesirable consequences. It would expose the Frank to responsibilities for which he is unprepared. Besides, it's in the private apartments that Suleyman wishes to enjoy his friend. So he names Ibrahim to positions whose holder enjoys unhindered access to these apartments. Head of the Privy Chamber. Chief Falconer. Head of the Palace Administration. This final office is usually held by a eunuch. Ibrahim is no eunuch.

The Sultan's bedchamber has no prepared bed, but in a corner there are three mattresses of crimson velvet, two of which are filled with cotton and one with feathers, with two covers of crimson taffeta and three similar pillows, from which hang a slip of green silk with a gold button attached. In the evening the pages spread these mattresses on the floor over the carpets, first the cotton mattresses, then the finer one with feathers, so that all three reach the height of a man's knee, and they arrange the sheets and the covers and the cushions, preparing the bed away from the wall so that one can walk around it; and at each corner of the bed they place a silver candelabrum, each with its white candle, and overhead, with silk cords, they hang a gold baldachin, which covers the bed, and when they have arranged everything they light the candles and call the Sultan.

Ibrahim sleeps with his lord, head touching head; alone except for two attendants who keep watch, one at the bed's head, the other at its foot, each holding burning torches. And in the daytime the Sultan writes him tender notes in his own hand and sends them using one of his mutes, and Ibrahim writes back telling him everything he has done, such that the lord cannot live without the slave, nor the slave without the lord. They are sometimes to be seen in a little boat, accompanied by an oarsman, landing beneath the palace and continuing on foot, or hawking on the Asian shore. And whatever Ibrahim wishes done, whether it is to be entertained by midgets, to be read aloud the medical treatise of Ibn Sina, or to partake of a peach, it is done.

If the Sultan orders an item of clothing for himself, he orders the same for Ibrahim. It is as if they are one and the same, the seed of the Conqueror and a boy from a beach, the Shadow of God on Earth and his shadow.

III

A generation ago, the Holy Roman Empire, Spain, Burgundy, France and England contended on terms of parity for dominance over Europe. But a succession of dynastic alliances and timely deaths has united the first three of these polities and brought Charles V of the House of Hapsburg to their apex.

In October 1520, Charles was enthroned at Aachen after being elected King of the Romans, the title that belongs to the Emperor-elect until he travels to Italy to be crowned by the Pope. Only then will Charles officially be Holy Roman Emperor. But the world already knows him by this higher designation.

October 1520 was also the month when Suleyman's subjects bound themselves to him with the traditional oath of fealty. Erasmus of Rotterdam wasn't alone in seeing a rivalry of brothers in this uncanny twinning, the two men locked in competition, as the humanist scholar put it, 'to decide the final outcome, whether Charles will be the sole ruler of the whole world, or the Turks. The world can no longer support two suns.'

The Sultan's possessions run in an arc from the Crimea to the Nile; the Emperor's, in an arc of comparable length and declivity, from the Baltic to the Atlantic. Algiers and Rhodes, Vienna and the Morea, are potential points of conflict. Sardinia and the Dardanelles. Almost anywhere along the arcs.

Little about Charles commends him to the Sultan. That he won his imperial title by bribing the Electors is unedifying. Then

41

there is his insistence on styling himself Prince of Jerusalem, a city which Selim captured in 1517 – and that from the Muslim Mamluks! – and which Suleyman, as Caliph or supreme ruler of the Muslims, looks forward to handing on to his heirs. Suleyman refuses to recognise Charles as Emperor of anything. He refers to him as the King of Spain, after his inheritance from his maternal grandparents, Ferdinand of Aragon and Isabella of Castile. As for Charles's younger brother and sidekick, Ferdinand, Archduke of Austria ... what exactly is his purpose in life?

Charles has been trouncing the Turk since he was a child, when little Ferdinand, forced into Saracen garb, would end the day's play with his brother's wooden sword across his throat. Ever since he came into his gigantic patrimony, the Emperor has been busy dealing with Christian mischief-makers. Their names are Martin Luther and Francis I. But what he dreams about at night, what he discusses with God when they are alone in the monasteries and hermitages to which he retreats whenever his outrageously heavy travel schedule and unflagging, back-to-back impregnations of his wife, Isabella, permit, is the recapture of Constantinople for Christendom. In the words of his Grand Chancellor, Mercurino de Gattinara, 'God has set you on a path towards the monarchy of the world.'

~

It was with joy that Pope Leo heard of Selim's unexpected death. Out of gratitude for God's mercy the pontiff ordered barefoot processions and church litanies and the cardinals chortled that a savage lion had been succeeded by a gentle lamb.

Amid the general relief, Leo shelved his plans for a Crusade and Charles and Francis resumed their struggle for northern Italy. Even Venice, which had so much riding on a correct divination of Turkish intentions, was preoccupied elsewhere. Doge Gritti was trying to extract advantage from the turmoil on the mainland, advising Francis how to defend Milan against Charles. And the Diet of Worms, at which the Holy Roman Emperor excommunicated Luther, who nonetheless made good his return to Germany . . . well, Bocaccio couldn't have made it up.

Yes, Christendom was distracted in the summer of 1521, when the peaceable new Sultan, that gentle lamb, marched seven hundred miles in a north-westerly direction and took Belgrade at the first time of asking.

In the autumn of the following year it was the turn of Rhodes, headquarters of the Knights Hospitaller and obstacle to smooth navigation between Ottoman Anatolia and Egypt. After a siege that lasted five months, Philippe de Villiers de L'Isle-Adam, Grand Prior of France and Grand Master of the Hospitallers, kissed the hand of the Sultan, the island's new owner. Suleyman let L'Isle-Adam and his surviving knights off the island before ordering the churches turned into mosques.

~

In less than three years, Suleyman has achieved two feats of conquest that eluded the Conqueror. His credibility as a warrior now established, he turns to the human resources at his disposal.

Ibrahim was along on the Belgrade and Rhodes campaigns – in the entourage, not in the field, where Selim's men were in control. But the Frank doesn't aspire to lounge in the throne tent counting buttons. He is watching how to wheel cavalry, exact tribute and administer justice. And he is opening the Sultan's eyes to certain shortcomings on the part of the Pashas.

Whenever Piri wishes to remind people of his indispensability to the State, he pretends to be ill and watches the quality of administration slide. Suleyman treats him with sweetness and consideration, as one might a respected uncle. But Piri's performance during the Belgrade campaign was disappointing. He also tried to prevent Ibrahim building his big new palace; and if you lose the goodwill of Ibrahim, that of the Sultan is sure to follow.

One day Suleyman says musingly, 'I want to appoint to a chancellery position a slave for whose service I am infinitely grateful, but I do not know which office I should appoint him to.' Realising what is expected of him, Piri replies cheerfully, 'it is my office that should be given to such a close and esteemed slave.' And he goes into retirement with a pension of 200,000 aspers.

On June 27 1523, Suleyman names Ibrahim to be Grand Vizier, one of the most powerful positions in the world that isn't passed from father to son. The Frank is also given command of the army of Rumelia, which is the most important military command in the Empire because Rumelia contains Thrace, the region of mainland Europe immediately to the west of the Bosporus – and Thrace is the Empire's windpipe.

No man has ever become Grand Vizier without proving himself beforehand in some administrative or military capacity. The Conqueror himself, for all his readiness to replace men who had outlived their usefulness, did not change personnel on a whim.

The Sultan's decision to sack an inherited subordinate and put in a man of his own raises two possibilities. The first is that, after three years on the throne, he is confident enough in his own judgement to step out of the shadow of his father. The second is that his obsession with Ibrahim has impaired his thinking. Some consider it unwise to exchange a colossus for a non-entity who under any prudent monarch would be kept out of the public life and reserved for private hours. The Sultan's two greatest triumphs to date, the Belgrade and Rhodes campaigns, were accomplished by his father's appointees. They were the triumphs of Selim, not Suleyman.

The new Sultan is perhaps a little sensitive to the achievements of his father. When Selim's mausoleum is completed, his son gives orders that there are to be no processions, and the body is moved quietly, attended only by a small circle of family members and former advisers, into the octagonal tower with its pallid emptiness. There the enormous catafalque rests, alone in the centre of the room, covered with embroidered velvet and surmounted by Selim's enormous shawl turban with its voluminous folds, like a swell of the sea.

~

The Frank would make an unhappy Lutheran. Membership of the dreary Reformist sect, garbed in shades of brown, fulminating in drab and joyless churches. It wouldn't suit him at all. What was it that Pope Leo said after his election? 'God has given us the Papacy; let us enjoy it.' Ibrahim is that kind of Muslim.

He receives a ministerial salary of 150,000 ducats. The Rumelian command brings him the same again. He can afford to dress his 6,000 slave soldiers in gold, silk and scarlet and top them with turbans wound in the exotic Moorish fashion.

The new Grand Vizier brings his mother to live in Istanbul. He places his brothers in palace service. For his father, a dilapidated fellow whose name has been changed to Yunus, he arranges the Governorship of Parga, with an income of 2,000 a year. Let no one say that the Frank neglects his kin.

A fuck-off statement has come up over the Byzantine vaults on the northern side of the Hippodrome. The Grand Vizier's palace, the palace that ended Piri Pasha's career. Two hundred thousand ducats' worth of masonry and stone dressed in the Italian style, the walls animated by cantilevered bays and slatted screens, the silhouette by domes and chimneys. Owing to its position up the slope, it is higher than the Hippodrome itself. Aya Sofya, the cupolas of the New Palace and the shining sea beyond are all overlooked by the terrace that runs the length of its inner courtyard.

After being dressed in the morning, he comes down to the courtyard and mounts his Arab stallion, black with a white muzzle and fetlocks, alert and well-proportioned. To get from the courtyard to the Hippodrome floor, he rides down an ornate ramp that runs flush to the facade. Then he crosses the Hippodrome preceded by slaves, guards and members of his ministerial and personal staff, all on foot. Pipers and drummers warn people to get out of the way – but please don't forget to stare. And the Grand Vizier is undeniably arresting in a green tunic, an azure kaftan embroidered with gold thread and a white turban as big as the Sultan's. He wears the 17-carat diamond that was a gift from his master against his skin.

45

Dismounting at the Gate of Salutations, he enters the Second Courtyard and walks along the diagonal path towards the Treasury. Startled by the attendants' unison cry of, 'May the Almighty protect the days of our Sovereign and the Pasha; may they live long and happily,' a falconer, who is drinking from a gold cup that hangs on a chain from the Executioner's Fountain, turns, sees the apparition, and drops to the ground.

The Treasury contains bag upon bag of ducats and pile upon pile of silk and woollen stuffs, gold brocades, furs of lynx and sable and sewn articles that have been presented as tribute, in addition to chests that hold the accounts of each province. Over these things the Frank runs his hand as if they are his own.

Few actions illustrate the ambitions of a ruler better than the selection of his ministers. If the minister is capable and loyal, it will reflect well on his master. And if a minister gains a reputation for venality or injustice it will be said that the fault lies with the ruler who appointed him. Both sides must handle the relationship with tact. A minister running a State must never think of himself, only of the ruler, and should concentrate exclusively on the ruler's business. And the ruler, for his part, must grant the minister wealth and respect, oblige him and share honours and appointments with him. That way the minister will have so many privileges, he won't go looking for more.

Machiavelli, author of these thoughts, is concerned above all with arrangements in Florence. But his assessment applies just as well to other jurisdictions.

~

The Sultan's son Mustafa is nine years of age. Showing some of the qualities one might wish for in an heir, he is brought by his father to live with him in the New Palace.

In the Third Courtyard, Suleyman likes to eat in a domed hall with a fountain at its centre and cushions arranged around the fountain. He eats with a wooden spoon. Good enough for his ancestors, good enough for him. One day, he, Ibrahim and Mustafa are due to eat together. Mustafa enters the hall and sits. The Sultan hands Ibrahim a wooden spoon and they start eating. Seeing Mustafa immobile, the Sultan also hands him a spoon, saying, 'Eat.' But Mustafa's face darkens and he snaps his spoon in two and tosses it away.

Ibrahim says smoothly, 'Lord Mustafa, you have done this because our master offered the first spoon to me. Do you not know that his slave is also yours?' And Mustafa replies coldly, 'I do not know what slaves you refer to, you eat in my father's house every day and you get a spoon before me.'

Boys are passionate and impulsive but they are also forgiving and logical. It isn't long since Ibrahim was one himself. So he smiles benevolently and takes care to show his partiality for the prince who may one day become Sultan. An occasion arises when Suleyman gives the Grand Vizier a beautifully ornamented saddle. When Mustafa shows jealousy at this gift, Ibrahim sends it to him, but he warns him to hide it from his father, for if he finds out, he will make him send it back. It will be their secret.

~

Up for reassessment are the younger Pashas from Selim's era, Ferhat and Ahmet.

Not long after Suleyman's accession, the former slave Jan-birdi al-Ghazali, whom Selim installed as Governor of Syria as a reward for deserting his Mamluk overlord, deserts his new Ottoman overlord. Ferhat Pasha is sent to crush the insurgents, which he does with exemplary efficiency. (This is when the question of what to do with Ghazali's head comes up.)

As a reward for subduing Ghazali, the Sultan gives Ferhat another of his sisters, Beyhan, in marriage, and a home in the New Palace. That's handsome. Ferhat is a man of superb and audacious nature, and the Sultan does not hesitate to give him other missions disciplining the extremities of the Empire, which he discharges with similar success.

Ahmet is also admired. An alumnus of the Third Courtyard, a veteran of the conquest of Egypt, Ahmet was Sultan Selim's second breath. Like Ferhat, he has done his best to ingratiate himself with the new man. During the Belgrade campaign, he celebrates his capture of the town of Sabacz, a rather costly victory, it must be admitted, by arranging the heads of the vanquished along Suleyman's route. At Rhodes he oversees the negotiations that lead to the Hospitallers' surrender, and interprets for the Sultan and the Grand Master as they exchange strained gallantries.

No one can accuse this pair of Pashas of not being bellicose enough. They are broadly speaking competent. It is their attitude to the new authority that is in question.

~

The Frank thinks he can make things up as he goes along. But the Ottoman Empire is built on procedure. Matters pertaining to Holy Law must be referred to the military judge. Those to do with the Sultan's finances are dealt with by the Treasurers, answerable to the Chief Treasurer. Decisions by the executive are taken by the Grand Vizier and recorded by the Chief Secretary in a book. The Frank disdains this basic division, the foundation, one might say, of just Islamic government, and trespasses into domains that aren't his. Then there is his habit of holding meetings of the Imperial Council in his own house on the Hippodrome, as if the New Palace were not the seat of government!

It is no disrespect to the late Sultan of blessed memory to recall that his subjects referred to him as *Yavuz*, meaning trenchant, inflexible, or grim. Selim wasn't running a puppet show. He would emerge after dark in disguise and sit with the people to gamble, a pastime abhorrent to God, and the next morning the wrongdoers would be taken away and hanged.

This Sultan is unsure of himself. Perhaps it is a fear of responsibility that makes him more of a delegator than his father was. Whatever the reason, it is Ibrahim, not Suleyman, who has taken charge of law and order. And the Grand Vizier's approach may be considered lackadaisical and excessively lenient. In the mosque courtyards and the lanes of the great bazaar, the people grumble that murderers, thieves and rapists are strolling about unimpeded and that a great peril awaits.

It is not a simple matter to bring these dysfunctions to the Sultan's attention. The Sultan is deaf. Ibrahim has come so far, so quickly, the best solution might be to wait for him to run out of road. But the Pashas are not the waiting kind.

Ahmet was expecting to step into Piri's shoes. He briefed against the old man, questioning his integrity in the Sultan's presence, and he is angry at being passed over in favour of the Frank. But an angry Ahmet is not an effective Ahmet. Reports of his indecorum in the Imperial Council, where he interrupts the Grand Vizier and passes sardonic comments, reach the Sultan's ears. In August 1523, Ahmet is ordered to Egypt as Governor. Although he is lying ill in bed he is told to get up and leave immediately. The Sultan won't let him kiss his hand before his departure.

Egypt is more like an empire than a province, and all that history is bound to encourage delusions of grandeur in a restless satrap. And sure enough, reports soon reach Istanbul that Ahmet is consorting with local troublemakers. Next he'll be minting coins and having Friday prayers read in his name.

And, whether because that has been his design all along, or because he feels the breath of the state assassin on his neck, Ahmet's insolence indeed becomes open insurrection. In the chill of the Cairo winter, his men creep along a concealed aqueduct into the citadel, where they put the unsuspecting Janissaries, who are steadfast for the Sultan, to the sword. Ahmet also seizes Alexandria and its lighthouse, blocking communication with Rhodes.

But even now the House of Osman inspires more awe in Egyptians than Ahmet's bogus new Sultanate. Two weeks after seizing power the usurper is surprised by a band of Suleyman's loyalists while he is being shaved. Escaping through the bathhouse window in nothing but a shirt, he seeks refuge among the Arab tribes, but they hand him back to the loyalists. Prior to his decapitation, Ahmed declares, 'I chose to go forward in this

49

direction not because I am a traitor. Rather, Ibrahim Pasha endeavoured to kill me.' And it cannot be denied that the Frank is the main beneficiary of Ahmet's death.

~

Ferhat Pasha's method of pacification is to put to death anyone he doesn't like and seize their land, even if by rights it should go to the Sultan. Ferhat believes that he is protected by his marriage to Berhan, the Sultan's sister.

On Ferhat's return to Istanbul from the Balkans, the scene of his most recent depredations, Suleyman won't see him. Berhan intercedes and Suleyman agrees to receive Ferhat at Edirne in Thrace. Ibrahim Pasha is in Egypt on his first mission of state, restoring order after the Ahmet debacle, and the Sultan is distracted with longing. Ferhat had better tread carefully.

The interview begins reasonably well. Ferhat presents the Sultan with a delicate box that belonged to al-Ghazali and is made of gold and crystal and covered in precious stones, as well as four gilded robes of Caspian silk. The Sultan gives Ferhat a thousand ducats and twenty caftans. Then Ferhat lets a little wind into his sails. He lists the services he has done for the Sultan, the rebels he has subdued, the nasty wounds he has sustained with his master's name on his lips and his sorrow at being denied even higher honours. He boasts and blusters, a combination objectionable to the Sultan, whose patience finally runs out.

Wherever you have been sent, the monarch replies, you have stripped the land for your own coffers and sent nothing to the Porte. What benefit did the Treasury see from these famous victories? And, on the subject of famous victories, what about your 7,000 men who were cut to pieces by a mere 1,500 Hungarians during the Belgrade campaign? Where's the peerless service in that?

Now Ferhat is furious. The accusations are coming out of the Sultan's mouth but he, Ferhat, knows who is speaking them.

'That whore Ibrahim is the reason for this.'

There is silence now. Silence in the palace built by Sultan Murat, whose great-great-grandson is now being accused by a former slave from Srebrenica of making a boy for rent the head of his government. Well. These are not words that the Shadow of God can accept under his own roof, from his own Vizier.

The Sultan orders Ferhat from his sight but he refuses to go, shouting, and the Sultan shouts too, for the guards, who drag him out. Ferhat plants himself on a stone bench and raves. The Sultan orders his guards to cut off the head of this disgraced man, his own-brother-in-law, raving on the stone bench. Ferhat has a knife concealed on his person and he puts up a strong fight before finally he is beaten with staves and beheaded, and they leave the corpse of Ferhat Pasha lying there on the ground, with his head nearby, knowing that news of this terrible scene will spread to the corners of the Empire and that anyone contemplating a similar course will have pause.

Who knows if Ferhat brought the knife anticipating that he might need to defend himself, or if his intention was to kill the Sultan? Such distinctions are immaterial to the dead man's mother, who arrives weeping. The Sultan apologises handsomely, saying his intention was to imprison Ferhat and that only the Pasha's contumacy rendered that plan inoperable, leaving him with no choice other than to have him killed. Next Ferhat's wife Berhan, the Sultan's sister, a very beautiful woman, arrives dressed in black and with a cart to take away the body, and she screams at the Sultan, you have killed my husband and I hope to wear these weeds for you in the near future. Believing it wrong to argue with women, the Sultan remains silent.

~

What distinguishes the Janissaries from other fighting divisions is their devotion to their master, their indifference to death and, perhaps most significant of all, that they are promoted on the basis of merit rather than patronage. A dedicated, celibate, convert soldiery, recruited exclusively from Christian captives and slaves, they have no home but the barracks and no family but their comrades. Among the Janissaries only officers may marry before their retirement, and then only with the Sultan's permission. A place in the Janissary corps may not be purchased or inherited. The Janissaries are also confirmed foodies and their commanders hang soup ladles from their belts.

When in camp the Janissaries are not allowed to bring their weapons out of their tents and if a member of the corps is unwise enough to draw the blood of his fellow, he is immediately killed. On the field of battle their habitual sobriety gives way to a savage inebriation. It is a kind of alchemy. Paolo Giovio – historian, aphorist, man of the cloth – contends that the Janissaries are like the phalanxes with which Alexander the Great subdued all the East. While defensible with respect to the Janissaries themselves, Giovio's comparison perhaps does the Sultan an injustice. Alexander's empire didn't survive the death of its founder, while the House of Osman strives for eternity.

This winter they are in arrears because the Grand Vizier is away in Egypt and the Sultan is mooning like Majnun for his Layla. Tipping over their cauldrons, they go on a spree, trashing Ibrahim's palace and killing Jews. 'There can be no government without a Grand Vizier,' they shout, 'and even if there is one, the soldiers cannot be controlled.' Suleyman coops his falcons, returns to the capital and executes the leading rioters with his own hands. But more than ever he feels lonely and he sends word to Ibrahim: come home.

~

Cairo has been good to the Grand Vizier. Following an entrance of exquisite ostentation, the Frank positively laminated, dripping in jewels and followed by five thousand gorgeously dressed soldiers, just a few executions are needed to bring the province to heel. After that it's all clemency and aspers. Poor debtors are freed from prison, orphanages are endowed and minarets are made taller. The new law code is a signal achievement. It imports Ottoman statutes and serves as a warning to anyone who may be contemplating rebellion: we Ottomans are here to stay. To the races of an international city, the Frank declares, 'let no one say, "I am Circassian and you are Turcoman." All are arrows from the same quiver and the slaves of his Majesty the Sovereign.'

Cairo teaches the Frank that he is a big-picture man and that the minutiae can be left to pen-pushers like Iskender Celebi. A lifelong Treasury bureaucrat, Iskender was much valued by Ahmet the traitor, but his attitude to loyalty is professional, that is to say, transferable. The Sultan himself has advised the Grand Vizier to use Iskender as a teacher and father-figure. And throughout Ibrahim's time in Egypt, whether he is setting import duties or discussing Muslim personal law with the sheikhs of the school of al-Azhar, the Treasury man is always at his side, camouflaging his inexperience, whispering the answer, great with figures.

After sorting out the mess left by Ahmet the traitor, the Ibrahim who answers his monarch's summons carries himself with a new authority. In Syria, on the way home, he renews Venice's most favoured nation status and assigns fiefs, until, four days shy of Constantinople, he gets another message from Suleyman: make haste.

A crisis has come up. Bustan, a Turkish sea captain, is saying that the Venetians have seized Turkish vessels and dishonoured the Sultan by dumping the Ottoman colours overboard. War is likely.

～

Ayas is the new Second Vizier. His mother back in Albania is a nun. He sends her one hundred a month, which isn't much when you take into account that he is on 50,000 a year. He likes the warring side of the job and keeps cannonballs in his garden. After hearing Bustan's allegation against the Venetians, Ayas threatens the Venetian bailo, Pietro Bragadin, saying, 'You have broken the peace; by sea and land we will make war with you.' And when Bragadin tries to give Venice's version of the story,

53

which shows Bustan to be the wrongdoer, Ayas won't listen because Bustan is Ayas's man.

To the New Palace, then, where the matter is brought before the Sultan, the envoy pacing nervously outside the Chamber of Petitions where the representations are being made. Luckily for Venice, Ibrahim Pasha will get home tomorrow. The Grand Vizier was born a Venetian citizen and does not conceal his affection for the Serenissima.

The following day after shaking the dust from his feet, Ibrahim is admitted to the New Palace. He gives his master a gold cup from Cairo set with a 58-carat diamond that is worth 18,000 ducats, an emerald worth 15,000 ducats and numerous pearls and rubies.

When the Sultan and Ibrahim are done, the Grand Vizier receives Pietro Bragadin. 'I am angry with everyone,' he says, 'but not with you.' *Son corruciato con tutti, non con te.* How nice it is to dispense with the interpreter and speak to the Turks' chief executive in one's own language. The envoy swears on his life that the version he has given is the truth, and Ibrahim, exercising his new, more bureaucratic mind, asks him if he wouldn't mind putting all that in writing. Ibrahim takes Bragadin's affidavit to the Sultan, who is convinced. Three state messengers are sent across the Aegean to Greece, where they find Bustan and drag him back in chains.

No sooner has Ibrahim got home than war is averted and the Sultan revives. It's not bad for the new boy who until recently was surrounded by bullies. Yes, when he first entered the Sultan's service half a decade ago many people hated the Frank. But seeing that the Sultan loves him and will not give him up, the court sycophants have learned to refer to him as *Makbul*, the loved one or favourite, and everyone takes care not to cross him.

~

The Frank is to be united with a lady called Muhsine, a member of the same family that purchased him all those years ago and turned him from little Piero into Ibrahim. Muhsine is less than enthusiastic. But it is the Sultan's wish and there is nothing more to be said. The bride will be peripheral to the public ceremonies, which will be enacted against the backdrop of Istanbul.

Even during Byzantium's decline the site of 'New Rome' was sublime. Now it is rising again. Standards of glory and magnificence are being set, worthy of a universal empire to eclipse that of the Caesars and inspire fear and awe in Charles V.

Schools, bathhouses and infirmaries are coming up, shoots of the new Islamic civilisation. From the detritus of churches rise fortress-like mosques, their minarets as sharp as lancepoints. A divine plan exists for Suleyman, for his friend. Let us celebrate it.

For seven days food is given out to the palace troops, the artillerymen, the infantry, the elders of the religious brotherhoods, the old, the young and their teachers, the poor, the bailiffs, the craftsmen and the great and the good who arrive from all around the Empire. There are six thousand different varieties of food. Eight thousand Janissaries are fed in a single serving. Cuts of camel and cows roasted whole on spits. Almond shortbreads steeped in syrup and sherbet made from tamarind and liquorice that have been shipped in by the hundredweight. The feasting takes place under canopies that were seized in war from the Empire's enemies and have been kept as trophies. The tent that Sultan Selim captured from Shah Ismail on the plain of Chaldiran is spread with cushions and throws, rugs and bolsters bordered with lace.

When the Sultan is conveyed from the New Palace to the Hippodrome, he is between walls of gold and silk, the streetfronts having been hung with carpets. Greeted by the bridegroom and ushered to the terrace of his palace, where a kiosk has been built for the purpose, the Sultan hears a debate between the venerable mufti, Ali Jemali, and the tutor of the royal princes, Shems Efendi, on the subject of the Quranic verse in which God addresses King David, saying, 'We did indeed make thee caliph on earth.' There is a parellel to savour between the Biblical King and the present Sultan, in whose domains lie the holiest sites of Islam. All the talking gives the Sultan a thirst that he quenches using a vessel which is made from a single turquoise and once met the lips of Anushirwan, King of the Sassanians. Afterwards the divines go away clutching preserves.

From his kiosk the Sultan watches the entertainments on the Hippodrome. There are wrestling bouts and horse races and competitions to knock a pitcher off a pole using a javelin. There are parades of paper tigers and monsters, Janissaries climbing the greasy pole, men on stilts pretending to be storks. Wrestlers grapple, acrobats somersault and sway, buffoons clown and topple, a foreign spy is pardoned. A strongman lies on his back, his pectoral muscles supporting boulders and an anvil while six men pound the anvil with hammers. For fourteen nights no one can sleep for the whistle of rockets and the explosions of tailed comets through the sky. On the ninth day comes the news that the Sultan has again been blessed with a son, who will be named Selim.

Each morning for the duration of the festivities, the groom's attendants, ten of them expensively dressed captives, come out of the palace and show off the gifts that he was given the previous day, including diamonds, walrus ivory and garments of lynx and white fox. It takes a full day for the bride's trousseau to be conveyed from her old home to her new one, like the supply train of an army. And when she herself eventually makes the same journey accompanied by twenty thickly swathed female slaves, it takes sixty mules and ten captives to bring the furnishings and other luxuries that the groom has set aside for her. Showing off to the in-laws, Ibrahim presents Muhsine with gold gifts worth 100,000 ducats. Then it is time for the night prayer.

IV

Now that Egypt is settled and the vizierates are assigned, the question that everyone is asking is where Suleyman will attack next. The Frank refers archly to a prophecy which says that the Sultan and his Grand Vizier, a man who has come from nowhere and happens to be called Ibrahim, will conquer the Empire of Rome. It is well known that the Sultan is looking forward to stabling his horse in St Peter's. If not Rome, then Hungary is a possibility, the continent's armour. If the armour is pierced – if Buda falls – Vienna will be next. Then the Rhine. Then Paris.

The Sultan has levied a war tax of 15 aspers on every one of his subjects. The foundries are forging cannons and the boatyard on the Horn is organised chaos as timber is sawed and planed, hulls are caulked and masts are hoisted into place. The Frank comes by to urge the workers on.

Men of fighting age are streaming in from the Asian provinces: Kurds, Arabs, Turcomans. To the west of the city, fifteen hundred tents go up. But the Janissaries continue to thorn the Grand Vizier. 'How can we go to war with two masters?' they demand. And the Sultan asks them, 'who are these two masters?' And they reply: 'You and Ibrahim.' The Sultan is angered by this and has Ibrahim strangled and hands his body to the Janissaries saying, 'Do what you will.'

At least this is the gossip that has spread as far as Corfu, where a shipowner shares it with the Venetian bailo, who includes it in his next dispatch to the Signoria. In the chaff of rumour may lie a seed of truth.

One spring day, on his way back from visiting his ancestors at Eyup, a little way up the Golden Horn, the Sultan stops for refreshments outside the old Janissary barracks, where the colonel of the sixty-first company hands him a cup of sherbet. After bringing the cup to his lips, the Sultan gives it to his sabre-bearer, who returns it to the colonel filled with gold coins. The Sultan takes leave of the Janissaries with the words, 'We shall see each other again at the Golden Apple.'

~

On the appointed day, when the Sultan and his commanders come out of the New Palace, Ibrahim, unappeasably alive, is dressed more splendidly than his master. Pietro Bragadin, invited along as an observer, regrets that he is too infirm for the rigours of the campaign. And it would certainly be awkward for the representative of a Christian power to associate himself so openly with the Mohammedan annexation of ... where, exactly?

At the tent city the army musters. After greeting their sovereign the troops join the cavalcade. While the army goes in a north-westerly direction, eight hundred riverboats, including artillery transports and double-decker galleys equipped with cannons, head eastwards along the Bosporus and into the Black Sea. Having reached the mouth of the Danube, these craft sail upstream through the Balkans.

The trouble with big empires is that the enemy is far away and there is weather in between. 'The army is suffering greatly from the rain,' the Sultan writes in his diary during the slog through Bulgaria, and at Sofia he flees his tent rather than get his slippers wet. After that experience, Ibrahim Pasha is sent ahead to scout for bivouacs and build bridges, and at Belgrade the Sultan's tent is pitched high above the raging confluence of the Danube and the Sava. The Turks are moving at an average of eighteen miles a day, not counting rest days, a rate achievable only through exacting levels of discipline. 'Two soldiers decapitated,' the Sultan writes, 'accused of stealing horses.' A few stages on: 'Execution of six Vlachs caught looting.'

~

A premature birth, King Louis II of Hungary and Bohemia was incubated inside a slaughtered pig. He married Charles V's sister Maria when he was sixteen. Divided between pro-Austrians and Hungarian patriots, Louis's court at Buda is far from the hive of useful activity it was under his illustrious predecessor, Matthias Corvinus, who defeated the Conqueror in battle and turned Hungary into a rich and powerful kingdom. The present monarch and his wife have little taste for high politics, Louis stuffing his prematurely aged little face six or seven times a day while his Queen veers between binge-eating, insomnia and equestrianism.

The Turks are on their way to destroy Louis but his coffers are empty, his nobles malinger and the bishops are late in sending the money that is needed for boats and guns. Of Christian solidarity there is little sign. 'I already have a tiresome Turk to deal with,' is how Charles V replies to his brother-in-law's plea for help. This is the Emperor's ironic reference to Francis. A league is forming that will be made up of the Papacy, France and Venice. But the league isn't against the Turks. It's against Charles and his younger brother Ferdinand, Archduke of Austria.

The Serenissima, meanwhile, is playing her usual double game, tipping off the Turks while promising His Holiness an armada against the infidel. The citizens of Buda need no convincing that every Turkish artillery piece is engraved with the lion of St Mark and that the Sultan's engineers have thick Venetian accents. In truth, Venice is a bird standing on the Grand Turk's shoulder and whispering in his ear. Of no other European power can this be said. At any rate, Louis knows it is the heart of Doge Gritti that he must move if his nation is to be saved.

'Most illustrious prince,' he writes, 'the Turkish Caesar is himself a three or four day journey away from Belgrade, and he doesn't delay, he will come against us and our kingdom with all his power, and your illustrious Lordship has understood how unequal we are to him on account of our much diminished forces ... for this reason we ask and appeal to your most illustrious Lordship by immortal God and by the safety of Christendom to come to our aid as we struggle in this present danger with whatever help and support is possible, and indeed without any delay. For it will be pointless if help is brought later, when the enemy power has penetrated into the guts of our kingdom.'

The Doge listens carefully to the King's plea and has it filed away.

~

From Buda, Pope Clement's nuncio is keeping the pontiff abreast of the Turk's manpower and objectives. The nuncio assumes that the River Sava will prove insuperable to the enemy, but no, they simply bring their bridges with them on wagons and take the army across that way.

Meanwhile, the Hungarian nobles are urging Louis to write to Clement to ask what is to be done and, specifically, whether Petrovaradin should be abandoned to its fate. Petrovaradin is a citadel on a bluff overlooking the Danube. The Turks must take it or risk the obliteration of their flotilla which is sailing up from Belgrade. Ibrahim brings up siege towers that his men scale so as to be on the same level as the defenders. There is strong resistance and he is obliged to send for reinforcements, but after twelve days mines open a breach in the walls of the citadel. Five hundred members of the garrison are beheaded and three hundred enslaved. 'We continue towards Buda,' the Sultan writes.

After slaughtering the garrison at Osijek, on the right bank of the Drava, near where it enters the Danube, and setting light to the town, the army crosses the river on a pontoon which the Sultan orders destroyed to stop homesick soldiers getting any ideas. They slog through the swamps of southern Hungary towards King Louis, who is waiting on the plain of Mohacs, called after a town of that name set amid vines and overlooked by a mountain shaped like an amphitheatre. It is on this plain, tomorrow, 30 August 1526, that the Turks plan to give battle.

But the Hungarians see their opportunity today. As the invaders rise from the afternoon prayer, they are charged by Hungary's armoured knights on their immense horses, which scatter Ibrahim's squadron on the Turkish left and force their way to within striking distance of the Sultan, who is saved only by the thickness of his cuirass. Having come through the hole they have torn in the Turkish left, the knights plunge into the centre – only by now this hole is filling with Janissaries who have descended onto the plain.

Over the next two hours the fate of Hungary is decided while Suleyman watches from a throne that has been placed on higher ground. 'Three or four times the Janissary division rake the infidel with gunfire,' he records in his journal, 'and at length, with the help of majestic God and the Prophet, the people of Islam hurl back the wicked ones, and when they no longer have the strength to throw themselves into a fresh attack, they are put to the sword like dogs.' An expected relief force led by Janos Zapolya, Voivode of Transylvania, fails to show up.

King Louis is dead. He drowned in a puddle under the weight of his own armour. His gold and silver plate, cups and trays, marten furs and German rapiers are stowed in Janissary knapsacks. The ancient Crown of St Stephen, which he showed to his troops that day in the hope that its depictions of saints would inspire them, is nowhere to be seen.

While Suleyman rests in his tent, his men build a pyramid made of heads, which greets him when he emerges refreshed. Then Mohacs is put to the flames. 'Order to kill all peasants in the camp,' he writes. 'The women alone are exempted.' Downstream, the people of Belgrade watch the bodies float by.

~

On, then, to Buda. The Turkish light cavalry, operating in advance of the main force, spares no village. Once they are done with burning and slaughtering, barely a piglet is to be found.

Queen Maria has fled the city, the people on her heels. On September 11, the Sultan occupies Matthias Corvinus's palace. In front of the palace stand two monstrous cannons that were captured by Matthias when he repulsed the Conqueror's assault on Belgrade, in 1456; they are loaded up for repatriation by barge along with bronze sculptures of Hercules, Apollo and Diana. Ibrahim Pasha knows just the spot for them. Two massive bronze lampstands are removed from the Cathedral of the Virgin to be embarked for Aya Sofya. And Matthias's great library is plundered in haphazard fashion of its Florentine manuscripts, the loot including a fine Horace and the *Satires* of Juvenal and Persius.

After throwing a pontoon across the Danube where it divides Buda from Pest, and securing it to the river floor using bells from nearby churches, the Turkish soldiers burn Buda to the ground, all except for the Imperial Palace, in which the Sultan's head rested, and which will remain his in perpetuity.

Trace the squiggle of the Danube north-west from Buda and you come to Vienna.

Refugees are pouring into the city and Maria is expected at any hour. The authorities are frantically building earthworks, the roads in and out are full of soldiers. Hungary's peasantry is reported to be turning Turk in their thousands. Further north the Rhinelanders have a new ditty on the invader. 'In Austria by break of day, Bavaria is just at hand, From there he'll reach another land, Soon to the Rhine perhaps he'll come ...' They sing this and peruse Durer's woodcuts which show Turks slicing up soft Christian children with scimitars. Even Luther, who used to consider the Turks a tool of God directed against his Papist enemies, is reconsidering.

But the road to Vienna is studded with fortresses, each one capable of holding up an advance. The rains have given way to an Indian summer; the flocks are dying of thirst and the soldiers have nothing to eat. Ibrahim is forced to divert southwards to find food. Meanwhile, back home a rising has broken out in the Anatolian province of Cilicia, a case of wolves descending on the fold while the shepherd is away. On 8 October, a resident of Vienna sends his Italian correspondent news of an 'infinite compassion . . . the Turks are returning to Belgrade by land and by sea with the entire army and infinite riches and prisoners, and you never heard of such good fortune in the world.'

From Belgrade the Turks go home. Vienna can wait.

~

'With the help of all-powerful God,' runs Suleyman's letter to Doge Gritti, which is brought to Venice by the Sultan's translator and envoy, Yunus Bey, 'I dispatched our first counsellor and commander, the worthy and valiant Ibrahim Pasha, with the Army of Greece, along with my governors and slaves of the Porte, to Hungary, which forces, having engaged the fortresses of Petrovaradin and Ulach, in few days put all to the sword, while a further fifteen fortresses surrendered and the rest were abandoned by their defenders, who fled . . . and on the first of September, with the help of all-powerful God, defeated [Louis] and cut to pieces his entire army . . . and for peace and friendship I have sent this slave . . . to bring the good news to your most illustrious Signoria that with the help of God the army of the Muslims has triumphed.'

Isn't it curious that the Doge of Venice is being encouraged to rejoice at the victory that the Muslim forces of the Sultan have scored over a Christian King? And yet, while Europe might disapprove of Venice's friendship with the Turk, it is Venetian territory, not that of the Pope, or Charles V, that lies contiguous to the House of Osman and is the most exposed to invasion. If Suleyman wants to, he can fold Venice up and put her in his pocket; her satellites are as rain drops on his handkerchief.

The other notable thing about the letter is its emphasis on Ibrahim.

The truth is that during the Mohacs campaign, the Ottoman

hierarchy showed little trust in the newcomer, and certainly not the Sultan himself, who fretted like an old woman whenever his favourite was in the field, conspiring to keep him away from danger. No, from the moment he set out from Istanbul, the contribution of the worthy and valiant Ibrahim Pasha was limited to a few low-intensity errands, scouting a camp here, mopping up stragglers there, and still he managed to misread the enemy's strength at Petrovaradin. The memory of his men scuttling for the trees at Mohacs remains the sole blemish on an otherwise flawless victory.

As anyone in the Turkish army will attest, the Hungary campaign was masterminded not by Ibrahim but by those experienced and knowledgeable frontier lords, the Governor of Belgrade, Bali Bey, and the Governor of Bosnia, Husrev Bey. Bali and Husrev plotted the army's advance and ensured that the supply train didn't come unstuck while crossing rivers and swamps. Procurement and supplies were entrusted to Iskender Celebi, who, following his success as Ibrahim's counsellor in Egypt, has been named army Quartermaster as well as the Sultan's Chief Treasurer.

But truth is no recommendation for a panegyrist. The chroniclers must depict Ibrahim as the engine of victory and the fount of wisdom. Kemalpashazade knows this. He knew it when he wrote his elegy to Selim, the one about the setting sun. Now he is the Empire's chief religious authority, the Sheikh al-Islam, the official face of the Hanafi school of jurispridence that is the basis of Ottoman law. He stayed in Istanbul to mind the shop in the Sultan's absence and having seen nothing of the campaign is considered the perfect man to set it down.

'His sword akin to the sun penetrates the entire universe,' he writes of the Grand Vizier. 'His wisdom, like the sky, governs the whole world. When he launches himself on the field of battle, he is a young hero full of heart; when he is in Council, he is a greybeard full of prudence; his soul is pure and his heart as limpid as running water; his natural inclination is to beneficence. He is an experienced general and as Vizier he is comparable to Solomon's Vizier Asif. His intelligence, which gets to the heart of everything, inscribes on the face of his luminous spirit concepts so admirable that they are impossible to express. Not since the sun first ascended to its brilliant throne, akin to a monarch resident in the sky amidst legions of stars, has such a man occupied the seat of the Vizier.'

Even by the highest standards of arse-licking, Kemalpashazadeh has his tongue fully inserted.

~

When news of Mohacs reaches Constantinople, Pietro Zen, the new Venetian bailo, has a fountain of wine erected outside his home, also sharing the happy tidings with Ibrahim Pasha's mother. Momentarily forgetting her conversion to Islam, she drops to her knees and appeals to the Virgin for her son's safe return.

The Venetian Senate also sends Marco Minio, Duke of Candia, back to Constantinople to convey the Serenissima's 'singular pleasure' at the Sultan's victory, as well as 'a fuller expression of our feeling . . . that the world may know of our loving disposition towards His Majesty.'

But having rejoiced at Suleyman's triumph, the Venetians are perplexed by his failure to follow it up. The Turks invaded but didn't occupy, the Sultan forgetting to leave behind an army, a governor or a client. Within a year the most promising candidate for the latter role, Janos Zapolya, Voivode of Transylvania and Mohacs no-show, is put to flight by Archduke Ferdinand. Then the Archduke is elected King of Hungary by a Diet of pro-Hapsburg nobles. If this travesty translates into reality and Hungary truly becomes his, the younger Hapsburg will squat on the Sultan's shoulder, able at a time of his choosing to descend on Thrace. All the while, the older brother is planning to strengthen his grip on the Italian peninsula. 'I will go to Italy,' Charles promises, 'and revenge myself on those who have opposed me,' by which he means Venice and the Pope.

Charles has been looking around for new targets ever since

he humiliated Francis in battle in February 1525. Intending to recover France's former possessions in Lombardy, the Most Christian King crossed the Alps but was overcome by an Imperial army at Pavia, in the Duchy of Milan. Francis himself was captured and imprisoned in Madrid, an ordeal that ended on terms detrimental to his exchequer and brought to a close his territorial ambitions in Italy – for the moment, at least.

Pavia has also ended the equilibrium that used to exist between France and the Holy Roman Empire, and from which the Serenissima derived much advantage. No longer can Venice count on Francis to keep Charles off her back. But for Venice herself to fight Charles, with his almost limitless resources, might be terminal for the Republic. She needs to find another big beast to hide behind.

And this is the real reason why Marco Minio, Duke of Candia, is back in Constantinople.

Will you, he asks his friends at the Porte, stand idly by while the Hapsburgs make your Sultan's northern marches their own? It is time to stop Charles before he becomes Sovereign of the World, the name by which the Spaniards and Germans already know him. Surely, as possessor of Constantinople, the Sultan already owns that title?

The Duke receives a sympathetic hearing. The Sultan himself is pained to know that advantages gained through superhuman endeavours – the immense campaign, the astounding victory at Mohacs – have been squandered through absence of mind. All that blood, all that zeal, only for Ferdinand to make off with the throne of Hungary like a thief in the night!

～

Then, in the spring of 1527: the unthinkable.

After laying waste to Montepulciano, Charles V's army of Spaniards, along with their German mercenaries, the Landsknechte, bear down on Rome. Venice makes a show of helping Pope Clement's defence. Doge Gritti's general, the Duke of Urbino, shadows and feints at the Imperialists as they zigzag south. Then he retreats to a safe distance like a lady removing her foot from the path of a carriage or a small dog barking at a big one from behind a wall.

Their entrance to Rome unimpeded, the imperial troops ransack the city from end to end, cutting to pieces friars, priests, nuns and anyone who stands fast in their homes. Invalids lying in the hospital of Santo Spirito are killed, except for a few who manage to flee. The same fate befalls the foundlings of the Pieta, some of whom are thrown out of the windows.

The sack of Rome was to be an Ottoman pleasure. That at least would make sense. Instead the Eternal City is defiled by avowed Christians who poke pikes into pregnant women and make free with the handkerchief of Veronica, which wiped the brow of Christ. The Pope cowers inside Hadrian's cylindrical mausoleum, the Castel Sant'Angelo.

Venice observes. It's a blotch on the Doge's soul and he is barracked by the crowd when the troubles on the mainland lead to food shortages at home. His problems are compounded when a ship bringing grain from Cyprus is hit by a great storm in the Mediterranean and breaks up. There can be no surer sign of the Republic's isolation than the spectacle of hungry Venetians falling on a consignment of emergency wheat that has to be sent from Turkey because none is available from the whole of Christendom.

The Serenissima's pains are only just beginning. With the war for Italy decided in Charles's favour, Francis skulking behind the Alps and the Pope a Hapsburg hostage, the Emperor grows doubly bold. Spain's prelates gather in Valladolid where they vote him 600,000 ducats to prosecute his war for world domination. The Imperialists' every success hastens the day when they will march on the lagoon and smash the Venetians who have always been the promoters of discord among Christian Princes and the abetters of the Turk. This is what Charles's ambassador to the Signoria is urging his master to do from his palazzo on the Grand Canal. The prospect of the Landsknechte shitting Lutheran turds in the Doge's palace is particularly unsettling when one considers Andrea Gritti's ambition to spend a fortune redecorating it.

After the sack of Rome the Doge takes a month to consult. The decision that he and his counsellors reach is that the Turks must launch a new invasion of Hungary. And this time they must do the job properly. They must instal a client acceptable to Venice. It is the only way to check Hapsburg ambitions and save the Republic.

But it is one thing to propose a common policy and another to achieve one. The Turks are relative newcomers to European diplomacy and in recent years many promising initiatives have been immobilised through misunderstanding and pride. The patricians of Venice, meanwhile, include influential men who hate Gritti's policy of appeasement, sympathise with the Emperor and want a united front against the heathen. Both parties will need careful handling.

For so fraught a marriage of opposites to come to fruition, a matchmaker of energy and discretion is required. Someone whom God has placed in a position equidistant to both sides. Someone who stands to gain as much as the parties themselves.

Act Two: The Beyoglu

V

The private apartments of the New Palace shine and scintillate
with an abundance of silver, precious stones and marble. In the
middle of the Sultan's porticoed balcony is a beautiful basin
worked in marble with colonnettes of porphyry and serpentine
and this basin accomodates fish whose darting movements he
enjoys watching.

Whenever the Sultan lifts his gaze and directs it between the
cypress-tips that intrude on his sightline from the garden below,
and across the Golden Horn, which, for comparison's sake, is
about as wide as the River Scheldt at the crossing from Flanders
into Antwerp, he sees another world: the tower which the Genoese built and the Conqueror coppiced because he didn't want
his Christian subjects looking down on him. Vines. Italianate
facades.

Pera.

The year is 1524, two years before Mohacs. The Venetian
merchants of Pera have set up a guild. Much thought went into
the livery which consists of scarlet and purple half-stockings,
green damask jacket and a cloak of green velvet and crimson
satin with gilt buttons. To mark the guild's inception the merchants celebrate mass in St Peter's Church before dining
substantially.

The Florentines of Pera are grateful for the Venetians' hospitality and declare their intention to give their own feast and to

blazes with the plague that's disrupting innocent pleasure. The Florentines come in a group to the house of the bailo, Pietro Bragadin. He came out the year before to replace poor old Andrea Priuli, who died of the plague. The envoy receives an invitation from one of them who is in the guise of the Zobia, the witch who is burned as a way of saying goodbye to winter and welcome to spring. It's a warming gesture to take the edge off the February chill.

Bragadin asks to be excused attendance at the feast. He has an understandable fear of the disease that carried off his predecessor. He also anticipates that the festivities will be long and draining, and, as is well known, sleep is the food of the old. But so charmingly and persistently do the Florentines press him that he feels he has no choice but to accept the invitation. And so, two evenings later, the Venetian population of Pera fetch Bragadin from his house and bring him by torchlight to the party; some 160 people coming along the lanes of Pera, also accompanied by two second-tier personnages from the Porte, Ali Bey and Kourosh Bey, in an excited, chattering cavalcade.

At the door to the house of the Florentine bailo, the Venetians are received by the envoy himself, two counsellors and the master of the guild of Florentine merchants. The sound of music draws the guests into a hall that has been decorated with gilt panels, golden drapery and arrangements of box trees. The painted ceiling depicts both night and day, with the moon and golden stars on one side and the sun on the other, and between them the Pope's coat of arms, five red balls and one blue on a gold shield, tastefully garlanded. The Florentines are naturally proud that Clement, who was born Giulio de Medici, is one of them.

After washing their hands and faces, the guests take their seats according to rank. The bailos and their countrymen, the Turkish lords, the gentlemen from Pera, the Ragusans and the Greeks set to eating venison, capons, peacocks and partridges, cakes, marzipans, tarts, mince pies and comfits. Two hundred women are at the trough in the next room.

After four hours there is no room for another crumb of honeyed *pignocate*. Hands rest on tummies, wind is discreetly expelled and attendants take away the tables. Then some Turkish ladies come forward, young and beautiful, who first play music, then sing, then begin to dance. They toss their heads, cross their arms and move their lips, their hair spreading over their shoulders or tumbling back and forth over their backs and their chests, while the box branches they hold clack like castanets. Taking up some Moorish poles they make wonderful leaps in the Slav style, arching their backs and employing such ravishing gestures as would melt the very marble, and their attire is so tight-fitting that one can easily spot their secret parts. Love flows through the marrow of the watching men.

After the dancing, a quartet sing beautifully about a young lady whose tyrannical parents are ruining her youth and who fears that death will overtake her before she can enjoy the pleasures of the world. The lady in question acts out her anguish before Death enters and cuts her down with his scythe, leaving her slashed and half-naked.

It's hungry work and there is a timely distribution of sugared almonds and Burano biscuits. Then the Portuguese ambassador enters accompanied by a giant gripping two Saracens in chains, gifts from the King of Portugal from the island of Taprobana. The Saracens dance a Moorish dance. And so from song to song and sweetness to sweetness, the evening exhausts itself.

Among the guests is a man whose complexion is dark, his black hair in waves over his ears. He has a thick beard and a single continuous eyebrow. His nose is a touch aquiline, his coal eyes aglow. He is built broader than average but being tall he works out as well-proportioned. He has kept better than many gentlemen of his age. His appetite is notably modest. And after each sip of wine he pours in a little water. That way a single glass lasts the whole evening, turning first mauve, then pink, then clear.

The torchlight glances off the ring on his bow-drawing finger, which is set with a pearl, and off his gold signet, which has been valued at more than 10,000 ducats and is inscribed with lettering in the Arabic script.

His quite outrageous suit of silk and gold hasn't been seen before. It would be surprising if it had, for he is prejudiced against familiar clothes and never wears the same set before and after lunch. After seven or eight outings he invariably tires of the item in question and passes it on to a servant.

The man with the pearl ring is an avid conversationalist, even if he is not scrupulous in following an argument to its conclusion, nor in listening to what the other person has to say. He tells the Florentine bailo that he is planning to stage a performance of Psyche and Cupid at his place on Carnival Sunday. He has high hopes of a reconciliation between the Pope and Luther. The muscatel is rather good if he says so himself. The bulk of the latest shipment went to the Hippodrome, which means it has met royal lips.

He speaks Italian to his host. To Ali Bey and Kourosh Bey, Turkish. To the servant who brings him aniseed to freshen his palate, Greek. His French is excellent but his Latin is rusty. Padua seems like an age ago.

His fellow-guests are openly pleased to see him. They include merchants for whom he arranged credit by putting a word in the right ear and a foundry-master who takes his metal. The servers and stewards smile also. Some of them feel warmly towards him because he helped them when they got into difficulties or were unable to make ends meet. He appreciates being thanked, even if it's just a nosegay or a leaf tied into a parcel with some mulberries inside. He doesn't like his wealth to be taken for granted simply because there is so much of it.

His presence at the bailo's party is a rarity because he doesn't often socialise away from his court of wives, concubines and eunuchs, his teams of children and slaves. He prefers to consult with his friends from business, politics and the arts within his own walls. Home is a palazzo guarded by private security and presented with Venetian overstatement. The top floor has one of the best views of the city: from there he looks down on Aya

Sofya, the memorial mosques dedicated to the Conqueror, Bayezit and Selim, and the three great bodies of water. His stables contain 100 horses of various breeds, 150 camels and 60 mules for the wagons that transport his wheat, cured and salt meats, silk, saffron, parmesan, wine, pelts and furs. The stones, of course, need more secure conveyance.

Shortly before dawn he begs his host's leave. One of his former slaves, whom he manumitted and set up with a wife from his own province, is a groom for the Florentines, and beamingly brings him his horse. He rides home with his Turkish and Christian servants following on foot.

The inscription on his signet ring is grandly self-abasing. It reads *Lovize bin-i mir-i Venedik el-haqir*, which means 'Lovize the worthless, son of the lord of Venice.'

Lovize is how the Muslims pronounce Alvise, the name Andrea Gritti gave him at birth.

~

Forty years before the feast in the vines, in 1484, the Senate decreed that no bastard may occupy high rank even if his father is a patrician. Any possibility that Alvise Gritti, then four years of age, might one day become Captain-General, procurator or Doge was foreclosed. If it was power and prestige the by-blow sought, it wouldn't happen in Venice.

After completing his studies at Padua, he returned to the city of his birth. No one in Constantinople seemed to think the worse of him that a generation ago his Greek mother stood weeping outside the grim fortress in which Andrea Gritti was imprisoned.

He set himself up in Pera, a merchant, a benefactor to the Italian community and a middleman between the Signoria and the Porte. Sound familiar? Yes, he was far from being the first Gritti to make his way on the Bosporus.

Then in 1523 two events outside his control raised him to a position higher than any his forebears ever attained in the city.

On 20 May, in Venice, the forty-one divided to vote. And when the father was elected Doge, the Turks gave the son a new name, *Beyoglu*, meaning Son of the Prince. The Porte realised that having the Doge's son in Constantinople was almost as good as having the Doge himself.

Six weeks later Ibrahim of Parga was named Grand Vizier. Surrounded by Pashas who wished him ill, Ibrahim needed an ally, someone older and better connected to make up for his inexperience. Not a rival who might try and usurp him. A non-Muslim, then. The Beyoglu was already an acquaintance. Why not make him a friend?

～

When Alvise was first admitted to the celestial presence, after handing his sable beret to a flunkey he hurled himself like a madman onto the carpet in the Chamber of Petitions, a sudden move that alarmed the Sultan into thinking he might be attacked. Composing himself, the Lord of Lords ordered the spreadeagled figure to get up. But Alvise was only warming up.

'Highness,' he said in his deep voice, his hands describing expressive circles, 'do not be surprised at this accident of mine, because the sun has so much power and vigour that when a man tries to stare at it his eyes are blinded and it is impossible to look at it, the more so if a man tries to look at the sun at its zenith, when not only is he dazzled but he falls to the ground as if dead.' The Sultan laughed with pleasure, and nowadays when Alvise visits the New Palace he is received by two state messengers who go before him holding his stirrup metal, not because he needs help or might have aggressive designs, but as a show of reverence.

What he desires more than anything is that after he is done living his long and superb life people will say that he ascended by virtue, while others relied on heredity. In that way he is what might be called a meritocrat.

～

He doesn't see commerce as separate from power but as its agent of propulsion, similar to the saltpetre that Ibrahim has licensed him to ship from Alexandria to Venice. (If only Venice were rich in grain and saltpetre she would want for nothing!) Having been barred from senior posts in Venice on account of his birth, in Istanbul it is his religion which excludes him. If he wants a formal position he need only convert. But he never misses Mass. And his life as a businessman outside the pyramid of government rather suits him.

Not just any businessman. The Sultan cannot make cannons without his tin. The Grand Vizier takes only his wine. Through a Venetian agent, the jewel merchant Vincenzo Levriero, he sends Arab purebreds to the Gonzaga stables in Mantua. When Vincenzo brings a jewel-inlaid gold box from Venice, Alvise finds a buyer for it at court. No one sees the angles quite like the Beyoglu. And when a visiting foreigner declares that Alvise is number three in the Empire, and that only the Sultan and the Grand Vizier are above him, he simply smiles.

He has many ears. One facing the Porte, another the Signoria, others cocked to Buda, Vienna, Transylvania. He is Argus, the man with one hundred eyes. Or a dozen mouths, communicating secretly with his father, informing the Grand Vizier of imperial troop movements, placing an order for a Nishapur turquoise. His borrowed tongue is Massimo Leopardi, a connoisseur of the Slav languages who is tutoring him on the extractive industries of Hungary. When the Sultan installs Janos Zapolya as King there, as he surely will, the Fuggers of Augsburg, Ferdinand's agents in the mining regions, will be expelled and the mines will be up for grabs. It was the Fuggers who financed Charles V's election back in '20, so that bit of business will also be a pleasure.

His secretariat is made up of every kind of chancer, pro- and anti-reform, heretical, humanist and crypto-Lutheran. They come at his invitation, all expenses paid. His secretary was born Catholic and Venetian and is now Muslim and Ottoman. His name is Muhammad. A frequent guest at the palazzo in the vines is the serial imposter and fugitive from justice Isidorus of Giliaco, who forged the seal of Archduke Ferdinand, sells property that isn't his and will be executed if he sets foot on Venetian soil. The Beyoglu's pen-pal Pietro Aretino, sinner and author of the *Last Will and Testament of Hanno the Elephant*, a satire of Pope Leo and his cardinals, promises to visit soon.

And while some of these incomers confess to a certain trepidation before stepping onto heathen shores, in the event they find the saddle of Pera more congenial than either Madrid or Vienna with their Catholic astringencies. Indeed, they are charmed, positively charmed by the diversity of its peoples, from Ragusans to Moors, from Tatars to Poles. And the place is crawling with Jews who were ejected from Spain by Charles V's grandparents, Ferdinand and Isabella, in 1492, speak better Castilian than one hears in Valladolid and are engaged in every kind of craft, profession and trade.

A Christian in Pera influencing the Sublime Porte calls to mind the image of a dog being wagged by its tail. When the dog in question is the Ottoman State, to the officers of that State there is something distasteful about the image. It would be wrong to assume that Alvise has a devoted following among the earnest converts who populate the Ottoman bureaucracy – this unrepentant Christian who is richer and more influential than they are. But there is nothing they can do because he is protected by the man who has been chosen by God to rule the earth, and the man who is helping him do it.

Alvise is the Empire's top dealer in gems, and every so often the Sultan and the Grand Vizier pay a nocturnal visit to the secret store he keeps in his palace. Suleyman has been interested in *objets de luxe* ever since Constantine the Greek taught him to work gold in Trabzon, while Ibrahim's collection, featuring rubies, pearls, diamonds, emeralds, turquoises and jewelled rings, is said to surpass that of the Sultan himself. The three men come together like adepts in the Beyoglu's candle-lit grotto. There's no bolder statement than a stone that has been sweated from a distant place. Power gleams from a cabochon emerald in Alvise's palm.

Some of the rocks are sourced by his younger brother, Lorenzo, a prior in Venice, who has connections with the Antwerp dealers. They arrive in Constantinople in the luggage of Zorzo Gritti, the youngest of the three. Jewels are in the transferable-but-speculative asset class. The Grittis might pay 12,000 ducats for a really sensational pair of rubies, but prices soften if a fresh consignment arrives from the East or a mine is discovered in Macedonia. It takes taste, timing and nerve to be a success in the international gem market.

~

When Pietro Zen arrives in Constantinople to replace Pietro Bragadin he immediately gets into a spat. Bragadin has an interest in the convoys that sail to and from Constantinople and he isn't keen on being distanced from his source of income. Where, he asks, is the Doge's letter instructing him to leave his post? And what about his going-away present? But Zen is already telling the Porte that Bragadin should no longer be treated as bailo because he, Zen, is bailo. This only makes the incumbent madder.

Enter the Beyoglu. With Alvise acting as honest broker, the parties fix a severance payment of 500 ducats, but at the last minute, as Bragadin is preparing to board ship, Zen decides that the sum is too much. More tergiversation, more uses for Alvise. In the event, 250 ducats passes hands and Bragadin sails for home where he entertains the Senate by making fun of Zen whom the Sultan is refusing to see because he isn't a bailo, or even an orator, but a mere vice-bailo, one who foolishly longs for his daughter to marry Giacomo Corner while this same Giacomo has scarcely 900 ducats to his name; not that he, Bragadin, has need of money, thank God; and the Senators fall about laughing before Bragadin's voice gives out at 3 a.m. and everyone goes home.

~

After Mohacs the tax take is off the scale and there is money for extra cutters, polishers, chasers and gilders, who arrive from

Bosnia, Moscow and Isfahan to join the Turks, Greeks, Armenians and Jews already at work in the palace workshops. The Sultan endows a manufactory for goldsmiths, equipping it with a fountain, mosque, bath and workshops arranged around a pleasant courtyard.

The Sultan's craftsmen make zinc jugs, pen-boxes of rock crystal and gold, jade boxes, mother-of-pearl plaques, saddles, head-collars, harnesses, aigrettes for the Sultan's turban, fastenings, ivory belts with links like squares on a chessboard, mirrors and tankards. They smother these objects in emeralds, rubies and turquoises and there are so many of them, of such fine quality, that people who see them think they are in heaven.

The New Palace is getting an upgrade. The Second Courtyard is an orchestra of carving, nicking, splitting and whetting as the workmen expand and embellish the Council Hall, grow the Treasury from a modest affair, deficient to the sovereign's glance, to an eight-domed Ala'ud-din's den. A new Chamber of Petitions is going up in the Third Courtyard, built of marble and set in a portico, also of marble. Invoices come in for cinnabar pigment and ostrich-egg shells.

One day the Sultan orders the bathhouse which Mustafa Pasha recently built at a cost of seven thousand ducats to be destroyed. Mustafa Pasha's wife is a sister of the Sultan who used to be married to Bostanci Pasha. Sultan Selim beheaded Bostanci after an unsatisfactory showing against Iran. Fearing that the destruction of his bathhouse means that he has angered Suleyman in some way, and that a fate similar to that of Bostanci Pasha awaits him, Mustafa sends his wife to ascertain her brother's intentions. She returns smiling; your bonce is safe. The bathhouse was standing in the way of the upgrade and the Sultan will give compensation for the wasted expense. Provided it doesn't slip his mind, of course. What's seven thousand to a man whose income is seven million?

During his trip to Constantinople to encourage the Turks to go to war, the Duke of Candia has occasion to enter the New Palace. He considers it to be much improved since his last visit.

The walls of the new buildings are spangled with azure and gold, the furnishings covered in gold brocade and pearls. The fireplace in the Chamber of Petitions boasts a hood of solid silver encrusted with pearls, rubies and emeralds. At the end of his garden the Sultan has installed a grotto covered with strips of gold and silver. The passage that leads from his apartments to the Tower of Justice isn't called the Golden Road for nothing. And his private apartments are said to shine and scintillate with an abundance of silver and precious stones.

Every glint, every wink, means more riches for Alvise Gritti.

~

Although Pietro Zen's geographical range never rivalled that of his father, the celebrated Caterino, who led an embassy to the then ruler of Iran, Uzun Hasan (who somewhat unexpectedly went on to marry Caterino's sister-in-law), the new bailo is weary after a career of travel. When news arrives in Istanbul of his cousin's death back home, Pietro feels every day of his 69 years. But if he goes back to Venice and leaves behind his friend Alvise, he will be leaving half of himself. So when he writes to His Serenity asking to be relieved of his post, he suggests that the Beyoglu accompany him. This is a neat hook on which to catch the Doge's attention. It is well known that Andrea Gritti longs to be reunited with the son he hasn't seen in a quarter of a century.

But Zen has no joy when he broaches the idea with the Beyoglu himself. And one can see why. To go back to the lagoon and accept the kind of ecclesiastical sinecure that keeps his brother Lorenzo happy, or to scurry around being useful like Zorzo . . . such activities would scarcely befit the third personnage of the Ottoman Empire, would they? And when His Serenity – may God postpone the day – relocates to the sepulchre that Jacopo Sansovino is designing for him at San Francesco della Vigna, what then for the man who will simply be the bastard son of a dead Doge?

'Noble sir,' Alvise explains to his friend, 'you have now seen how I am accustomed to live here and have seen my affairs, so it is not necessary for me to speak of them – and if I should go to Venice, abandoning these matters I have at hand, where is my sustenance? Fortune doesn't always smile, and when opportunities are lacking I would be very dissatisfied. Then the customs of that city are such that one is required to live according to the standards of others, and if not, one is disdained. I find myself in great anguish because I wish to satisfy His Serenity the Doge, who loves and wants me, and thus I live in the gravest discontent.'

It's not common, even in this age of declining respect for authority, for a son to defy the fond wishes of his father. But the case of Andrea and Alvise Gritti has characteristics that are shared with no other. The trouble in this relationship is Venice itself. Andrea Gritti is no bigger than Venice and it is to Venice that he has returned. Alvise's illegitimate birth, on the other hand, has obliged him to consider himself more globally, to be a patrician of the world. The Beyoglu is a proud man and he is reluctant to set foot in a Republic that while needing his services refuses to recognise him. Nothing pleases him more than when his daughter Marietta is married to Vincenzo Cicogna, of *the* Cicognas, an alliance that stitches her back into the patrician fabric from which her father was torn. But a desire for acceptance and a desire for revenge are not necessarily strangers. How satisfying it would be to outgrow the homeland that spurned him all those years ago!

~

A Pole of active mind, as deft with his quill as he is with his sword, Jerome Laski, Palatine of Sieradz, is one of those international men of negotiation who trickle along the grooves of Europe like water in a clepsydra. Jerome was recently in France to win the Most Christian King's help for Janos Zapolya. Since he bought his freedom from Madrid, Francis has been trying to come up with new ways of needling Charles without getting into another pitched battle he might lose. Politics by proxy has much to commend it. Charmed by Jerome, Francis gives 5,000 in gold with a promise of 20,000 to come.

But in September 1527, Archduke Ferdinand and his army dispossess Janos of most of Hungary, including Buda, and drive him back to Transylvania. Around the same time, the Venetians, Janos and Jerome come to the view that a second Turkish invasion is the only solution to Ferdinand's aggression. Thus, in December Jerome arrives in Istanbul, charged with winning the Sultan's support for such a venture.

But it takes two to truce. In Turkish eyes the Diet of Hungarian nobles that acclaimed Janos as King was no more legitimate than the rival Diet that elected Ferdinand. Neither met with the permission of the occupying power. Janos is an upstart who lacks the basic good manners to send the Sultan regular pouches of money. And with his expulsion from central Hungary into the semi-detached principality of Transylvania, Janos is reduced to the status of a failed usurper lying low. It's not an encouraging position from which to demand an alliance.

Not just an alliance, but territory. After their withdrawal in '26, the Turks held onto Syrmia. This province runs from the southern bank of the Danube to the northern bank of the Sava and extends as the confluence of the two rivers at Belgrade. Syrmia is well known for its vines and it is painful to the friars and squires that their refreshments are in Ottoman hands.

It costs Suleyman 56,000 ducats a month to hold Syrmia down. Janos would be doing him a favour if he relieved him of it. But mosques have been built in the province and the doctors of the law would judge harshly any Sultan who abandons them.

What can Jerome offer? He can offer a negative. Janos is not Ferdinand. And he can offer a Hungarian buffer between the Sultan and the Archduke. An opportunity for the Turk to ring-fence Austria and turn eastwards to the perennial problem of Iran and the Shah's trouble-making in Ottoman territory. Jerome Laski wants an accord wrapped up before Ferdinand hears what is going on and sends spoilers.

But Mustafa Pasha is testy when he receives the Pole on 23

December. 'So,' he says, 'you have come empty-handed to ask not our friendship but our help. Tell me: how did your master dare to enter Buda, a place trampled by my master's horse, and the royal palace, which he only left intact to await his return? You come on behalf of one of the Sultan's slaves and yet you bring no tribute. Are you not aware that our lord, as unique as the sun, rules the sky and the earth?'

It is not the value of the gifts that is important, Mustafa explains. 'If you want honour, that is to see our master and to kiss his hand, you ought to bring gifts; but your master doesn't act like a king, because he is not in fact a king.' And waving him away Mustafa warns, 'A man learns most about himself in adversity.'

Christmas Day is a chance for Jerome to think on these words. In the stableyard the guards rough him up a bit. The next day he is transferred to another house with a state messenger stationed outside his room, barring entry to all, and Jerome is forced to pay for his food and his horses' fodder as if he was a common wayfarer and not the honoured representative of a Christian monarch.

He would receive better treatment if he accepted the Grand Turk's demands, but for Janos to become Suleyman's formal tributary would arouse the disgust of the other Christian princes. Even the French would feel obliged to withdraw their support. Francis takes very seriously his title of Most Christian King, which derives from the holy oil, the chrism, with which he was anointed at his coronation, and which, after being borne to earth by a heavenly dove, has been used ever since to anoint his predecessors as King of France.

On Boxing Day the door of Jerome's cell opens and in comes a splendid specimen. On his arrival in Constantinople, the Pole managed to send a letter to the son of the Venetian Doge. Disregarding the quartan fever that has been laying him low, Alvise has bestirred himself from the palazzo in Pera, carrying coins that are now jingling in the pockets of Jerome's guards.

The Beyoglu begins the interview by boasting about the

influence he enjoys over the Ottoman government. It was he, he says, who dissuaded the Sultan from invading Hungary again last summer and teaching Janos a lesson. He gives some blunt advice: don't think about a peace with the Turk without tribute. And don't think about getting Syrmia back. But his tone is consoling.

'My master has understood that you are doing business here,' Jerome replies cautiously, 'and that you have influence with the Pasha: and he asks that you might advise me in the areas in which I am not experienced.' Specifically there is the matter of the 25,000 ducats that Francis has promised Janos. Will the Turks cooperate in making sure this money doesn't get lost en route through the Balkans and actually reaches him?

Jerome is barely thirty years of age; Alvise is two decades his senior. But the Pole is experienced enough to understand what the silence of the man opposite means. 'As soon as there appears a possibility of achieving my objective,' Jerome goes on smoothly, 'I will have another talk with you about the reward you are to receive for your good services.' The best diplomats are unafraid to be bold. 'Explore the minds of men for me and submit your findings to me; if you do not get permission to come and see me, you should write.'

The following day, Jerome receives a note that Alvise has sealed using his thumb, which confers more anonymity than a signet. The note tells Jerome that he should visit Ibrahim Pasha tomorrow but if he comes without tribute he may be mistreated and will certainly not be admitted to see the Sultan. When speaking to the Pasha he should press his case without fear. 'I dare not write more.'

～

When Jerome is admitted to Ibrahim's presence, power attained meets power desired. By whichever measure you employ, revenue, territory or political influence, the Ottoman Empire is a sow next to the Hungarian flea. Every word the Grand Vizier utters is intended to emphasise the disparity between the two.

'We killed King Louis. We took his castle and ate and slept there. His kingdom is ours. It is folly to imagine that a crown makes a king. It isn't gold or precious stones that allow a man to reign. It is iron. The sword teaches obedience. What has been won by the sword must be protected by the sword. We know that Hungary has exhausted its money and resources, that your master recognises the Sultan as his lord and implores him to lend his help. Were it not for Doge Gritti and his son we would by now have destroyed the power of both Ferdinand and your master; for war between two enemies who destroy each other is always favourable for the third who remains. What would have happened if I had marched against Ferdinand with the Janissaries and the Army of Thrace and Ayas Pasha had fallen on your master? We have stayed tranquil all summer at the entreaty of our friends the Venetians; but we are very much awake.'

And the Frank begs Jerome's pardon for not speaking in the Turkish manner, that is, briefly, for as is well known the Turks speak little and act much.

After Ibrahim's speech Jerome must restore his master's dignity. Is that so hard? Hungarian kings have received tribute from Venice, subjugated Bohemia, Austria and other provinces. Only fifty years ago Matthias Corvinus defeated the Turks and the Germans and enlarged his kingdom at their expense. Nor does Jerome feel any personal sense of inadequacy. He isn't the first Laski to achieve prominence. Son of an ancient and noble family, nephew of the great Jan Laski, Chancellor of Poland, he didn't emerge last autumn from behind a cabbage plant. Unlike others he could mention.

Laski lays out some of Hungary's achievements and chides Ibrahim for conduct unworthy of a great empire. 'If you had wanted to have Buda you ought not to have left it in the way you did leave it. By burning it, by carrying everything off from there, by leaving nothing there, by not fortifying the garrisons, by not rebuilding what had been destroyed, and by suddenly pulling back; who would not say that you did this out of fear? In this kind of occupation, nothing great has been achieved. The fact is that Buda was captured easily; nothing would be more disgraceful than if on account of this the Kings of Hungary were obliged to recognise your Emperor.'

Time now for a dig at the hospitality he has received. 'You assign as many guards to me as to one who was planning to flee. I have not come here in order to flee, I have not come to investigate anything. I have come, as I said, in the hope that I might be welcome.'

It's a spirited conversation between two people who understand how the world works, using words designed not so much to sting one's opponent but stir him from his complacency and set him up for a talk about chattels and cash.

~

Between spasms of quartan fever the Beyoglu spends the next few weeks going between Ibrahim and Jerome, carrying proposals and counter-proposals, with tweaks and amendments of his own devising. One day he invites Jerome for lunch at the shipyard on the Horn where he is sometimes to be found conducting his business. And Jerome looks in on Mustafa Pasha, mentioning that he, Mustafa, was less than welcoming the last time they met, but there's no hard feelings and God willing the gout will pass. They talk of the joint military campaign they will undertake as soon as Alvise has guided discussion of the outstanding issues to a successful conclusion.

Under the treaty that eventually emerges from the Beyoglu's efforts, Syrmia is returned to Hungary. Each year an ambassador will come to the Porte from Janos carrying presents worth 10,000 florins. This is not a tribute. It is a gesture of goodwill from one monarch to another. The Turks pledge fifty cannons, fifty quintals of powder and 8,000 cavalry for Janos's war effort. 'I accept with pleasure the devotion of your master,' the Sultan tells Jerome when he receives him. 'Not only do I cede him Hungary, but also I will protect him so effectively against Ferdinand of Austria that he will be able to sleep on both ears.'

Jerome leaves Istanbul on 29 February 1528, taking with him a treaty of accord, a squadron of cavalry and a wardrobe of turbans and caftans. He has become quite Turkish in his habits. Before his departure, he names Alvise as Janos's official representative at the Porte. The Beyoglu is also promised the bishopric of Eger, which was established by St Stephen himself, as soon as the invasion has taken place. When Jerome gets back to Transylvania, in recognition of sterling service, he is made Count of Szepes and awarded Kesmark Castle. Not that King Janos currently has control of either place. They will need to be prised from Ferdinand's forces.

~

When he hears that his enemies have come to an accord in Constantinople, Archduke Ferdinand sends two ambassadors, Janos Habardanecz and Sigmund Weichselberger, to undo the damage and negotiate a three-year truce with the Sultan. But their manners lack finesse. They demand that the Sultan recognise Ferdinand as King of Hungary and restore Belgrade and other fortresses taken in the campaign of 1521, and Ibrahim asks why the Governor of Vienna doesn't ask for Istanbul while he's at it, before concluding the interview with the warning, 'We will deal with Ferdinand in Germany.'

Habardanecz has the grating habit of referring to his master as 'all-powerful'. How does your master have the pride and audacity to call himself 'all-powerful', Ibrahim retorts, here at the seat of the Sultan, under whose protection Christian princes gather? Further discussion thus demonstrated to be impossible, Alvise Gritti devises a way out of the impasse and declares that Habardanecz and Weichselberger are spies. During their incarceration they hear Istanbul erupt in joy at the news of Charles V's death. This turns out to be false.

After nine months the joke wears off and the pair are admitted to the Sultan for dismissal. They get 500 ducats apiece and the Sultan says, 'Your master has yet to enjoy the amicable relations of a neighbour with us, but soon he will. You can tell him that I will come to find him with all my forces and that I will give him exactly what he wants. So tell him to prepare well for our visit.'

VI

Four years after he was elected, Doge Andrea Gritti is the embodiment of Venice. The ceremonials of the Serenissima have never been grander. The Gritti coat of arms has made its way even onto the surface of a festive dessert. On Ascension Day, His Serenity weds the waves in a plush new barge slathered in gold.

He still holds to the conviction that no cause is more sacred than patriotic self-interest. And whatever indignities were heaped on him following the sack of Rome, even his critics concede that the Holy City isn't Venice's main concern and that he may have been right to save the Duke of Urbino's army for another day.

The Cunctator continues to strive not for victory on the battlefield but for peace and a favourable balance of payments. A peace that will allow Venetian convoys to sail unmolested in the Mediterranean and the Black Sea, and whose dividend enables the Republic to build and improve. Planners are examining designs for a stone bridge to replace the wooden one that burned down at the Rialto. In the Piazza plans are germinating for a vast arcaded building that will run the length of its northern axis and cause anyone who sees it to gasp and yawn at once. Forests are being planted on the mainland to stop the lagoon silting up.

Aspects of Gritti's personal conduct continue to give cause

for concern. The boundary between his financial affairs and those of the Republic is a matter of indifference to him. He seems unfamiliar with his oath of office, which pledges him to meet foreign diplomats only in the presence of his counsellors. He generally holds these meetings one-on-one. Entitlement and process seldom see eye to eye.

His practice of receiving buffoons sits uneasily with the solemnity of his office, and he allows unusual liberties to an old crone who has been in his service for many years. With this servant, who is called Marta, he fights a constant war over the garlic and sweet onions he loves to eat after supper. If she catches him biting into a clove she simply snatches it out of his hand.

His vigour is undiminished. It suffices for a woman to be moderately attractive for His Serenity to make an approach, offering money if necessary, presumably the more so on account of the garlic and onions. Far from showing contrition for the indiscretions of his youth, he's gathered the lesser bastards to his side: holy Lorenzo, who lives with him at the Palace when he's not taking care of the Priory, and Zorzo, purveyor of objects with a market value, such as Flanders cloth, or strategic value, like Alvise's informative letters. Zorzo also keeps the Doge informed about the Beyoglu's elevated status, his friendship with Ibrahim Pasha, his fine house, etcetera.

Diplomacy is like ducks and drakes. You skim your stone without being sure it will reach the other side. One that didn't carry was the envoy King Francis dispatched to the Grand Turk. He never reached his destination and the ruby in his luggage somehow ended up on Ibrahim Pasha's finger.

With all these vagaries in mind, it is undeniably useful to have an informant on the ground, one who won't get murdered or caught in a landslide whilst travelling along some Balkan road, and whose news keeps on coming regardless of the rotation of bailos, vice-bailos and orators. Not that it would be fair to Alvise to consider him solely an information-gatherer. He is more like a wheel on the Sultan's cannon, a precious wheel owned by Venice. They have so much to discuss, father and son.

The Doge's family feeling is an axiom. His first son, Francesco, whose birth was the death of poor Benedetta, himself died young. He was already on the Senate's maritime committee. After Francesco's death Andrea transferred his affections to Francesco's daughter, Viena, and took a close interest in her upbringing. Viena's wedding to the Pisani boy lasted ten days. When it was time for the bride to go to her new home she threw herself at the Doge's feet and he wept from within his fountain of gold brocade. Anyone who is anyone attended the nuptials: the widow of the late Vincenzo Gritti (looking very much the poor relation); gazillions of Vendramins and Corners. The lone absentee was Alvise, the closest of all the Doge's sons to him in ambition, temperament and aptitude.

The Doge does not hide his partiality for Alvise. One day he rebukes a member of the Collegio for referring to Lorenzo with a flurry of honorifics, noting that such titles are appropriate to someone of greater distinction. Ah! another of the city fathers cuts in gleefully, but you are happy for members of the patriciate to call your other son, the one in Constantinople, 'Most Illustrious' and 'Most Serene'. Isn't it odd that His Serenity wants one son born out of wedlock to be handled with kid gloves and not the other?

Andrea merely smiles and points out that the Beyoglu should not receive less respect in Venice than he does in Istanbul. A case of reflected glory, similar to that of the Senator's own wife, the daughter of a concubine, who is called 'Magnificent' in deference to her husband's position.

~

When the Doge is informed about the successful conclusion of Jerome Laski's mission to Constantinople and the imminence of a Turkish invasion of Hungary, he writes to Alvise expressing his satisfaction at the way things have gone. That his son was able to influence the negotiations in the Republic's favour gives him a keen sense of satisfaction. But he is adamant that any Venetian involvement in the forthcoming campaign must remain a secret. He instructs Alvise to avoid signing his name whenever he writes to King Janos. It goes without saying that the Beyoglu should resist the temptation to join the Turkish army on the push north.

So it comes as an unpleasant surprise to His Serenity to learn that Alvise will not only take charge of provisioning Suleyman's forces during the forthcoming campaign, but will also have fighting men under his command. The participation of the Doge's own son in an Ottoman war against Ferdinand is a scandal that can only strengthen the desire of both Hapsburg brothers, and particularly of Charles, to annihilate Venice. The political crisis is all the more upsetting for the personal humiliation it entails. Doge Gritti can no longer move the world with a flick of his mane. His son has embarrassed him in the most public way possible.

The news, the Doge writes wearily to Alvise, 'has given incredible pain and anxiety to our person, for, being elevated to this rank by the grace of God, we know we are surrounded on all sides by hatred ... everyone attributes this venture to us alone and maligns our honour and person.' If, however, Alvise docs the right thing and desists from his reckless plan, his father promises to reward him with either a knighthood or an abbacy worth 1,000 ducats a year. He can take his pick.

Finally, the Doge lowers himself to beg. 'We wish to see you once more in our life.'

Andrea Gritti does not understand that he is dealing with someone whose ring finger is worth 10,000 ducats. There is a gap between the son the father remembers and the man the son has become. A knighthood or an abbacy – not even both at once! – cannot be considered a serious inducement for someone whose eyes have been opened to vistas of limitless wealth and influence.

~

Before giving the order to march Suleyman names Ibrahim Pasha Commander-in-Chief for the campaign. The Sultan's subjects are to obey his every word and thought as if they are orders coming from Suleyman's own mouth which causes pearls to rain from the sky.

Along with the Sultan he possesses full rights over the life and death of any subject. He may name, dismiss or execute any of the ministers and other agents of the sovereign's will. He proclaims and implements laws. He is the supreme chief of justice, albeit with the assistance of the doctors of the law. He represents the King in all his dignity and potency not only within the Empire's borders but also in its dealings with foreign states. At one stroke, the Sultan has solved the problem of the division of powers that so perplexed Ibrahim at the beginning of his vizierate.

'Should anyone disobey the order of my Grand Vizier and Commander-in-Chief,' the Sultan proclaims, 'those responsible, no matter how numerous they may be, will be duly punished.' And appended to the letter are a number of helpful sayings in Arabic. They include, 'When God wishes the best for a King, he gives him a loyal minister who reminds the King of his duties when he forgets them, and helps him when he fulfils them.' And, 'We have raised some by degrees to be above others.'

~

In May 1529 the army goes north. The rain is never-ending and men and beasts of burden are washed away or struck dead by lightning. From Philippopolis in Thrace to Osijek in Croatia, a distance of 600 miles, the rivers are in revolt. The plague is also rippling through the ranks. Janos Zapolya, who is marching to join the Turks from Transylvania, orders all Hungarians to be prepared to provide food to the invaders. The Sultan gives the Beyoglu 30,000 ducats towards the purchase of provisions.

On the banks of the Drava, Ibrahim orders the marshes filled with faggots. A bridge is thrown across the faggots but the pack animals rush onto it and fall into the marsh and drown. Six more days are needed to get the army to the other side, harried by the infidels. His men safely across, the Sultan orders the bridge to be destroyed, just as he did three years ago.

In the meantime, there is news from the world of diplomacy.

Margaret of Austria, Charles's aunt, and Louise of Savoy, Francis's mother, have been negotiating on behalf of their quarrelsome charges. The result of their discussions is a treaty that fixes the tear that has been running through Europe and confirms Charles as master of Italy. The Republic of Venice is the only major European power to be excluded from this 'ladies' peace', which involves not only Francis, Charles and Ferdinand, but also Henry of England and the Pope. Charles is in Italy with a large army with which, among other measures to 'pacify' the peninsula, he intends to punish the Venetian Republic, that 'head of the serpent.' In addition to Venice's dishonourable alliance with the Turks, the Republic has become a refuge for Lutherans and other heretics whom the Doge refuses to extradite, intoning piously, 'Our State and Dominion are free.' Gritti's Venice is not simply an affront to the Empire. It is an affront to Christ.

From a Venetian point of view it is now doubly imperative that the Hapsburgs be distracted from their designs on Venice, an objective best achieved by tying them down elsewhere. The Ottoman advance mustn't stop at Hungary but must strike deep into Ferdinand's home territory, forcing him to sue for peace. For all the distress that Alvise has caused him, old Doge Gritti recognises that there are certain advantages to having his son in the retinue of the Ottoman Commander-in-Chief. Now is not the time to dwell on questions of filial insubordination. The Senate instructs Alvise to 'urge his Excellency the Pasha to advance into Austria'.

As Voivode of Transylvania, Janos Zapolya's forces were too late to save King Louis at Mohacs. Now that he is a claimant to the throne of Hungary, he is more punctual in answering the summons of his new master to the same place. On 19 August, between two high walls formed of Janissaries, Janos and his ambassador Jerome Laski are funnelled into the Sultan's tent on the Mohacs plain. Suleyman accepts the allegiance of his new vassal.

Then the Turks march northwards and lay siege to Buda, which falls easily. Alvise Gritti and some soldiers are left in the city to keep an eye on King Janos, while the great army advances into Austria. By late September, Suleyman is under the walls of Vienna. He intends to breakfast in the city's great cathedral at Michaelmas.

~

Ferdinand has assigned the defence of Vienna to Nicholas von Salm, a veteran of the siege of Rhodes who also distinguished himself in the Battle of Pavia. Von Salm has razed the houses outside the walls in order to clear fields of fire, also bricking up the city's gates, except one, the Salz Gate, facing the Danube. When the fighting starts, his arquebusiers prove as lethally effective from the ramparts of Vienna as they were in the parkland outside Pavia. And the Turks possess no heavy artillery, having been forced to abandon their big cannons further south in waterlogged Hungary. Mining operations are the only way in.

Repeatedly the Sipahis and Janissaries throw themselves at those stretches of wall which the Turkish sappers have undermined, swinging their maces and axes, and each time they are met by von Salm himself, who, at 70, shows a relish for the fight that one would associate with a man half his age. At unexpected moments the defenders sally forth from the Salz Gate, slay a few of the enemy and slip back in again. Four German soldiers are quartered after taking Turkish bribes to sabotage the defence; their limbs are exhibited from the walls. And gradually the Turks' ardour cools.

As summer becomes autumn, provisions run down. The light tents which the Turks have brought from Istanbul are inadequate against the biting frosts. Michaelmas goes by and the Sultan receives a message from the defenders to say that his breakfast has gone cold. He will have to make do with gruel from the Austrian guns. And Ferdinand is on his way from Prague to relieve the city.

On October 15 Suleyman orders a final assault. Exceptionally for an Ottoman army, some of his men stay rooted like horses beyond the limits of their endurance and have to be whipped into unwilling motion. After the attack is repulsed there is nothing to do but save face. Ibrahim writes to assure the defenders that it was never the Turks' intention to take Vienna, but rather to 'fight your Archduke; that is what has made us waste so many days here, without being able to reach him.' On 16 October the Turks turn for home and the defenders, for lack of pay, loot the city they have spent the past three weeks defending.

What the campaign fails to provide in glory, the Austro-Hungarian marches make up for in flesh and lucre. Of those towns and villages that are visited by the Sultan's irregular cavalry on their way south, Gritti informs the Signoria, 'neither a cock nor a hen sings there, nor is a single house intact, nor even a tree.'

When Suleyman reaches Buda, King Janos comes out of the city to congratulate him on expelling Ferdinand from Hungary.

No one mentions Vienna.

～

In his previous guise, Janos Zapolya was Hungary's second most powerful man. Under his Voivodeship, Transylvania enjoyed much autonomy and its Magyar, Saxon, Szekler and Vlach or Romanian populations were competently ruled. Janos was considered a potential monarch long before he was propelled to the throne by the disaster of Mohacs, the death of Louis and the Sultan's demand for a Hungarian proxy. But real power will be less easy to acquire, let alone exercise, than it was in Transylvania.

It's not just a question of subduing the nobles who voted for Ferdinand and continue to run their estates as Hapsburg satellites. Janos owes his throne to the enemy of his people and from the day he kisses the hand of the Grand Turk he is tainted in their eyes. There is no hiding the reality that the cavalry maniple left by Suleyman in Buda and the well-armed craft that patrol the Danube, flying a crescent flag, are instruments of subjugation. And yet Janos wouldn't forego the Turkish presence even if he had the chance, for he has no money for a cavalry or a flotilla of his own. Hungary's wealth is underground and its biggest concentrations are found in northern pockets of the country, known as 'Royal Hungary', that are loyal to the Hapsburg crown. And Ferdinand, made bold by Vienna's deliverance, is plotting to come south again and recapture the rest of the country.

The borders that divide Janos's territories from those of Ferdinand are far from static and the Beyoglu is perversely comfortable working where the two sides rub, a place where people are sometimes Hapsburg and sometimes Ottoman, a bit Christian and a bit Muslim and perhaps a bit Jew. In these fickle borderlands, cooperation can usually be bought or coerced.

It was Alvise Gritti who put Janos on the throne and it is Alvise Gritti who is asked by the Sultan to deliver the Crown of St Stephen, which recently came to light after being mysteriously lost at Mohacs, to the new King. After receiving this sacred object, the new King confirms the kingmaker as Bishop of Eger. The bishopric will bring in 36,000 ducats a year. Janos also awards Gritti the Dalmatian towns of Clissa, Segna and Poglizza, not that they are yet his to award. Somehow they will need to be taken from the pro-Hapsburg forces that are currently in possession of them.

'Besides the harbour of Clissa being the best in the world,' reports one of Charles's diplomats, 'it is only 100 miles from [the Italian port of] Ancona, and if the Turk only continues his successes, it is to be feared that he will soon take possession of the two fortified towns which the Venetians have on the [Adriatic] coast. There is still another circumstance which makes the advance of the Turks on that coast more formidable than ever; instead of attacking with fury and massacring the inhabitants, as is their general habit, nowadays they proceed slowly, with greater caution, promising people liberty of religion, privileges, franchises, and all manner of good treatment, which would show that they intend perpetuating their dominion in those parts.'

In the autumn of 1529, Janos names Alvise High Treasurer and Councillor of the King of Hungary. He does this after receiving the gracious permission of the Sultan to keep the Venetian in his employ. The Beyoglu immediately sends his men to relieve the Fuggers of their concessions in the north of the country, including the mines at Besztercebanya, which are rich in copper and silver. Alvise also sends his men to take over the salt mines of Transylvania. One can quite imagine the Doge seasoning his bigoli, and the Sultan his pilaf, with rock salt extracted by their shared servant the Beyoglu!

At the cost of the father's disquiet, the son has become number two in Buda, in addition to being number three in Istanbul. He's considered the leading candidate for the throne of Naples when the Sultan invades Italy, which is only a matter of time. He has a canny way of making himself indispensable to whichever sector of the economy he favours with his attention. As the Fuggers' chief agent in Hungary writes to his employers in Augsberg, 'Nothing can be done without him.'

~

Depending on who he is speaking to, the Beyoglu describes himself as a servant of the Sultan or a footsoldier of the Redeemer. If there is one claim he is a little sensitive to, it is that he has turned Turk. This calumny is aired with tedious frequency in Hapsburg and Papal circles. A collaborator he may be, but a knowing one, manipulating those who believe they are manipulating him, working under cover for the Christian goal of Hungarian independence. And yet the new High Treasurer of Hungary has no affection for the country or its intractable inhabitants. For Alvise, Hungary is a question of power.

Observers of Alvise at the Porte and the Serenissima, the crowned heads of Europe and undoubtedly his own father would all love to know what his real intentions are. He probably doesn't know himself; versatility is his watchword.

Machiavelli would have derived enjoyment and perhaps instruction from meeting him, for the Beyoglu exemplifies the opportunism and want of scruple that the Florentine admired in the modern statesman. Sad to relate, Machiavelli has been dead these two years and the encounter will only happen at the discretion of God.

VII

Rarely one to insist on the maximum, usually content with the possible, Charles V becomes positively demanding when he learns that Andrea Doria, the most successful admiral in the Mediterranean, is unhappy with his master, Francis I. The Emperor declares that he will do 'anything to persuade the said Andrea Doria to enter my service, whatever it may cost me'. His agents promise Doria 60,000 ducats a year, two palaces and the title 'perpetual magistrate' of Genoa, the harbour city that is gate and key to the Italian peninsula. Fortunately for the Imperial party, for three nights, a man appears to Doria just before dawn and tells him, 'Go and serve the Emperor.' In the summer of 1528, this sailor of fortune whose forebears have commanded their native Genoa on land and sea for centuries duly goes over to Charles.

Doria's first act as Charles's Captain-General is to withdraw his galleys from the Bay of Naples, putting an end to a debilitating French blockade of this important seaport, for years in Spanish hands, and its fertile hinterland. Then Doria sails back home to Genoa and drives his former French allies out of the city. Refusing the Dogeship that his fellow Genoans offer him, satisfied to be honoured as 'Liberator and Father of the Nation', Doria now becomes Charles's strong arm in the western Mediterranean, his galleys a menace to French shipping and a defence against Muslim pirates from North Africa. And in 1529 he sails to Barcelona to escort Charles back across the Mediterranean to Genoa in triumph, accompanied by a fleet of one hundred sail carrying twelve thousand infantry, two thousand cavalry and two million ducats in American gold.

On August 12, the Emperor disembarks at Genoa's Old Pier. Marching eastwards through Italy with his army and his treasure, he receives delegations from the various city states, the cheerful ones claiming a reward for having supported him against Francis, the sheepish ones mumbling apologies for backing the wrong side, while Mercurino de Gattinara, his Grand Chancellor, rhapsodises on the unceasing train of defections, triumphs and submissions that follow each other in apparently pre-ordained synchronicity. It is, he writes, 'almost as if Caesar's affairs had been directed miraculously by God'.

~

When Charles enters Bologna on 5 November, the troops accompanying him are arrayed like one of Alexander the Great's phalanxes, marching two abreast and carrying verdant branches as a sign of victory. At the gates to the city he replaces his helmet with a cap which he doffs each time he sees a beautiful woman at her window, in the process exposing his golden hair which hangs down to the middle of his ear like a Roman Emperor. Two minions go in front of his horse, scattering coins while the crowd shouts, 'Charles, Charles, Empire, Empire, victory, victory!' The Emperor's pages exhibit four plumed 'helmets of Caesar', one of which is surmounted by the Hapsburg eagle and another by a cross. The city has been decked out to resemble Rome, or rather, Rome before Charles's troops sacked it, with arches for the emperor to look triumphant against.

Pavia established Charles's military dominance of Italy at the expense of Francis, a dominance reinforced by Doria's defection and formalised in the Ladies' Peace. At Bologna the Emperor shoehorns most of the peninsula into a league, with him in control. Pope Clement forgives him for trashing Rome. And at

Charles's insistence Clement excommunicates Janos Zapolya, a *filius iniquitatis* whose encouragement of the Turk has not only led to the conquest of Hungary, but has exposed all of Europe to the peril of attack.

It is impossible for Venice to stay aloof from a general peace imposed by so overwhelming a foe, and on 23 December 1529, Doge Gritti's negotiators in Bologna cede the Republic's Apulian ports to Charles's own Kingdom of Naples, and the cities of Ravenna and Cervia to the Holy See. Venice also pays Charles a big indemnity and makes peace with Ferdinand.

After the successful conclusion to the negotiations, on 22 February 1530, the Emperor kneels in the chapel of Bologna's Palazzo Pubblico wearing an ermine-collared mantle of purple satin inlaid with gold over a robe of white and gold brocade. Clement places a small crown, iron on the inside and gold on the outside, on his head. This is the Crown of Lombardy, which St Helena, mother of Constantine the Great, ordered to be forged for her son using an iron nail from the True Cross. Whoever wears it is King of Italy.

Charles carries on kneeling. Clement hands him a sword which the Emperor sheaths before raising it over his head and lowering it, four times. Then the pontiff takes back the iron crown and puts an octagonal one made of gold, that of the Holy Roman Emperor, on the same golden head. He hands Charles a golden orb with a cross on top, signifying his dominion over the world, and a sceptre, and after more prayers the Emperor receives the body of Christ with the greatest devotion.

Two days later, which happens to be Charles's thirtieth birthday as well as the fifth anniversary of the Battle of Pavia, he again receives the octagonal crown, this time in the Cathedral of San Petronio, which has been modified to look like St Peter's in Rome. Afterwards he and the Vicar of Christ parade around for the crowd, the Emperor in his octagonal crown, the Pope in his triple-tiered tiara, amidst banners emblazoned with the Imperial and Papal insignia. A few days after this the Holy Roman Emperor leaves for Augsburg to confer with his brother

Ferdinand. The Archduke is elected King of the Romans, meaning he is Charles's heir.

In the aftermath of Bologna the Holy Roman Emperor is hard to avoid. The images that pour out of the workshops following the coronation – frescoes done in Florence, Rome, Verona, Pesaro and Bologna itself; a frieze commissioned by the magistrates of Tarazona – make sure of that. Every groom and milkmaid has seen the woodcuts that show the Emperor's entry into the city in full armour, his tour with the pontiff under a single canopy, or the Emperor alone in half profile and gripping his orb, and while these depictions cannot entirely disguise the Hapsburg jaw which resembles a coping stone or the lips jammed open like an unwell oyster, the splendour of the occasion, allied to the miraculous deliverance of Vienna from the Turks, do his image much good.

~

Venice's participation in an alliance that is aimed at unifying Christendom as a preamble to the liberation of Constantinople leaves her with some explaining to do on the Bosporus. When Thomas Mocenigo, the Secretary of the Senate, visits Istanbul, he wheedles about how the Serenissima was forced into the new alliance by her diplomatic isolation which was caused by the capitulation of France, and that her devotion to the Sultan remains undimmed. The word of a Christian is written in snow, Ibrahim sighs, and that of the Sultan in marble, though he revives at the sight of a Badakhshan ruby that is sent to him on Alvise's suggestion.

Cries of 'Charles! Empire! Victory!' are disturbing the Sultan's sleep. 'How can there be an Emperor other than my lord?' Ibrahim demands of Pietro Zen. And the Pasha scoffs at Charles V, who claims to be a Christian and yet sacked Rome, the holy of holies. In fact, he speaks so rudely of both the Emperor and the Pope that, when transcribing Zen's report of the conversation, Marino Sanuto leaves suggestive dots rather than sully his manuscript with the Grand Vizier's words.

The Republic of Venice is as neutral as the tide. The tide turns where the word 'but' comes in a Venetian sentence. The Senators are resigned to the Bologna peace accords containing hostile references to the Turks, but ask that these references be kept from Ottoman ears. Doge Gritti informs Charles that the Turks are preparing to attack the Italian coast, but . . . would His Majesty mind keeping the source of this information secret? When Pope Clement asks Cardinal Grimani if Venice will contribute to the cost of a Crusade, the son of the former Doge replies, 'We shall never dare do that, owing to our vicinity to the Turk; but we may secretly contribute some money.' All the while, Venice is giving Ibrahim Pasha intelligence about Charles and his intentions.

Not just intelligence. The Venetians make sure that their gifts to him are more to his liking, and arrive more frequently, than those of any other state. A typical haul of Venetian largesse consists of cheeses, candles, five golden jackets and two expensively wrought iron chests. The Grand Vizier calls for the chests to be brought forward so he can examine their workings. Are they Venetian work? No, comes the response – German in actual fact. One of them contains a surprise bonus of 8,000 ducats and some silken robes. This prompts Pietro Zen, who even after his retirement is often in town for business or pleasure, to praise the Pasha for having so much money. Yes, the conversation on these occasions is rarely very profound. It turns on money and who has most of it. (The Sultan, of course.) And Ibrahim finds the Venetians' flattery very congenial. It excuses them their superficiality, cynicism and lack of influence.

Calling for his wine which is made from the Soltani grape, he urges his guests 'Drink! For now is the time to refresh oneself!'

Ibrahim likens the King of Spain to a lizard pecking here and there at a bit of weed or some grain found in the dirt, while the Sultan is like a dragon which gulps down the world when it opens its mouth. But the owner of the Netherlands, Burgundy, Franche-Comté, much of Germany, Austria, Bohemia, Spain,

Naples, Sicily, Sardinia, Algiers, Mexico and the West Indies cannot be seriously compared to a lizard. Perhaps one of the gargantuan reptiles that Portuguese mariners have reported seeing in the Spice Islands, capable of swallowing a deer whole, but not a European darter the length of an asparagus tip. Suleyman owns Anatolia, Greece, Bulgaria, Serbia, Bosnia, Hungary, Moldavia, Wallachia, the Crimea, Syria, Egypt and Arabia. Both men possess a lot of real estate. Their subjects cannot be counted. But the Sultan's image among the Christians he considers his natural subjects could do with some improvement.

Act Three: The Pride

VIII

One day Suleyman pays Ayas Pasha the honour of a visit. Entering the Pasha's house near the Hippodrome, he tells him to open the special room he has heard about. Having spent hours in the Beyoglu's chamber of marvels, the Sultan is intrigued to think that Ayas may have a similar, but undisclosed, taste for bling.

Suleyman is somewhat taken aback when Ayas's secret room turns out to be empty except for some dusty old garments. No gold. No gloss. Just a tunic and a hat of the kind that peasants wear in Albania. The Sultan asks him, what is the reason for this? And the Pasha explains that these garments belonged to him in the old life. He has kept them as a reminder of the favour that God has shown him, which may be taken away at any time, and he adds that whenever he enters this room he sheds all pride and conceit. The Sultan is pleased with these words and praises Ayas for his modesty.

~

When he was Governor of Manisa, in his father's reign, Suleyman became intimate with a Montenegrin of base extraction called Mahidevran. She was given an income of four aspers a day, neither the top rate for a woman of the harem, nor the lowest, but somewhere in between.

In due course Mahidevran gave birth to Mustafa, his first son. She got a raise, a kitchen budget and ladies to help with her toilet. When Suleyman inherited the throne, Mahidevran followed him to Istanbul and took up residence in the Old Palace along with Mustafa, the Queen Mother, the other concubines and the concubines' offspring.

Mahidevran is no longer welcome in the Sultan's bed. Her procreative functions are at an end and she concentrates on preparing Mustafa for the day when he will compete for the throne. She does this with his tutor and the specialists who teach him war, religion and the decorative arts. Apart from ensuring that each of the Sultan's sons has his mother's undivided attention, the practice of limiting each concubine to a single princeling stops her forming a clique that might upset balances at court.

Mahidevran will need to avoid the fate of Cicek Khatun, poor Cem's mother, who tagged along during that prince's fruitless tour of the courts of Europe and died unhappily in Cairo. Instead she will try to emulate Suleyman's mother Hafsa. She stayed alert during her son's apprenticeship, supervising his education and ensuring her own good reputation by endowing pious foundations in Manisa. She also saved him from the poisoned gown.

In the autumn of 1521 the plague carries away two of the Sultan's children by other women: Murat, a son, and a daughter, Raziye. News of Murat's death reaches him as he is returning from the siege of Belgrade and, as the hired chronicler puts it, 'The wheels ground out their desolation on earth and the clouds wept over the waning of this charming moon.' Ten days after he gets home, another son, Mahmud, dies of smallpox. Suleyman buries his children next to his own father on the city's Sixth Hill.

No Sultan has been succeeded by other than his own son. The Ottomans aren't the Mamluks, they draw the line at letting former slaves near the throne. In the absence of other healthy male children, the deaths of Murat and Mahmud have made it more than likely that Mustafa will one day accede to the Sultanate.

~

The seraglio's inmates consist of the concubines and trainees, the Lady Steward or superintendent of palace operations, ladies-in-waiting, wet nurses, laundrywomen, fire-layers, scribes, harp and needlework teachers, women astrologers and doctors of the law, and eunuchs, the seniormost of whom is in charge of security and may beat any trainee who misbehaves. The majority of the trainees will never be chosen to consort with the Sultan. They will become servants and attendants. Over this locked and gated community with its factions, constellations and satellites presides the Queen Mother. A position of immense power awaits Mahidevran, should Mustafa attain the throne.

But soon after his own accession the Sultan gains a new favourite among the concubines. She is of Russian origin. Her spirit wasn't broken by the Tatar slavers who drove her through the winter in her native Ruthenia, nor by the auction at Caffa, where women are severed from their daughters and sons amid pathetic cries, nor by the arduous voyage across the Black Sea to Istanbul. Lucky enough to preserve her virginity, smart enough to give her best profile to a man dressed with incomprehensible opulence who comes looking for a gift. Ibrahim wants something to please his master who recently came to the throne of the Ottomans. The Russian girl.

She hasn't Mahidevran's beauty but she has undeniable charm, sweetness of temper and is amiable, graceful and petite. She has ambition and intelligence and is making quick progress in Turkish and needlework and the right way to pray. Her name is Hurrem, which means joyful, and if the memory of her abduction occasionally gives her cause for regret, she isn't alone in that. Every girl in her dormitory is a convert, girls from the Slav regions of Europe, from the Caucasus, Africa and the North Sea, all dreaming in their own languages while learning the rules of this stud farm whose windows look in – only in – onto the finest amenities. Everyone wants to please, everyone is trying to forget. And everyone needs to get on the right side of Hafsa, the Lady Steward, and the beating eunuch.

In due course she finds herself seated in a grand carriage,

with a bodyguard of eunuchs, being driven along the Council Road from the Old Palace to the New where the Sultan keeps a smaller, second court of damsels. There she is washed and dressed, rehearsing in her mind the phrases she has been taught, before being brought to the door of the Privy Chamber.

More nights follow. She is in the Sultan's eye. While he is away taking Belgrade the sound of cannons tells Istanbul of the birth of a son. Hurrem has left the dormitory. She has a suite of rooms with a governess for the child and a richer wardrobe for herself. The palace accountants no longer refer to her by her name but as the mother of Prince Mehmet.

Hurrem has done her bit to alleviate the chronic mortality of Suleyman's heirs presumptive. Ordinarily she will not receive a further invitation to the Privy Chamber. Other women will make their contributions and the rest is in God's hands.

But Hurrem is not an ordinary concubine. Having enjoyed the Sultan she wants to enjoy him more. And Suleyman is not an ordinary Sultan. He is running from triumph to triumph, he has established Ibrahim Pasha, a favourite of his own discovery, at the crest of the State in defiance of convention, his power makes men tremble. And then there is the Sultan's pleasure to consider, his personal taste and peace of mind. It cannot be argued that an existence encircled by pyramids of skulls is an emotionally fulfilling one.

There is something he likes about this Hurrem. Something he does not want to resist. If he is to spend his time between foot rot and sieges making heirs, it suits him to do so with someone he likes, someone fertile, someone who brings him joy.

~

The newcomer received Mahidevran's kindness and she, proud and beautiful, the mother of the Sultan's oldest son, had no reason to feel threatened by the Russian baggage.

Now she hears that the Sultan is much pleased by Hurrem and that he never tires of her. Mahidevran seeks her out where they can be alone. And so, from words to deeds, and the encounter ends with Mahidevran scratching Hurrem's face, pulling clumps of hair from her head and shouting, 'Traitor! Sold meat! You want to compete with me?'

When the Sultan next sends for Hurrem, she tells the eunuch that unfortunately she isn't fit to come into her lord's presence, being sold meat and half bald with a face all spoilt. The eunuch delivers this message and the Sultan repeats his summons with greater urgency, to which Hurrem, with a reluctance most becoming, accedes.

Sliding shyly into his presence, shedding a tear or two, she relates how she came to be in this state. The sight of her scored cheeks and plucked scalp moves the Sultan and he comforts her before sending her back to her quarters.

Hurrem already understands the Sultan and his nature better than her rival. Suleyman is sentimental; when arbitrating a dispute he usually sides with the injured party. His libido can be tamed by appeals to his honour. But Mahidevran is not thinking coolly about how she might win the contest for her future and that of her son. She is thinking of the injury that has been done to her pride.

The Sultan summons her and flashing defiance she confirms Hurrem's account of events. The Russian got what she deserved. In fact she got less than she deserved! She and the other concubines must yield to her, Mahidevran, and recognise her as their senior. These words inflame the Sultan, who won't see Mahidevran again.

In time Hurrem's hair grows back and she returns to the Privy Chamber. She calls him her Yusuf; after a prophet so handsome that a married woman called Zuleikha ripped his shirt, such was her desire to have him, a prophet so virtuous that he rejected her advances.

～

When they aren't in bed he's at war. As the sieges succeed each other, so too do the births.

Rhodes, Buda, Vienna. Mihrimah, his second daughter; Selim,

born during Ibrahim's wedding celebrations; three further sons, Abdullah, Bayezit and Cihangir. A tradition is being trialled. It's called fidelity.

Like a puppy the Sultan is enthusiastic but clumsy. He loses his way when a provincial governor sends two beautiful maidens for the seraglio. One is addressed to Hafsa but she has more than enough ladies-in-waiting so she passes this second maiden on to her son.

Hurrem will not make Mahidevran's mistake. She will not stimulate the Sultan's sympathy for the new girls by tyrannising them. Better to work through his mother for whom he has such love.

She brings the subject up in Hafsa's presence and throws herself onto the ground sobbing. Alarmed by Hurrem's exhibition, the Queen Mother immediately sends her maiden to be the wife of a governor in the provinces. And Suleyman follows Hafsa's example, fearing that Hurrem might die of sorrow if even one of the girls stays at his side.

~

When campaigning he sends her presents to remember him by: furs, money, a hair from his beard. A shirt arrives in Istanbul brought by a holy man from Mecca. It's by no means straightforward to deliver an unsolicited item of clothing to the Sultan's beloved who is never seen and is guarded by vicious eunuchs. But the holy man manages to do so through the intercession of an Istanbul saint called Emre. Hurrem immediately recognises the value of the shirt, which lies not in the ordinary cotton from which it is spun but the Quranic verses, sacred numbers and the names of God, all ninety-nine of them, that are written on its surface. She sends it on to her lord, begging him to wear it in battle for it will turn aside cannonballs.

And when she receives his letter she replies to it by return.

'My soul's fragment, after rubbing this ugly face of mine in the dust under the blessed feet of Your Highness my Sultan, my dear soul, my existence, my prosperity – my Sultan, thanks be to God, whose name be exalted, that your auspicious and noble letter arrived bringing light to eyes and joy to hearts. May God allow your perfection an old age, and not part me from you until the Day of Judgement, and allow me once more to rub my face in your noble face. My soul's fragment, my life's work, Sultan of my existence, in your auspicious letter you conveyed news of your good health. Thanks be to God, may He protect you from all mishaps. If you enquire of this feeble, helpless concubine of yours, I swear to you, my soul, I have neither night nor day. When I am denied the conversation of a King such as you, what else is to be expected?'

Sometimes she composes with the help of one of the seraglio scribes.

> O, morning breeze, let my lover know that I am devastated,
> Tell my lover that I cry like a nightingale because I am
>   deprived of his rose-like face.
>
> Do not think that your medicine is a cure for my
>   heart's yearning,
> Tell my lover that no one can cure my woes.
>
> Since the hand of grief pierced my heart with the sword
>   of my loving for you,
> Say that I have become diseased and am groaning and
>   moaning like a reed-flute from separation.

When he is away on campaign she doesn't fail to remind him that he's a family man now.

'Now my Sultan, this is enough, my soul is too affected to write more, especially as your servant and son Mehmet and your slave and daughter Mihrimah weep and wail from missing you when your noble letters are read. Their weeping has driven me mad, it is as if we were in mourning. My Sultan, your son Mehmet and your daughter Mihrimah and Selim and Abdullah send you many greetings.'

$\sim$

He writes.

My solitude, my everything, my beloved,
My gleaming moon,
My companion, my intimate,
My all, lord of beauties, my Sultan

My life's essence and span, my sip from
The river of Paradise, my Eden,
My springtime, my bright joy, my secret,
My idol, my laughing rose

My happiness, my pleasure, lantern in my gathering,
My luminous star, my candle
My oranges bitter and sweet, my pomegranate,
The taper by my bed

My green plant, my sugar, my treasure in this world,
My freedom from woe
My Potiphar, my Joseph, my existence,
My Pharaoh in the Egypt of the heart

My Istanbul, my Karaman, my lands of the Byzantines,
My Badakhshan, my Kipchak Steppes,
My Baghdad, my Khorasan

As if I were a panegyrist at your door,
I sing your praises, I wish you well
My heart filled with grief, my eyes with tears,
I am your lover

You bring me joy

~

Pavilions have been put up among the Pharaoh's needles to
accommodate the great and the good. Clustered around

Ibrahim's Buda statues are spoils of war which include the tent that the Conqueror captured from Uzun Hasan and those that Selim took away after he defeated Sultan Qansawh al-Ghawri in Syria. In front of the ruins of Constantine's lodge, a palatial building has come up in which birds and beasts will be slaughtered, butchered and cooked. The biggest area of all has been left empty for performers and spectators.

The diplomatic corps are assigned tribunes from which to watch. The Venetian contingent includes the current bailo, Francesco Bernardo, his predecessor, Pietro Zen, and Thomas Mocenigo, whom the Doge has deputed to convey his regrets at not being able to attend in person. Alvise Gritti, now the reverend Bishop of Eger, is present in his capacity as minister plenipotentiary of the King of Hungary. The surfeit of Venetians is camouflage for the lack of other foreigners. No one from Charles or Ferdinand. No one from Francis or Henry. Among the more ambivalent guests are Qansawh al-Ghawri's son and a scion of Uzun Hasan, who, while they are treated with the utmost consideration, won't be going home any time soon.

Under a blistering sun Ayas Pasha and Kasim Pasha take their positions near the Lion House, at the entrance to the Hippodrome. Ayas, well-built and handsome; Kasim, orotund and red; both converts, both mediocre. Kasim was Governor of Rumelia but then Mustafa Pasha left the stage and everyone moved up a step.

Ibrahim has no other step to go up.

The Grand Vizier is last to arrive and goes to his designated pavilion. The Sultan's soldiers are in glittering lines, while around the perimeter stand his subjects of all confessions.

At a quarter past three the Sultan makes his entrance. He is on a Morello bay so massive it would shatter a lance if one was hurled at its flank. Silence descends over the old circus, disturbed only by the rustle of the plane trees' scorched leaves. If one shuts one's eyes one would be forgiven for assuming that the place was empty.

Then the military musicians strike up and the gnash of

cymbals and the trumpets' fanfare are so loud that they carry across the Straits to Uskudar. The sudden cacophony panics the Sultan's stallion and he prances frantically. Those who haven't witnessed the Sultan's equestrian skill fear that a mishap is about to happen, which would be inauspicious in the extreme.

But the Sultan is a Turk. His ancestors were born in the saddle and as a horseman he is at least the equal of Charles V. Using his calves and thighs, his seat and his upper arms, his voice of command, he controls his mount without the large white turban on his head so much as slipping this way or that.

His horse once more under control, the Sultan acknowledges the Pashas. Then he rides further into the Hippodrome while his subjects admire his satin Limoges jacket and crimson kaftan with Persian hem. At the spine of the old race course he is met by Ibrahim Pasha, on foot, who takes his master's bridle and leads him to the royal belvedere. Suleyman dismounts, a signal for his soldiers to shout fervent wishes for his health and happiness. Then he climbs four steps to the throne which sits on columns of lapis and is sheltered from the sun by a gilded baldachin, its summit floating with rich fabrics.

Now Janissaries and palace gatekeepers come forward to accept gifts on behalf of the Sultan from the slaves and servants of the VIPs who are giving them. The gifts are spread over the ground in such a way that they are visible to the largest number of people. By evening the centre of the Hippodrome is a trove of Egyptian cotton, Indian muslins, Syrian damasks, silver plates containing gold pieces, gold plates containing gems, crystal cups, blue and white Chinese porcelain, Tartary furs, Turkmen stallions and bevies of Mamluk, Ethiopian, Greek and Hungarian slaves. The Grand Vizier alone gives 160 gifts, including precious books, a golden caftan encrusted with jewels and twelve boys. The total number of presents given is 1,100.

Each giver climbs the four steps to kiss the Sultan's hand, including old friends like Piri Pasha, who has taken on the government of Edirne as a retirement hobby. And the grandeur of the occasion, allied to the natural grace and handsomeness of the Sultan, give him the aspect of an idol being adored.

Every morning for the duration of the festivities the subjects of the New Rome come back to the Hippodrome to see what marvels they will see. A man lifting nine men into the air on his shoulders and then standing on one leg, men climbing to the top of the needles so that from the ground they are as small as sparrows, pantomimes put on by Jews, Greeks, Persians and Armenians. Music and dancing and comedians smashing pots over their heads for laughs. There is jousting, each pair bowing to the Sultan like gladiators before rushing at each other, each combatant with his slave to pass him a fresh lance if the one he is using should snap.

The Sultan's elephants are saddled with iron palanquins with three mahouts apiece. The elephants are playing football. Donkeys and baboons perform tricks and bears dance to trumpet blasts. Lions and leopards are teased. A mechanical snake twelve feet long spits fire.

And at all times, whether from his belvedere or the palace of the Grand Vizier, where he goes every now and then for a change of perspective, the Sultan gives out money, sugared almonds and other titbits. The VIP pavilions are served trays of sugar figurines: lions, pine cones, melons and apples.

The garrisons of two fortresses constructed on the Hippodrome, one of them Hungarian and the other Turkish, fight and skirmish before the Hungarian fortress surrenders and the Hungarians reveal themselves to be Janissaries. They bow to the Sultan, who won the castle in question during the Mohacs campaign. Sultan al-Ghawri's Mamluk army is also defeated, his general being played by a former Mamluk now in Suleyman's service, the son of the defunct Sultan looking on stonily.

The nights are pyromaniac heaven. The fortresses spew out thousands of rockets while carts are pulled across the Hippodrome from which fireworks whirr into the sky amid tremendous cracks and explosions. Then the fortresses are delivered to the flames which rise so high the sky itself appears to have caught fire. And the following day when the spectators return they are surprised to see no sign of the charred fortresses, but two new ones, just as good, that will meet the same fate this evening.

The food palace in front of the Byzantine lodge belches out wood smoke. The VIPs eat off porcelain while for the poor, a thousand stone dishes are arranged on the floor of the Hippodrome, each one replete with rice and honey and flatbreads. The poor rush to put as much food as they can into their sacks so they can take it away, and not only do they fight over the food but they also use the bread to biff and buffet each other, much to the merriment of the persons of quality watching from their pavilions, who throw down more goodies for them to fight over. On another day pyramids of whole cooked oxen are built on the Hippodrome floor and when the people approach them all manner of live birds and animals spring from their flanks, crows, magpies, jackals, foxes, cats, hares, curs and wolves, and there is a toothsome mayhem which, again, delights the spectators.

The Sultan knows that the stomach of a Janissary is not to be trifled with. Two thousand stone dishes are placed before the corps, piled with ox meat. The men stand immobile and soundless before their plates. Upon a sign they fall to eating with the same unanimity of action as if firing a volley.

An unknown poet called Figani becomes the talk of the town after delighting the Sultan with a command performance. Figani's poem compares Suleyman to the greatest Persian and Seljuk Kings, the epic heroes of the *Shahnameh* and the Prophets of Islam. And Figani praises the Sultan's hospitality such as no one has ever seen.

Each tent you set up like a throne in the Hippodrome,
The awning of Atlas's sphere is base and paltry in comparison.

From your table is pledged daily the bread of all Creation,
The salt can never be extracted from the seven
seas of your kitchen.

One day there is a debate for the Sultan's enjoyment between the doctors of the law. The subject of the debate is the first verse of the Quran, which contains the essence of the Holy Book, the essence of Islam, the essence of a good life. It's a tournament as brutal as any with lances. One of the divines, finding his words with difficulty and sputtering banalities that are greeted with embarrassment, has an attack of apoplexy and dies shortly after being taken home.

The news from Pera, meanwhile, is that the plague is killing indiscriminately.

~

The morning of the fourteenth day of the celebrations finds many officers of the State standing outside the gates to the Old Palace to greet the boys as they come out decked in jewels, velvets and brocades.

The boys ride along the Council Road on identical greys that their father has sent them. They wear jewel-encrusted bonnets, each with a fissure in the fabric. The tuft of hair that has been threaded artfully through this fissure will be cut off at the appointed time. While all three are angelic it cannot be denied that Selim is more than usually beautiful, six or seven years of age with an adorable little scimitar hanging by his side. He most resembles the father while the older two, Mustafa and Mehmet, are thought to resemble their mothers, not that many in the crowd have seen their mothers.

As they come into the Hippodrome and the spectators shout praise and thanks to God for the princes' well being, the Janissaries direct their passion and affection at Mustafa alone and he graciously inclines his head towards them showing reciprocal friendliness. The Janissaries show no such love for the younger princes.

Bowed and scraped to by the Pashas and the High Governors of Rumelia and Anatolia, ushered with an excess of deference up the four steps to kiss the hand of the Sultan their father, the boys are exposed for the first time to the almost infinite resources of the Ottoman State. But they are not thinking about the money and ingenuity that have been spent in their name. They are concentrating on their mothers' instructions. Hold your chin up. Do not cry. Do not smile.

To be born the Sultan's son is to be abstracted from the ordinary run of human relations and naturalised into an ocean of divine will and cosmic alignment. It is the breaking of these forces over the human qualities of intelligence, strength and cunning that produces a Sultan.

The parading of three contenders for the sabre of the Ottomans is the greatest concentration of dynastic potential the city has witnessed, one that may never be repeated as the boys enter adolescence and are sent off to their provincial governorships, henceforth to be rivals unto death. The air in Istanbul today is light with joy and choked with dread.

The brotherly fellowship on display is an interim arrangement, pending fratricide. The people looking on in admiration are all too aware how the Ottoman royal family trims fat. Those princes who do not become Sultan will face one of a range of unpalatable outcomes. One may become another Korkut, Sultan Selim's brother who was run to ground in a cave and strangled, another a son of Korkut, killed by his uncle in a palace bedroom. A third may find himself emulating Sultan Bayezit's brother Cem, who died in Naples, lonely and dissipated, while his mother pined for him on the other side of the White Sea.

Of the royal brothers, only Bayezit isn't available for inspection. He is too small to take part in events. But his cadet status will not necessarily rule him out from one day occupying the throne. Sultan Selim of blessed memory made it despite being his father's fourth son. Primogeniture is Christendom's oddity.

Hurrem is here behind the lattice that screens the Grand Vizier's terrace, along with the woman who scratched her face and in doing so made herself odious in the Sultan's eyes. Mahidevran has the Janissaries on her side. Hurrem has the

Sultan on hers. The Russian already has the bigger pack from which to draw a King. And she is pregnant again.

On the final Thursday the boys process again, this time with musicians playing tambourines, castanets, trumpets and other instruments. Arriving at the palace of Ibrahim Pasha, they ride up the ramp and into the Pasha's courtyard before dismounting and going inside.

One by one they enter a room and are undressed. In the room are a sheikh and some eunuchs. One puts the naked boy on his lap, the boy's hands are squeezed reassuringly and he hears encouraging words until the sheikh decides that everything is ready. Saying the bismillah, he grabs the prepuce's epithelium and presses it well together, then he squeezes the epithelium with a silver cutting pincer and the boy cries and trembles. Then the sheikh cuts away the excess prepuce with a razor; over the cut he sprinkles a powder that dulls the pain, allowing the boy to stand and run into the next room where his mother is waiting to examine the damage and make him laugh through his tears. Then she helps him into loose garments and sends him running proudly to his father.

In the afterglow, Suleyman turns to Ibrahim and asks which were the more sumptuous celebrations, the Grand Vizier's for his wedding, or those the Sultan put on for the circumcision of his sons. The Pasha replies, 'There have never been, and never will be, finer festivities than mine.' This isn't the answer that Suleyman was waiting for and he tells Ibrahim to explain himself. 'My nuptials,' the Grand Vizier goes on, with the self-assurance of an acrobat executing a flawless parabola high above the earth, 'were honoured by the presence of the King of Mecca and Medina, the Solomon of our epoch. Your Majesty's celebrations were not attended by the guest I had at mine.' Suleyman laughs and says delightedly, 'A thousand praises on you for reminding me of this fact.'

For an intimate procedure, a circumcision can have surprisingly public ramifications. In the months that follow, the reports from the Hippodrome reach the Christian powers just as reports from Bologna reached the Porte. And Marino Sanuto and others write them down and the continent's Secretaries of State nod and smile at the way Suleyman plays the ancient game of one-upmanship. He is spending his way out of the humiliation that befell him under the walls of Vienna; he is peacocking into the sightline of Charles V.

IX

Marino Sanuto is an abundantist. His attention is drawn to too much of everything. He dumps the news into his diary with the same matter-of-factness as his neighbours emptying their bedpans into the canal. His public career, being low-powered and marred by slights that he overcomes with heroic over-sensitivity, has left him a lot of time on his hands, which he spends with his diary, his monument while he breathes. Well, he declares, I have written so much that it is impossible to believe how I have managed it, given that I have been perpetually out and about seeking every occurrence, no matter how slight.

Every day he comes out of his little palace in Santa Croce and makes his way amid street vendors, pawnbrokers, sweepers, water-carriers and beggars to the Rialto where he looks in on the tavern-cum-hostel that is his family business, or passes the time of day with the bankers who assemble in the portico of the church of San Giacomo. His destination is the Piazza, where, speaking to his fellow patricians in the Doge's chancellery, he gathers his material.

On this particular morning, having walked his usual route through San Cassian, perhaps thinking about his late wife Cecilia Priuli, his daughters from subsequent unsanctified liaisons, Candiana and Bianca, or chuckling at Doge Gritti's refusal to get his feet muddy following an *acqua grandissima* – thinking these thoughts, or listing in his head the names of every candidate for the Senate and the votes they received, he enters the jeweller's shop in question.

The Caorlini brothers, Luigi and Marco; the sons of Pietro Zen; the Levriero family of Levantine fame and some other merchants and master craftsmen on the Rialto make up the Venetian end of the consortium that is financing the project. From time to time during the piece's assembly, the craftsmen have been to Istanbul to receive directives from Alvise Gritti, whose technical and political nous make him the ideal project manager.

Whether it can ever be worn is in doubt. The Sultan's swan-like neck would probably bend under the weight. But it will look fabulous on a cushion held by a page. It will leap out from the woodcuts.

Marino does what he always does when he is confronted by something quantifiable. He makes a list.

On the face of the crescent-mount: one diamond, two rubies, one turquoise.

On the reverse of the crescent-mount: one diamond, one ruby, a rose with with eight diamonds.

Sprouting from the crescent-mount: an aigrette of plumes of various colours.

On the skull: five pearls, one large emerald, four diamonds, three rubies.

On the reverse of the skull: a bejewelled, upturned vase-shaped mount, three rubies.

On the pommel of the skull: three rubies, three emeralds.

On the uppermost crown: three pearls, three diamonds, three rubies, two emeralds.

On the second crown: twelve pearls, four diamonds, four rubies, four emeralds.

On the third crown: four diamonds, four rubies, four emeralds.

On the lowest crown: twelve pearls, four diamonds, four rubies, four emeralds.

On the circlet: seven pointed diamonds.

On the apex: three rubies, two emeralds.

On the lappet at the apex: six diamonds, seven rubies, seven emeralds.

On the neckguard: eight diamonds, eight rubies.

Price (including velvet-lined gilt ebony presentation case): 144,000 ducats.

After the private view it will go on display in the Doge's Palace. Then the consortium's courier, Marco Antonio, will sail to Ragusa where he'll be met by one of the Pasha's best men with a large and showy escort to wind through the Balkans into Thrace. By this time half of Venice will have seen it and every chancer from Innsbruck to Algiers will know of its existence. Discretion might work better from a security perspective, but then discretion isn't what this is about, is it?

~

In times of need, the Turks hastily build an armada. The autumn of 1530 is such a time. A letter from Alvise Gritti advises the Signoria that Ibrahim Pasha has twice been to the shipyard to check on progress. Suleyman, Alvise continues, is planning to advance by land and sea to put an end to the arrogance of Charles V. And Gritti reports a victory that King Janos has scored against Ferdinand's forces on the Danube, sinking or capturing twenty-seven shallow draught boats that the King of the Romans dispatched in an unsuccessful attempt to retake Buda. The Signoria is keeping Alvise abreast of events in Italy so he can pass on the information to Ibrahim. And Alvise convinces the Pasha to allow the sale of more saltpetre to Venice.

On the surface the old alliance jogs along. But ever since the Venetians went behind his back and made peace with Charles, Ibrahim has been pointing out to them how small and powerless they are. Showing a capriciousness they haven't seen before, he insists that the Venetians send a certain horn of a unicorn as a gift for the Sultan for whom they profess such esteem; no more Venetian presents will be accepted unless this rare and valuable alicorn, known to be a treasured possession of the Venetian state, is among them.

Ibrahim also decrees that luxury goods coming from Alexandria may no longer be shipped directly to Italy but must come first to Istanbul. The Porte allocates 600,000 ducats to buy up all the Alexandrian merchandise, anticipating healthy profits from the secondary market. Unease spreads among investors in the Venetian galleys, which, having put into Alexandria, are unable to load their usual cargo of silk, sugar, pepper, ginger, cloves, cassia, mace and perfumed amber.

Venice is being supplanted by Istanbul as the clearing house for commerce across the White Sea – which the Europeans know as the Mediterranean. Alvise Gritti saw this coming and has reserved space for 70,000 ducats' worth of silk aboard the Turkish convoy from Alexandria. He is building a warehouse in Pera to handle the new inventory. But Alvise is his father's son and when the Venetian merchants ask him to get the Pasha's decree overturned, he acts against his own interests and negotiates on their behalf. Thanks to him, Venice's merchantmen are eventually able to set sail from Alexandria fully loaded. But next time his charm may not work. The Sultan loathes ambiguity in an ally, and what, if not institutional ambiguity, is the Venetian policy of being all things to all men?

A new Turkish economy is being built, reaching from Egypt into the Balkans and waiting to be sprung across the Adriatic into Italy. It is on show at the caravansaray that Ibrahim has built at Tatar Pazarjik, three hundred miles from Istanbul on the great road west. Cleverly situated before the road forks, the caravansaray is used both by caravans that will continue along the Via Egnatia towards the Adriatic and those turning northwards through Sofia and Belgrade into Hungary. The caravansaray contains two hundred well-appointed rooms and eighty substantial suites for the most important merchants and their families. The accommodation looks in on a courtyard shaded by a great tree, while the outer courtyard, with a pond at its centre, holds more than five thousand horses. Security is first class.

~

After the circumcision ceremonies Alvise goes north, a small town on the move. With him are three hundred mounted men, two hundred camels, two hundred slaves and wagons loaded with sixteen commodious pavilions, a more extensive train than either of Hungary's rival monarchs can afford.

On reaching Buda he writes to pro-Hapsburg nobles who have been slow in giving loyalty to the Sultan's client King Janos. 'We have been sent out and commissioned by the mighty Emperor of the Turks,' runs his letter, 'to ascertain the actual state of the Hungarian Kingdom, to find out who are obedient to King Janos, who are faithful to him, and who are not, and also to make all this known to his Imperial Majesty, who promised us: if the high priests, barons and nobles of this country do not go over to the side of the mentioned king, next spring he will start out with all his armed forces – and not so mercifully and moderately as he did last summer – and will not only destroy those who are unfaithful, but will also devastate and put to fire and sword their estates and subjects.'

He is keeping a close eye on negotiations towards a truce that are taking place in Poland between representatives of Janos and Archduke Ferdinand, a settlement that might hand Janos, and by implication Alvise, the Dalmatian town of Clissa. Not only Clissa, but also Isabella, daughter of King Sigismund of Poland. The Beyoglu can see her by his side as a future Queen of Naples. Then he sets off for Poland to take charge of the peace negotiations himself.

Not long into his journey he learns that a Hapsburg army under General von Roggendorf, who distinguished himself in von Salm's defence of Vienna, is approaching Buda. Von Roggendorf is offering 10,000 ducats for Janos alive and 1,000 for his corpse. Alvise retraces his steps and joins Janos inside the citadel before the encirclement is complete.

Hapsburg messengers are riding out to spread the word that the Voivode of Transylvania, an excommunicant, and the Doge's bastard, a traitor to his religion, are trapped in Buda Castle with no chance of escape. 'This piece of intelligence has been received at Rome with great joy,' reports the Imperial ambassador to the Curia, 'as it is considered that if the two above-named individuals fall into the hands of the King of Hungary all cause of alarm will disappear forever. Here, at Rome, they would much prefer the capture of Alvise Gritti to that of the Voivode, for they say the former is much more dangerous, owing to his influence over Ibrahim Pasha, and if taken he ought to he drawn and quartered.' By 'King of Hungary', the ambassador means Ferdinand.

Shortly afterwards, news arrives in Venice that Ferdinand's men have taken the citadel of Buda and slaughtered all inside, including Gritti. Another report says that he has survived the massacre and is in captivity. None the wiser, the Doge says, 'Let the will of God be done,' and moves on to other business.

It is not the will of God that Alvise should die. This Gritti is a fighter. Like his father Andrea at Vicenza. Like great-uncle Battista on the ramparts of Constantinople in '53.

He's the spirit of Buda's defence, setting up his tent on the walls and distributing gold florins to distract his men from the 10,000-ducat bounty on their master's head. When the Austrians try to storm the castle, he's in the thick of it, shoulder to shoulder with his Turks and Serbs.

An assassin conceals himself among a band of defenders returning from a sortie and creeps into the castle, a dagger hidden in his sleeve. Approaching the King's room, he is given away by the barks of a dog prowling the royal threshold, overpowered and identified as Janos Habardanecz, who was in Constantinople only two years ago as a member of Ferdinand's embassy. Habardanecz is put in a sack and thrown into the Danube.

By mid December the walls of the city are rubble and the defenders are eating their horses. But the besiegers have been weakened by sickness and the cold. Mehmet Bey, the Ottoman Governor of Smederevo, in Serbia, is approaching the city with a relief force. When he learns of Mehmet's imminent arrival, von Roggendorf packs up his artillery and siege engines and goes away.

King Janos spends the days after the victory finding new ways to reward Alvise. The Beyoglu is dubbed 'Defender and Saviour of Hungary' and is authorised to incorporate a lion in his coat of arms. On December 23, he signs a letter to Sigismund of Poland with the initials GR. *Gubernator Regius*. An office created specially for him. The nobles are not impressed. Men like the brothers Pal and Balazs Artandy, who have the salt monopoly in the Maramures region, and Imre Czibak, Bishop of Oradea. In past wars Czibak fought with distinction against the Turks. He observes that the Beyoglu, being not quite Christian and not quite Turk, must be pagan.

These men cannot accept that the country of Matthias Corvinus, with its abundance of men and horses, its full seams and giving soils, must submit meekly to the foreign yoke. Is Janos a child that he must have a governor to teach him kingship? The country already has two kings. Does it need a third? If so, should that person be an Italian in the pay of the Turk?

On 25 January 1531, the Artandy brothers are arrested and their heads are cut off on the orders of Alvise, while King Janos is conveniently away on a hunting trip. Along with the mines, Alvise pockets the family title, Count of Maramures. The Bishopric of Eger is becoming a chore so he gives it to to his fourteen-year-old son, Antonio.

Castle by castle, mine by mine, Alvise Gritti's tribe of men, the so-called Grittiani, mostly Italian-educated non-entities of uncertain loyalties, are taking control.

When Janos asked the Sultan if he could keep Gritti, was it a despot he had in mind? But Janos has few options. If he submits to Ferdinand, Hungary will become another entry in the Hapsburg log. To alienate Gritti would precipitate the Kingdom's annexation by the Sultan and its formal incorporation into the

Empire. In neither case could Janos, a fallen traitor, expect to avoid a nasty death at the hands of his countrymen. He has been warned by his nobles that Gritti has designs on the throne. But what choice does he have, other than to keep the Beyoglu close?

After the deliverance of Buda, Alvise writes to Charles V. He advises his majesty not to believe any false opinions that have been circulating on the subject of his faith, which is constant and should be esteemed all the more because he is in the camp of the Turk. In fact, his unique position means that he is the only person who can save Christendom, and he warns the Emperor to take very seriously the 'huge and inestimable preparations for war that the said Turk is making both on sea and on land, such that our epoch has never seen'. Turning to possible solutions, the Beyoglu recommends that the Emperor tell his younger brother to renounce his claim to Hungary. That would obviate the need for a Turkish invasion, while leaving Hungary safely in the hands of a Christian administration. And should the Emperor show such a willingness, the Beyoglu concludes flirtatiously, he will 'undertake to do and entertain whatever action is appropriate in this affair'.

The Beyoglu is between adversaries, promising everything and nothing, exhibiting what his critics call an excessive disposition to render service to whomever seeks it. But there is something incomplete about this assessment. It is by rendering service that Gritti serves himself.

He is already the richest private Ottoman. He receives 40,000 ducats annually from collecting excise on goods passing through three Thracian ports, including Gallipoli, and 80,000 from the Hungarian mines. Then there is his income from Hungary's episcopal sees. He collects the tribute that the Ragusans pay the Ottoman Treasury every year. Not forgetting his warehouse of luxury goods in Pera. His secret gemstore. His private fleet, commanded by Zorzo. His debtors include Ibrahim Pasha, Hayreddin, a pirate, and Antonio Rincon, a Spaniard in the service of the Most Christian King.

King Janos is supposed to be his employer; in fact he is his debtor, too. With the Kingdom bankrupt, the King is in the disagreeable position of having to borrow 300,000 ducats from his own Treasurer. And he mortgages him the city of Szeged for 15,000 florins.

In Istanbul, if the King's messenger comes knocking at an odd hour, the minister bows his head and goes docilely to die. But Buda is not Istanbul. In 1526, it was burned to the ground and left for dead. The Kingdom is on its third King in six years. Not having been elected by his peers, answerable to a man he owes a sum equivalent to more than a third of the revenues of Egypt, Janos has no choice but to allow Gritti to determine the prerogatives of the *Gubernator Regius* as he sees fit.

~

In the spring of 1532, Alvise sends Nicolo Querini, another Venetian bastard, to take possession of Clissa and the other Dalmatian fiefs from the Hapsburgs. On hearing that Querini has set out, the Doge cannot bring himself to contribute to a Senate session on Turkish affairs, such is his agony on account of his son, although he doesn't consider Alvise his son, inasmuch as those who don't obey their fathers cannot be regarded as sons.

One evening Charles V's ambassador calls on the Doge. Will Venice come to Clissa's aid, he asks, now that the Beyoglu's force of Turkish and Venetian mercenaries is bearing down on it? Will the Doge defend the possession of his ally against the treachery of his own son? And the ambassador informs Andrea that a letter recently sent by the Emperor to the beleaguered town was intercepted by one of Alvise's vessels, hardly the act of a friend, which Venice claims to be. The Doge says something about Venetian neutrality being sacrosanct, and he will look into the question of the intercepted letter. Then the ambassador goes away and the Doge faces his fellow patricians.

The Doge is angry, as any father would be, but his love for his son is stronger than any revulsion he may feel for Alvise's

133

irresponsible conduct. It is true, he admits, that Alvise has never fought under the Venetian flag, but he has served it in many other ways. Even now he continues to perform critical services for the Serenissima in Constantinople – not unlike Antonio Grimani lobbying for Venice while he was in exile in Rome. Some of the patricians see through Gritti's nepotistic defence of family. For them the sentence of death which was passed on the imposter Isidorus of Giliaco would be too good for the Beyoglu.

The Doge has never had greater pain, Marino Sanuto observes of this lion whose career he has followed since his incarceration in the Seven Towers of Constantinople, whose mane is coming out in tufts, a prince of shot nerves. 'The Doge can do no more,' the diarist writes with emphasis and fellow-feeling, one father to another. 'His son does as he wishes, and nothing can be done about that. On one side is the Turkish Sultan and on the other the Emperor and the King of the Romans; and his son is in the middle.'

~

He is ready for power. Power over vast tracts and numberless beasts, including those of the two-legged variety. Power to enact the will of God or violate it, depending on the circumstances. Alvise Gritti's relationship with his Maker is more discretionary than that of an ordinary person.

As Querini is setting out for Clissa, Alvise rides with his army through Wallachia and Transylvania, convening Diets, levying troops and awarding taxation rights to anyone who pleases him. To his current secretary, a linguistically gifted Dalmatian called Tranquillus Andronicus, he dictates letters addressed to the Pope, the Emperor and the King of the Romans, reminding them of the futility of trying to resist the Sultan. On his way to Buda, he is received with every honour by Imre Czibak, Bishop of Oradea. This is particularly gratifying in view of Czibak's past opposition and his highly offensive 'pagan' joke.

And at every stop, whether he is met with gifts of silver plate or, as also happens, attempts on his life, the meaning is the same: go away.

The aldermen, magistrates and bishops of Buda are out in force when he enters the capital riding a handsome chestnut with a gilded harness and wearing a cloak whose crimson fabric is embossed with golden moons circling a golden star. Alongside him is Janos Doczy, unofficial commander of the Grittiani, a former judge who fell out of the King's favour and has been rescued from obscurity by the Beyoglu's patronage. After meeting with King Janos, Alvise emerges from the palace in possession of the Captaincy-General and a Marshal's baton. He addresses a Diet in the city in Italian – Hungarian isn't his thing – and announces a punitive tax on nobles, urbanites and clerics amounting to half their assets. After promising everyone immense riches from the mines he has discovered, he is folded once more into his coterie of hangers-on.

While Alvise was away in the interior, in Buda a group of highly placed Hungarians were entertained at luncheon by some actors who made fun of his Italian manners and way of dressing and described him as the author of crimes and misdeeds. Around the same time, a malicious rumour was spread, by persons unknown, that the Beyoglu has been killed on the Sultan's orders and his body stuffed with straw and hung from a tower.

Shortly after Gritti arrives back in Buda and is informed about these disagreeable events, one of the guests at the luncheon is found hanged in his house. Another loses his position as chief steward to a prominent Cardinal. Justice on a third is administered through his fiancée, a member of the distinguished Kanizsai family. An imposter arrives, claiming to be a long lost Kanizsai, forces himself into the bosom of the family, and does not rest until the bride-to-be has been disinherited.

X

On 10 May, while Alvise is still in Transylvania Suleyman goes to Aya Sofya. He is preceded by fifty mounted mace-bearers, thousands of Janissaries, Sipahis and archers and fifteen or twenty led horses, all with rich head-trappings and adorned with carbuncles, diamonds, sapphires, turquoises and great pearls, though their saddles are invisible because they are covered with housings of scarlet velvet. Around the Sultan, no one is mounted, but four grooms walk a pike's length away on either side, to keep off the people, except when he calls to one of the Pashas or another of the officers to come closer so they can talk.

Nothing else is heard but the sound of feet and hooves. The numberless throng of people along his way, composed of Istanbul's different nations – Turks, Greeks, Armenians and Jews –- remain silent as a way of showing respect and reverence. They bow to the Sultan as he passes, and he, very pleasantly and good-naturedly, returns the greeting, with a slight, but clearly perceptible tip of the head.

In the courtyard blood runs for the success of his forthcoming enterprise in Europe. The objectives of the campaign are, as usual, kept vague, but it is well known that the Sultan directed the Emperor's diplomats to tell their lord to expect a call from the Ottoman army. The long-awaited pitched battle between the world's most powerful monarchs has gone from a remote contingency to a distinct possibility. And with that, the future of Christendom must be considered in the balance.

After the sacrifice, the Sultan performs his ablutions using scented water from a golden bottle. Then he enters the mosque and the officials go ahead and shoo from his path a dishevelled person who was found curled up behind one of the pillars. Facing the tiled niche that the Conqueror installed at an oblique angle in the apse, flanked by the lampstands he himself brought back from Buda, the Sultan says the bismillah. Then he kneels to Mecca and his forehead meets the thickly knotted pile. Behind the plaster in the conch of the apse, the Virgin and Child are shielded from this scene.

Five days later he goes to the Old Palace to take his leave. And he kisses his old mother Hafsa with great reverence and she weeps the feeble tears of one who doesn't know if there will be another time, and tells him of her vision, which she has seen more than once and which tells her that if he goes on the campaign he will be putting his life in grave danger and will almost certainly die. At this he laughs and kisses her the more before going away again. That night he permits a little variety into his love life, sleeping with a most beautiful Macedonian. Then he goes to work.

～

On 9 June the consortium's courier Marco Antonio reaches Edirne where the army is mustering, and on the next day he sits with Ibrahim. The Pasha is delighted with the product but the price is a little high. According to what measure exactly? Andrea Doria is spending 150,000 ducats on an armada at Genoa. Forty coins will buy you a slave. What is a fair price for the crown of the world?

Iskender Celebi, Ibrahim's former mentor and the current Chief Treasurer and Quartermaster, isn't hiding his unhappiness that an outlay of this size is being entertained just as the army begins a costly campaign. The tax harvest from Aleppo and Tripoli has yet to arrive and the bags nestling under the eight domes are fewer and slimmer than usual. There have also been murmurs of disquiet among the doctors of the law. Opulence is a quality the Sultan can only benefit from being associated with. But the aping of Christian kings shows the Caliph of Islam in an ambiguous light, to say the least. On the other hand, having come this far, it would be perverse for the Grand Vizier to haggle over an object whose function is to proclaim his master's wealth. Even Iskender sees this.

The consortium is aware of the nuances and Marco Antonio has permission to come down. It's not as if another buyer is about to appear. Its market is precisely one. After an amicable enough conversation the parties settle on 116,000 ducats and Marco Antonio travels to Istanbul where Iskender hands over 100,000 ducats and later on, after the Syrian revenues arrive, the difference. The Treasurer frees three Christian slaves, two male and one female, as a gesture of goodwill. Pietro Zen's sons and the other members of the consortium have made a 100 per cent return on their investment. The proud father declares it an excellent result under the circumstances.

～

At Edirne the Sultan hands out punishments to flock-owners who have been breaking the sumptuary laws by dressing their servants in velvet and have refused the army's requisition demands. The leaders of the sedition are dragged by horses till they are limp, two others are hanged, four are decapitated and two lose a hand apiece. Fifteen escape with a beating on the soles of the feet.

After feasting the townspeople for the bayram holiday, the Sultan journeys sixteen days to Sofia via Philipopolis and Tatar Pazarjik. His army now includes the legions of Anatolia, Rumelia, Thrace, Serbia, Bosnia and Dalmatia. He has 100,000 men under his personal command. The High Governor of Rumelia commands 90,000, Ibrahim 50,000; a further 50,000 are under Kasim and Ayas and 14,000 under the High Governor of Anatolia.

The Sultan's personal camp is being transported by two caravans of two hundred camels apiece, which take it in turns to go forward, like the legs of a human being. At any given time one of the legs is with the Sultan and the other is a step ahead so that when the court arrives at its next stop, the tents and pavilions are already up.

Suleyman isn't ducking his head into some marginal lands that may shortly be lost or bartered away. He is taking a leisurely tour through some of the territories that lie at the heart of his Empire, making sure that all is in order and that his governors are doing their jobs, just as the epistles he studied as a boy recommended he should. The towns are being equipped with mosques, baths and bazaars. And the old Roman road northwards is in good condition, the broken sections having been relaid by locals in return for tax breaks.

As he comes through with his viziers and bags of silver, a State in motion, as he enters each town by its southern gate, the army unfurling against a hillside before being folded up again, the faces that stare at him do not show the bruised, guileless loathing of the rebel. For these Orthodox Christians, Jews, shaman-followers and a growing number of Muslims, themselves a mix of Anatolian incomers and local converts, the Turk – his garrison, his judge, his engineer – is a known quantity. He is a bulwark against the war and misery that are endemic to the borderlands between Janos's territories and those controlled by partisans of Ferdinand. It is a curse to be liminal. And down here, where everyone knows who's in control, trade is booming.

It is commonly believed that people make up their minds whether to serve their lord on the basis of a prejudice or sometimes a principle. They do not. They look for weakness and, if they don't find it, compelling reasons for loyalty present themselves. Dissent is a warning that the seams are already split. Suleyman has not known dissent on any meaningful scale and does not mean to. Aside from his immediate objective of getting to the battlefield, he wishes to convince his subjects of the strength of the House of Osman and the impossibility of its ever being removed.

~

Nis is a town in Serbia full of Byzantine junk. Sultan Murat took it for the Ottomans in 1385. On this June day Suleyman will process through Nis for the edification of the townsfolk. Not with the whole army. Nis would sink. But with enough.

Two men in German clothes stand unwillingly on the balcony of a minaret looking over the town. Their names are Leonard von Nogarola and Joseph von Lamberg. Last year Lamberg was in Constantinople to talk peace with the Turks, an abortive venture tainted by treachery elsewhere. On the same day that Ibrahim and Lamberg were engaged in their discussions, Lamberg's comrade in the Austrian diplomatic corps, Janos Habardanecz, was sneaking into Buda Castle to kill the King. Not that the Porte itself was anticipating a successful conclusion to the diplomatic initiative. When Lamberg entered the New Palace to see the Sultan, he was greeted by ten chained lions and two leopards, evidently hungry.

Nis is to be a fresh start. Lamberg and Nogarola have instructions to extend the truce and offer the Sultan an annual pension in return for Hungary. Negotiations are to open at an optimistic 20,000 ducats, but the ambassadors may go to 100,000 if necessary. And if the Turk says no, they are to propose that Janos may keep Hungary on condition that he end his days in celibacy, at which point the country will go to Ferdinand and his heirs. Under a side-deal the Austrians may offer Ibrahim 10,000 ducats yearly.

The Pasha is keeping the ambassadors waiting. It took weeks for their safe-conduct to be issued. And now, after several days spent in conditions of near imprisonment, instead of being ushered reverentially into his presence . . . this minaret!

From their vantage the Ottoman army is like an enormous snake whose head is miles from its tail, slithering along and inspecting some corner of its lair.

Fifty carts are being pulled through Nis. They are so gorgeously caparisoned that the townspeople looking on from the roadside speculate that they contain the harem's beauties. People are stupid in this way. They let their imaginations get the better of them. The harem isn't a travelling circus. Behind the carts, men walk abreast with hawks on their gauntlets. Keepers lead ferocious hunting dogs, as docile as lambs. Thousands of camels pull artillery pieces and wagons laden with gunpowder, cannonballs and crossbow bolts. The procession goes through triumphal arches that have been put up specially, referencing Bologna.

The clump of the camels' feet and the grinding of their teeth. The horses' farts, the flap of the standards, the music of the head trappings. The murmur of a watcher: Glory be.

Then come the provincial governors with their men and banners of different colours denoting the force to which they belong, each emblazoned with a crescent moon. So monotonous, so unending. Ayas Pasha is followed by 25,000 men on horseback holding lances. The tall stature of the Sultan's archers is further accentuated by their long turquoise satin coats and their high bonnets, not unlike the cap worn by the Venetian Doge, with a tall white crane feather rising in the middle which makes them seem snow-topped. The Sultan's pages carry his accessories, including a skinful of water drawn from a well two thousand miles away in the Meccan desert, the one which God caused to gush in order to save the Prophet Ismail and his mother Hagar from dying of thirst.

Suleyman is twelve years into his reign, twelve years older and surer than the day he came ashore at the Palace jetty, his loins and bow arm proven to all the world. He has loved and punished. He has adjudicated and forgiven, he has lost daughters and sons. He has thought about the burden that God has put on him. But the crowd is encouraged to sense precisely nothing of the experiences that – allowing for a certain difference of emphasis, a certain difference of scale – make them and him the same.

The intention of Ibrahim of Parga, the director of this mise-en-scène being enacted on the streets of Nis, is not to bring the Sultan closer to his subjects, but to take him further away. The people's eyes are riveted to Suleyman's tight-fitting robe made of finely woven crimson cloth embroidered with gold thread and embedded with pearls and sapphires. They are transfixed by his turban covered in diamonds, his bejewelled and dama-scened saddle, the browband of his horse, set with a turquoise the size of an egg and encircled by precious stones, and his sword whose jewels alone must be worth 80,000 ducats. But they do not see Suleyman himself. He is an icon on the scale of Aya Sofya, so big, so incomprehensibly big, as to be invisible.

And the climax of the spectacle is yet to come.

Behind the Sultan walk a selection of his most beautiful pages, their hair in long braids hanging from red caps, each of them carrying a jade-green celadon vase. And behind them, the most beautiful page of all carries a cushion on which rests a golden sugar cone embedded with preserved fruit of different colours.

That would be a child's interpretation. In fact it is a stupen-dous helmet made of solid gold. It is a solid gold helmet so big and heavy that no one could ever wear it. The fruit are gemstones.

Superficially it resembles Clement's tiara. But the papal head-gear has three tiers while the Sultan's has four. The helmet sits within these gold crowns. The surface of the helmet, the circlet, the neck guard and the crowns themselves are saturated, drip-ping with jewels. Another distinguishing feature is that where one might expect the cross to be – where it is on Charles's octagonal mitre crown, for example – is a gold mount shaped like a crescent. From this sprouts an aigrette of very soft feath-ers that come from the chameleon, a native animal of India that is said to live in the air.

The helmet's existence has long been rumoured. It came from Venice to Thrace and the Grand Vizier paid for it using his Syr-ian revenue. That it is should be so tall and beautiful is a matter of surprise, however.

Ever since he procured the holy Crown of St Stephen for his vassal Janos Zapolya, the Sultan has been calling himself the 'distributor of crowns to the monarchs of the world', in his letters to European rulers. Now he has one of his own.

The Ottoman approach to regalia is cosmopolitan to say the least. The Abbasid caliphs of Baghdad adopted the Persian practice of wearing a taj, or crown. In their case, the taj was a turban adorned with gems. Suleyman's throne, transported through Nis in one of the caparisoned carts, is, again, of Persian inspiration. The Venetian mirror that is a companion piece to the helmet is an allusion to the mirror of Alexander the Great, reflecting the whole world that was his and is now the Sultan's.

That the Sultan puts himself about so eclectically reveals something of the civilisation of Istanbul–Constantinople. Yes, to refer to the city of the world's desire by just one of its names would be misleading, for it has two selves. It is Mecca and Rome, Persepolis and Corinth, East and West. And these two selves are both healthy, crawling over each other like crabs in a bucket.

∼

Archduke Ferdinand claims to want peace. But still he plots to recapture Buda and he has been talking to Shah Tahmasp of Iran, Ismail's son and successor, about a possible anti-Turkish alliance. Brother Charles is in Germany raising a vast army. That this army will include Lutherans is Charles's reward for his new, more flexible attitude towards the heresy, essentially a policy of toleration in exchange for cannon fodder. Suleyman, meanwhile, who is forever saying, 'to Rome! to Rome!' and who detests the Emperor and covets his title of Caesar, is camped at Nis with the biggest army ever assembled by an Ottoman Sultan. War for mastery of Europe is weeks away. But Nogarola and Lamberg have their instructions.

Ibrahim Pasha has never relished his dealings with representatives of the Archduke. They behave as if their employer is the

Sultan's equal; they are surly and self-righteous and have tried to assassinate the Turks' good friend in Buda. If Ibrahim were in Ferdinand's place, he would be embarrassed to call himself the King of Hungary and the King of the Romans while possessing neither place.

Diplomacy is as much about generating unease as it is about winning friends. Charles and Ferdinand must be left in no doubt of the Turks' contempt for Hapsburg arms and their confidence in victory, sentiments that Lamberg and Nogarola will have the goodness to convey to their masters.

The morning after the Nis parade finds the two Austrians waiting for Ibrahim Pasha to speak. The Grand Vizier is not his usual, talkative self. He is silent and frowning. He barely glances at the six gilded goblets which the Austrians have brought as gifts. It is a long time before he opens his mouth.

As a diplomat the Frank has two registers: winning and derisive. For Austrians it is always the second and never the first. 'My Emperor,' he begins, 'has heard how three or four years ago a King of Spain came over the sea and at one time travelled back and forth, doing great harm wherever he went and making enemies of many a nation; he wished to bring Christendom together but never succeeded; he also sent messengers back and forth to the monasteries, abbeys and patriarchs, and tried to extort money from them, proclaiming that he wanted to advance against the Turks.'

And so on, in the manner of someone stating the obvious to people of limited intelligence, regretting that his time is being wasted. Finally getting to the point, Ibrahim tells the Austrians that the Sultan's business is with the King of Spain, not with Ferdinand, whom the Sultan does not consider a king but a low fellow who does not keep his word. Then Ibrahim asks: is it really true that the Pope crowned Charles with his feet? And while the Austrians are trying not to combust from distress and consternation at the Pasha's insults, he sends them away.

The following day, Lamberg and Nogarola deliver Ferdinand's proposals to the Sultan. They also give him two wine jugs, not even made of gold, but of gilded silver, two biggish bowls and six cups. After dismissing the pair, the Sultan receives diplomats from Ragusa whose gifts need two dozen brawny men to carry them. How curious, Suleyman observes, that a place the size of a pimple gives him fine and copious presents while the supposed King of two vast countries sends such indifferent stuff. What is he going to do with this rubbish? And Ibrahim Pasha dives into the basket of sweet aubergines which the Ragusans have also brought with them, gobbling up at least ten without even having them tasted beforehand.

On 12 July the Sultan writes a letter to Ferdinand. 'The King of Spain has long been proclaiming that he wants to take action against the Turks, but it is I who by the grace of God am advancing with my army against him. If he is a man of courage, let him await me in the field.' And the Sultan confesses to doubts over the Emperor's manhood. 'When we shall have reached his German frontier,' he writes, 'it will not be fitting for him to abandon his provinces and kingdoms to us and take flight, for the provinces of kings are as their wives. And if they are left by fleeing husbands to fall prey to aliens, it is an extraordinary indecency.'

The following day, the servant of one of the state messengers comes to Nogarola and Lamberg's lodgings and tells them that the Sultan has departed for Belgrade. They are to follow immediately. That the state messenger himself did not deliver the news is one more insult to add to the others. The envoys cut short their lunch, pack disconsolately and spend the next few days schlepping to Belgrade, where there is another interminable parade. They are lodged in a house below the castle that belongs to a Turkish merchant who has no more than ten wives. There they are forgotten.

After two weeks the Sultan sends them each an underskirt and an overgarment, along with several other pieces of velvet and silk that are patterned and coloured in the Turkish style. They also receive six silver bowls and four jugs between them. If you were to put all this crap together and try and sell it, you wouldn't get two hundred ducats. When it comes to delivering insults through the medium of gifts, the Turks are in a class of their own. Nogarola and Lamberg are expected to wear their Turkish fancy dress for their final audience. Ibrahim has an ordeal planned for them.

On 5 August a state messenger escorts Lamberg and Nogarola across a pontoon that straddles the Sava. Cresting the hill on the far side, looking down on a plain that falls gently away into the distance, they are confronted by a remarkable sight. The entire Turkish army is arrayed before them in perfect order, maces, swords, lances and axes glaring in the sunlight. The messenger escorts them up between the forces of Rumelia, Anatolia and Bosnia, up and down avenues formed by heavy cannons, ordinance carts, squadrons of purebred chargers and thousands of Tatar horsemen baring their teeth over bows of seasoned willow.

Emerging from a forest of bonnets and caps, horsetails and aigrettes, Lamberg and Nogarola approach the Sultan's tent along a tight corridor of Janissaries who shout abuse at them. As the pipes and kettledrums of the military band merge and become an undifferentiated roar, the Janissaries discharge their arquebuses into the air, producing flashes of fire and whorls of bitter smoke.

On an imperceptible sign the tumult ceases, its last wave breaking over the distant hills.

In his royal tent Sultan Suleyman sits on a golden throne with four columns. Hanging from each of the two foremost columns is a golden sabre, a golden bow and a quiver filled with arrows. The columns are studded with gems and pearls, no more than a thumb's width apart, as are the quivers and sabres. On a stand next to the Sultan rests his golden helmet.

Only a sadist would not feel some sympathy for Lamberg and Nogarola. The past few weeks have been a trial. Worse than a trial; they have been a crucifixion. And now, whether it is from exhaustion or nausea at the excess of magnificence in front of them, or the knowledge that the soldiers outside who have been reviling them are coming to possess their homes and everything they love, the diplomats lose their ability to stay impassive in the face of provocation. For a few moments they lose all power of speech and motion, becoming as corpses whose souls have left them for the inferno.

After their audience Ibrahim tells them that their master will get his answer in a sealed letter which they are to take to him. Nogarola and Lamberg object bitterly, saying that the King of the Romans has given them full powers and that it pains them not to know the contents of the letter. Ibrahim merely smiles and says, come, come, you already know the Sultan's answer. And just a few days after the Austrians are dismissed, Alvise Gritti lays siege to Esztergom, a Hapsburg-held citadel north of Buda, to distract the enemy from the main Ottoman thrust further west.

~

Guns. A non-place in north-western Hungary less than six leagues from Vienna whose name no one can agree on. Bers. Koszeg. Gins. Grinas. Schrips. An unimportant little fortress to roll over en route to the meadows of Austria, there to do battle with the King of Spain and his brother.

The garrison is headed by a Croat, Nicholas Jurisic. He writes to his master, Ferdinand. 'I have volunteered to fight against the Turkish Emperor and his army. I fight not because I presume to equal his force, but only so as to delay him a little while to give time for Your Royal Majesty to unite with the Christian Holy Roman Emperor.' The specialist soldiers under Nicholas's command consist of ten knights and 28 light cavalrymen. His other assets include 1,000 local men of fighting age, a ring of low-slung walls and a moat.

Nicholas Jurisic is not the kind of commander who hands over the keys to his castle and asks to be left alone. The Turks have met several such tacticians on their way north. He is a warrior in the mould of Philippe de Villiers de l'Isle-Adam at Rhodes and Nicholas von Salm at Vienna. When the Sultan and

Ibrahim arrive outside Guns with their 70,000-strong expeditionary force, they find the fields black and smoking, the wells poisoned and the neighbouring villages aflame.

Defending castles is about walls: holding them up or knocking them down. The Turk's superabundance of men is less significant than the calibre of his cannons. In this respect, Jurisic is in luck. In the course of its northwards advance the Turkish baggage train took a wrong turn into the mire near Lake Balaton and the heavy guns that were shown in so formidable a light on the plain of Belgrade got stuck and had to be abandoned.

Hostilities start as they always do, with a barrage. Missing their big guns, the Turks bring up small artillery pieces which lob out gunpowder-charged Biscayens the size of goose eggs. They bounce off the walls. Jurisic has drilled his men well. Whenever the Turks mine a section of wall the defenders immediately sap the mine with a countermine. The Turks bring up their siege engines, towers of faggots leering over the defenders. But Nicholas's men have had the foresight to fill barrels with sulphur, tar and tallow, which they set alight and tip onto the engines, turning them into infernos. Inside the castle supplies are running low but Turkish casualties are heavy and the besieg ers are running out of bread. And the rain isn't helping.

This is ridiculous, they're thinking in the Sultan's tent, worse than Vienna: a river stopped by a thumb.

After two weeks of fruitless assaults a Turkish delegation comes to tell Jurisic that Ibrahim Pasha is feeling kind. Pay an annual tribute of a florin per household – that or a one-off payment of 2,000 ducats to the Janissaries – and Guns will be spared. Nicholas replies that there's no money and it's not his castle to surrender. The attacks resume and the Turks manage to plant a standard on the walls before they are hurled back by defenders whose demographic is changing, as the men are killed and are replaced by women and children. When the fighting is at its most intense, a knight appears on the ramparts, stabbing his flaming rapier towards the Turks. It's St Martin, patron saint of nearby

Szombathely, who once shared his cloak with a beggar and brandishes the same sword he used to split it in half. The Janissaries flee in terror and the mood amongst the besieged turns ecstatic.

Again the Turkish delegation comes, this time bringing news that Guns is to be left unmolested. But its commander must come out of his castle to discuss a ceasefire. Nicholas looks at his surviving followers, out of powder, out of puff, and realises he can't hold out another hour. He himself is close to collapsing from his wounds. The Janissary chief and his men take him to the Pasha's tent. They are still holding out for their 2,000 ducats.

Jurisic was with Lamberg on the mission last year and he fell ill in Constantinople. Ibrahim doesn't miss much; the first thing he does when the Croat enters his tent is to inquire if he is quite recovered. Then, after clucking sympathetically over his wounds, the Grand Vizier tells Nicholas that he has convinced the Sultan to give him Guns. And the Sultan will honour him with a meeting.

There is something about this Ibrahim. In his own depiction he has a softening influence on his severe master. And perhaps he does. Certainly this is the impression he likes to convey. Last year in Constantinople, Nicholas also heard rumours that the Frank is prejudiced in favour of his fellow Christians, or perhaps that should be former fellow Christians.

Even in his weakened state, Nicholas is alert to the dangers of lost prestige. If he goes to Suleyman's tent, the Turks will announce to the world that the Sultan has accepted the surrender of Guns and shown magnanimity to its commander. But Jurisic has the measure of the man before him. Dropping to his knees, he kisses the hem of Ibrahim's robe and says, 'I know how much power and credit you enjoy with the Sultan.' Then he asks to be excused from the meeting on account of his injuries. Not a problem, comes the reply, and Jurisic realises that Ibrahim derives much pleasure from his reluctance to go in front of the Sultan, and his expressions of respect and esteem.

∼

Later on, when making out his report to Ferdinand on the great triumph, Nicholas writes, 'Even the Turks say that not once since Suleyman's accession to the throne have they been dealt such a blow by so vile and low a place as this.' And the margin of victory is indeed far greater than the score, 2,000 Turks dead to 400 defenders, would suggest.

What happened to the definitive meeting of the great armies, the massive leaders, that was promised on the plains of Belgrade? The answer is Nicholas Jurisic and the three and a half weeks he spent holding up the Turks at Guns.

For it is autumn now. Who would invest Vienna as the frosts start, without food for the men, without cannons? The gateway to western Europe is better fortified and its garrison more formidable than was the case the last time the Turks were in these parts, three years ago; and events at Guns have made the Turks doubly allergic to siege warfare.

As for Charles, it is clear to him that castles, scorched earth and winter are his most effective weapons. He would be confident in his ability to humiliate Suleyman from a position inside the city walls. But to take on the Sultan in a pitched battle, winner-takes-all . . .

That would be a gamble unworthy of the leader of the Christian world.

Throughout September Charles studiously avoids the Turks, allowing Suleyman's men to vent their fury on the unfortunate province of Styria. It is telling that Styria isn't in the direction of Vienna, but away from it, evidence that Suleyman, like Charles, is reluctant to enter into combat on the enemy's terms. And in due course, but not before losing thousands of men to ambushes in the gorges of Lower Austria, and all the while expressing continued scepticism over the Emperor's virility, Suleyman turns for home.

His arrival in Istanbul is met with the usual festivities and illuminations, but the truth is that the northern front has confounded Ottoman intentions for a second time. Not many at the Porte want to recognise this fact.

A minister running a state must never think of himself, only of the ruler, and should concentrate exclusively on the ruler's business. To make sure he does so, the ruler, for his part, must take an interest in the minister, grant him wealth and respect, oblige him and share honours and appointments with him. That way the minister will see that he can't survive without the ruler. He'll have so many honours he won't want any more, so much wealth he won't look for more, and so many appointments that he'll guard against any change in the status quo. When rulers and their ministers arrange their relationships this way, they can trust each other.

As Machiavelli goes on to explain, a ruler shouldn't be morally good, at least not all the time, because that would mean following different standards to his rivals. He must seem and sound wholly compassionate, wholly loyal, wholly humane, wholly honest and wholly religious. But he mustn't actually be these things. Indeed, if he is, he is putting himself at risk. Machiavelli would call himself a realist, not a cynic. He deals with the way people behave, not the way they should behave. A ruler should be both fox and lion, he says, because the lion can't avoid the snares and the fox can't defend itself against wolves.

Accustomed to a more socially stratified society than that of the Ottomans, Machiavelli has given no thought as to how the elevation of a poor man to ministerial rank might go to his head. And when we look at the example of Ibrahim of Parga, we see that it reveals a flaw in the Florentine's theories. If a minister is given an abundance of privilege, this may not have the tranquillising effect that Machiavelli foresees. It may foster a sentiment that is as dangerous to the ruler as the resentment and jealousy his actions are designed to prevent.

Ibrahim Pasha also has a lion theory, one at variance to the hierarchy that is integral to Machiavelli's view of the world. According to Ibrahim, the lion does not bear full responsibility for its actions. That lies with its keeper in the Lion House. The keeper gives the lion lots of meat but he also has a stick to hand, to impress the lion and make it cringe, and if necessary as a weapon of self-defence. In the scheme that Ibrahim has built, the lion is Sultan Suleyman, the tamer is himself and the Ottoman Court is the Lion House.

~

Ibrahim is walking along one of the stone paths in the Second Courtyard, towards the Council Hall.

He enters through the portico and takes his seat between the two army judges and some of the provincial governors. Also present are the Chief Treasurer, Iskender Celebi, and the Keeper of the Royal Monogram. Secretaries are poised to take records.

The defendant is Mulla Kabiz, who claims to be a man of religion but spends more time in coffee houses than he does with qualified doctors of Islamic law. Recently Kabiz made an assertion, founded on an erroneous reading of the Quran and the sayings of the Prophet Muhammad, which has reached the ears of the Council. Kabiz's assertion is that the spiritual status of Jesus Christ is higher than that of Muhammad.

The present Sultan's father fought wars for less. To the East the infidel Persians disrespected the messenger of God and gave Shah Ismail a bogus divinity, and Selim was obliged to crush them in warfare. Not a rebellion breaks out but some seer, citing a relationship with God of peculiar intensity, is acclaimed by the credulous as a Messiah. The distance that separates the true faith from wrong doctrine is critical and must be maintained. This is especially true in the case of the Hebraic monotheisms that preceded Islam. To allow Christians and Jews prosperity is one thing; to indulge their errors is to threaten society, the Sultan and the world with confusion.

Today in the Council Chamber the army judges are Muhiddin, who is simply stupid, and Kadri, who is both stupid and corrupt. After hearing Kabiz twist the Prophet's words, the judges do their best to refute him. But they are not masters of theology, they haven't the telling verse or saying to hand, and they end up running out of argument and shoutily sentence Kabiz to death. It's not an edifying scene, a charlatan out-arguing two of the Empire's pre-eminent jurists, but the conclusion is correct.

Not to the Grand Vizier, it now becomes clear. Stepping into proceedings, rather than congratulate the judges on their ruling and urge its speedy implementation, he reprimands them for their lack of sound evidence, which, he says, brings the judiciary into contempt. The way the Frank speaks, one would be forgiven for thinking that this is not a trial but a humanist debate – a debate, furthermore, that Kabiz has won. And the Grand Vizier tells the apostate that he is free to go.

Ibrahim has unsettled the Chamber but his intervention is hardly out of character. He came back from Buda with brazen images of three Greek deities which he installed in the Hippodrome, insulting Islam which forbids artists from mimicking the human form. Recently Flemish weavers were in town, hoping to interest the Sultan in a series of epic tapestries about kings hunting, but they went away disappointed on being told that such subjects are banned under Islam. Does the Grand Vizier consider himself exempt from a rule that the Sultan obeys?

Then there is the Pasha's wine-drinking, his flaunted affection for the Catholic Republic of Venice. His father, a notorious drunk, has brought disgrace on the office of Governor of Parga.

Whenever the old man wishes to emphasise a point, he swears not on the Quran but the Virgin Mary!

Suspended above proceedings in the Council Chamber is a golden globe with a chain hanging down. This is an allusion to King Anushirwan, whose chain of justice needed only to be pulled by an ill-used subject for the monarch to direct his undeviating will at righting the wrong that had been committed. At the same elevation as the globe, on the wall above the Frank's head, is a curtain which hides a latticed window. Behind this curtain, behind this window, sits the Sultan, listening to the trial of Kabiz.

What is each window, but an eye opening to the whole world, to watch ceremonies and spectacles? What is each tower, but from head to foot a tongue to praise and eulogise the just King? So wrote the Conqueror's poet.

For those who are present in the Council Chamber the Sultan is a tingling on the nape, a bubble of sweat in the declivity of an upper lip. He is both there and not there.

The Sultan may at a time of his choosing pull back the curtain and fire an arrow at the globe, spreading his justice around the whole world. It is as if now that arrow has been fired. Descending from his position at the window, the Master of the Celestial Conjunction enters the Council Chamber.

In the stunned silence that follows he addresses Ibrahim.

'Why has the heretic who dared to prefer Jesus to the Prophet not been punished?'

Ibrahim replies easily. 'The army judges condemned him from anger rather than basing themselves on healthy reasoning. This is why I have thrown the case out.'

No. The Sultan corrects his favourite, itself an event without precedent. Then he decrees that the case will be retried tomorrow by a higher religious authority. Mevlana Semsettin Ahmet is the son of the late Kemal Pasha and is a man of learning.

The following day Kabiz again explains why Jesus is higher than Muhammad and then, very quietly, very politely, Mevlana Semsettin dismantles Kabiz's argument. Again very quietly, with all kindness, Semsettin asks Kabiz if he will return to the path of the pure faith. But he will not. And when the trial ends his head is cut off with a sword.

~

The poet Figani has been dining out on the ode he addressed to the Sultan during the circumcision ceremonies. It is quoted even now, and rightly so, for it is as good an example as any of the art of buttering up one's sovereign using ladles of verse.

That command performance bought Figani some prominence. He has since dedicated poems to certain pillars of the state, but the rewards in terms of commissioned work and income have been modest. Iskender the Treasurer, who has a poetic soul as well as a full purse, is his only regular patron.

No one denies Figani's aptitude. According to his fellow versifier, Latifi, whatever Figani reads in Arabic or Persian is engraved on the inner page of his soul. But irregularity of income has forced him to accept a clerkship in the tax office, drudge work that takes him away from the inner page while not even making him comfortably off.

And he is prone to other distractions. For him the tavern, cup-bearer and wine flask are not simply poetic images of the divine, but fully material realities. Figani and his pals can often be seen cruising for prostitutes around the Hippodrome or taking a boat across the Horn to the hostelries of Galata, where they spend the night talking about rhyme and metre and shouting for wine. After staggering back to his digs in the grimy and vertiginous port neighbourhood of Tahtakale, the poet sharpens his reed pen and writes verses deploring his lack of funds.

It isn't clear who started the rumour that he wrote the couplet in question. Enough people wish him ill on account of his flaunted royal connections, his nights of sin. But it is Figani's bad luck that all of Istanbul is whispering these two lines, simple in form and glittering with unpunished insolence.

Do Ebrahim amad be deyr-i jahan,
Yeki bot-shekan u yeki bot-neshan.

Two Ibrahims drank from the world's cup,
One knocked down idols, the other set them up.

Once in the deserts before Islam, disgusted by the idolatry that was being practised by his people, the Prophet Ibrahim, or Abraham as they call him down there, entered the temple and smashed the idols to smithereens. This is the Ibrahim who knocked down idols.

The one who sets them up is in this very city.

One night there is a gathering of literary types. Figani isn't his usual mirthful self but at dawn he agrees to accompany the rest of the party down to the Bosporus to carry on drinking. Figani's host asks him why he is out of sorts. Figani replies that in his dream yesterday he was at the top of the minaret by this very jetty, singing out the call to prayer, but when he awoke he was seized by a strange dread.

A few days later the officers come for him in Tahtakale. First they bind him, then they put him on a donkey and walk him around town so the people can revile him and draw the appropriate conclusions. Then they take him down to the jetty at the foot of the minaret and hang him.

~

Public diplomacy is about show. Private diplomacy is about gifts. The best kind of gift is long in the waiting, benefits the recipient in tangible ways and is extremely rare.

One must beware of fakes. Only genuine alicorns detect poisons and cure diseases. A tiny fraction of the declared ground horn on the market is real. An entire horn – certified – is the gift of kings.

The arrival of Venice's alicorn in Pietro Zen's luggage puts the Grand Vizier in an excellent mood. Pietro takes the horn out of its case and hands it to the Pasha, who, holding it to the light and admiring its hue and curvature, exclaims, 'This is beautiful and very precious. Did you know,' he goes on, 'that the Conqueror himself bought the horn of a unicorn from a Christian seafarer returning from India, along with a very old book covered in wax, explaining its provenance? That alicorn is in pieces now, broken up to make dagger hilts and belt buckles and bow rings.'

Ibrahim observes that the Conqueror's specimen, being bigger than this one, must have belonged to a bigger beast. Not, he reassures his guest smoothly, that his intention is in any way to belittle the Venetian gift. 'On the contrary, it is a great sign and demonstration of his lordship the Doge's supreme benevolence towards the Sultan, particularly as this alicorn has for so long been among the most precious possessions of the Venetian State. And this gift is the more worthy because no one has ever heard of such a rare gift being sent by any prince at any time. His Imperial Majesty wants it noted in the chronicles that are being written about his deeds that the Venetian lords sent him an alicorn of singular beauty and great value, a gesture that will be preserved for posterity.' And he ends with one of the aphorisms that he, as Grand Vizier of the Ottoman Empire, is surely entitled to coin from time to time. 'Cloths and comestibles, like the flesh of men, wear out rapidly, whereas certain gifts leave eternal memory of themselves.'

In response to the Pasha's outpouring, Zen graciously declares that the Signoria is pleased to make the Sultan a present as rare as the Lord of Lords himself. 'He is the supreme Emperor and Master of the World, and just as his power is infinite, so is the reverence that the Signoria feels for him.' Later on the Venetian is fetched by the state messengers who bring him to the New Palace to present the alicorn to the Sultan. And Pietro kisses the hand of the Sultan whose face glows with satisfaction while examining the alicorn.

This episode is a good example of gifts by the weaker party earning the goodwill of the stronger. While no one is happy to give away an object of such good omen as an alicorn, Ibrahim Pasha's insistence on having it presented to the Sultan turned a trivial issue into a crisis of protocol, and the Doge had no option but to make a gift of it. Once that decision was taken, there was nothing to be gained from withholding the kind of praise that engenders the fondest recollection of the giver. It costs nothing to call someone King of the World.

While the Bologna accords have left a crack in the relationship of trust that used to exist between the Porte and the Signoria, the alicorn has acted like lime plaster over the top. It is impossible to say how long the lime plaster will last before it too cracks. Provided gifts are made with sincerity and their effects are not compromised by some act at variance with the interests of either party, they buy time.

These caveats were disregarded by Ferhat Pasha, who gave the Sultan an exquisite box of gold and crystal and a mere half an hour later lost his head. His present didn't help him because it was given in a spirit of rancour and distrust. And a gift offered in such a spirit is worse than no gift at all.

~

The Grand Vizier has a diamond that was prised off Clement's tiara during the pontiff's incarceration in Castel Sant'Angelo. He bought it for 60,000 ducats. The ruby set in his ring was on Francis's finger when the Most Christian King was captured at Pavia. Ibrahim's authority is so great that he can buy the intimate possessions of the princes of the world. His network is so good he is informed the moment such trophies come to market.

But wealth is pointless without munificence. Today he is giving a banquet for the doctors of the law. Next week it will be the turn of all the women of the palace. And two days after that the entire court will dine at his expense. All in honour of his nephew who is to be circumcised.

He and his wife are endowing pious foundations in Istanbul, Mecca and other places. It may be Muhsine's influence, she has perhaps warned him that it is dangerous to underestimate the power of religion.

~

The Austrian diplomats who arrive to negotiate the truce first cleave a crowd of hangers-on before they pass through a gate in the picket fence that runs from one side of his audience chamber to the other. After bowing once, they bow a second time, standing with their toes in the rich pile and waiting for the seated figure to speak.

To hear the Frank talk is to solve the problems of the world in light, easy steps. It is in his gift, he says, to convene a council of the Christian Church to end its divisions. 'I could immediately put the Pope on one side of the room and Luther on the other.'

Whether he believes his own boasts cannot be known. Certainly it is no less plausible that he should broker a Christian peace than become Grand Vizier in the first place. Men like him believe whatever turns out to be possible. That way they are never surprised.

Holding a letter that the diplomats have brought for the Sultan from Charles V, he examines the seal and declares, 'My lord has a seal which he takes with him. I have a seal similar to his, which I carry with me, for he does not want there to be any difference between himself and me.'

He can invade Italy – or not, depending on his mood at the time. 'I have 40,000 Tatars at my disposal,' he says airily, 'sufficient to destroy the whole world, out of a force totalling 300,000 men, but I didn't send them to Italy where they would damage and destroy everything.' He has no great love for violence. After Guns, while the irregular cavalry were trashing Styria, Ibrahim's force marched abstemiously south without committing notable atrocities.

In truth, his generalship will never be of the first order, for it is rhetorical swordplay that interests him. There is in him an irony, a verve, a desire to be in the pit of world affairs, puffing his chest and flashing his spurs.

~

'Take me,' he goes on (he has never been stuck for things to say), 'I am his slave, and yet he has given me all his realms and his empires and I alone do everything. Above all the governors and the high governors and the Pashas, stand I. Everything I want done is done, I can make a Pasha out of a groom and give territories and provinces to whomsoever I please, and he will not say a thing. No matter how much he wants something done, if I do not give my assent it will not happen. And if he orders something and I order the opposite, it is my order that will be carried out. I can make peace or war, I can spend whatever is in the Treasury. He isn't better dressed than me, we are equally well dressed.'

He is naturally pleased when the Austrians tell him that Ferdinand wants nothing more than to be a brother to him; would he, Ibrahim, do Ferdinand the honour of being his elder brother? Little Piero has come a long way, hasn't he?

Diplomats learn from each other. Even Austrian ones. These ones have learned from their predecessors that it pays to bite their tongues when Ibrahim is being rude about their master, that a present of rubies does marvels for his mood and that if they follow the guidelines he will not only treat them to a lunch of assorted fowl and sugared rice that is eaten with dinky wooden spoons, but also tell them which phrases to use and which to avoid during their audience with the Sultan. And finally, in a transport of goodwill, he will exclaim, 'Now that we have taken bread and salt together we cannot be enemies!'

~

To the Palace. The Sultan is forty years of age, tall, dark and well-proportioned, with a pleasingly oval face, a narrow upper lip, the beard on his cheeks barely speckled with grey, with an acute, piercing gaze, a nose tending to the aquiline, long hands and a gracious way of telling you that he will grant your master the peace that no fewer than six earlier embassies were denied, and that this peace will not last seven years, or twenty-five, or a hundred, but two or three centuries or all of eternity, provided Ferdinand, whom he considers his son, does not break it.

All this is conveyed to the Austrian envoys by the translator,

Yunus Bey, whose father was a George Taroniti of Modone – with what degree of exactitude, one cannot be sure. And the Sultan's words are subject to the constant mediation, interpretation and rhetorical embroidery of the Grand Vizier, who is standing by.

They are no longer young men, Suleyman and Ibrahim, no longer exchanging tender notes via deaf mutes, but potentates with paunches and the world at their feet. And still the Sultan, while he shows great pride in the majesty of his office, is susceptible to influence. And still his friend is hated.

Ibrahim of Parga is not bloodthirsty. He is not incompetent. He is skilful enough to convince the King of the Romans to trade Hungary for a father figure. And yet the people at large, the Ottoman wife and soldier, do not love him for the services he has performed. Their feelings have nothing to do with Figani's death. They understand when severe measures need to be taken to protect the dignity of the State. But the couplet in question is both damning and revealing. It exposes the contempt that the Grand Vizier feels for the people, their traditions and their prophets. And this is why they hate him.

~

As is often the case when it comes to sensitive questions of internal dysfunction, the outsider may be the person with the clearest head. On the other hand, outsiders know less and draw their conclusions based on limited data; and there is no guarantee that their analysis will be free of prejudice.

The position occupied by Daniello de Ludovisi, Secretary of the Senate, brings him into frequent contact with the Doge, who sets much store by his opinion. And Ludovisi knows the Turks well, having visited them in Istanbul and Cairo. He is not, however, one of the Republic's Turcophiles.

Part of the novelty of Ludovisi's reading of the Ottoman situation lies in his indifference to the charms of Ibrahim Pasha. The Pietro Zens of this world swoon at the kisses blown by the Pasha in the Serenissima's direction, they are charmed by his

Italian, they love his money. But Ibrahim's Italophile pretensions leave Ludovisi cold. He has a weakness for the Teutonic sense of order, which he sees as essential to the German soldier, who imbibes it in the womb.

Back in 1517, when Ludovisi was an ambassador to Selim in Cairo, he had dealings with Ahmet Pasha, the late Sultan's second breath, who was later beheaded for insurrection there, having been sent back to the same province as Governor by Suleyman. Believing Ahmet to be incapable of pre-meditated treachery, Ludovisi holds to a revisionist account which argues that the Governor only rebelled against his monarch after learning that the Porte was planning to assassinate him. Suleyman went on to kill his ablest general, Ferhat Pasha. These two acts Ludovisi attributes to Ibrahim's plotting. Suleyman's approach to capital punishment is in general more collegiate than that of his late father, who needed no accomplice to chop off heads! But Suleyman is made of softer clay than his father.

To cap it all, Piri Pasha's recent death is widely believed to have been caused by poison. 'With what stratagems did [Ibrahim] engineer his own rise!' the Venetian sighs, 'and with what arts does he maintain his position!'

It is a mistake, in Ludovisi's view, for the Republic to repose much confidence in a double murderer, perhaps triple.

The Grand Vizier is indeed suspicious of anyone gifted enough to become his rival. The measures he takes to protect himself explain why the army generates no brilliant new leaders and the court no promising new bureaucrats. Whoever has talent hides it for fear of attracting the wrong kind of attention from Ibrahim. The fact that he has left Ayas and Kasim unmolested says nothing about his humaneness or compunction. It is testimony only to the ordinariness of the Pashas themselves.

The Frank prefers to be alone among weaklings he can dominate rather than share with others of aptitude and means. His instincts to hoard power and monopolise opportunity may have strengthened his position, but they have also destabilised the State. Its surface is as firm and burnished as a rice pudding; dig your spoon in, however, and what you find is half-baked ingredients that haven't mixed.

~

Ludovisi is the kind of Venetian who takes a discerning view of the national interest. And the memorandum he writes for the Senate in the aftermath of Guns is the threat assessment of a sceptic.

To begin with the differences. We Italians are in hock to mercenaries. The poor reputation of all Italian armed forces may be attributed to the bad faith and feeble willpower of paid soldiers, who deprive city states of their best warriors and behave as if they are the arbiters of the nation, bringing ruin, desolation and servitude in their wake.

By contrast the Turk's men are his own, gathered in childhood from a variety of sources. Continuity of pay and firm discipline engender obedience, while bonds of loyalty form between captains and their men. Furthermore, all are united around one language. And it is certainly a remarkable if under-appreciated aspect of the Sultan's military apparatus that men of so many linguistic backgrounds have adopted the Turkish tongue and reach for it when they are in mortal danger.

That said, Ludovisi has yet to see much evidence for the Turks' famous military prowess. Their victories over the frankly primitive Iranians and Mamluks are no guide to their future performance against top-flight European opposition. Belgrade and Rhodes were also uninformative. Those campaigns didn't prove the superiority of Turkish arms, only the superiority of Turkish numbers.

The Ottoman army remains a steppe army, overwhelmingly horse-borne, with foot soldiers and gunners added as an afterthought. Ludovisi doubts the ability of such an army, which lays emphasis on the handling of bows, lances and maces, to fully exploit the opportunities presented by the arquebus, the quintessential modern infantry weapon. 'More than at any time in the past,' he writes, 'the Christian armies have become infantry armies. The most Serene Lord of the Turks entirely lacks this kind of infantry. I say entirely, for the Janissaries have neither order nor discipline, nor the cunning of the Christian armies.'

Ludovisi's assessment of the Janissaries should be treated with caution. He didn't see them annihilate the Hungarians at Mohacs, nor has he visited one of their camps, as silent as a Carthusian cloister. What is true, however, is that the Janissaries number just 12,000 and are not characteristic of the army as a whole. Furthermore, Ibrahim Pasha is diligently undermining their effectiveness by dispersing them around the Empire. One can see why. They trashed his palace. They view his advertised conversion with scepticism. He owes them 2,000 ducats from Guns. All in all, it is hard for an elite infantry to operate effect-ively if the Commander-in-Chief treats them as a threat.

That Suleyman's most recent offensives against the Haps-burgs ended in failure is further fuel for the Venetian's misgivings. And when he tots up the forces of the Emperor, the King of the Romans and the other German states, he arrives at a number superior to anything the Sultan can ever hope to command.

Although the German princes are not prepared to help Ferdi-nand prosecute his claim to Hungary, they draw the line at letting him lose Austria. While the Sultan can live without Aus-tria, he will not give up Hungary. In these distinctions may lie the germ of peace.

The Ludovisi memorandum comes with two take-aways. The first is that the Turks' northward push is over. The second is that in order to continue to express their mutual loathing the Sultan and the Emperor will need to find a new theatre of war.

Act Four: Royalty of Sea and Land

XII

An unwelcome piece of maritime news reaches the Sultan while he is tied down at Guns. Andrea Doria – 66 years of age but still with palaces to fill – has sailed south with his fleet and invested the port city of Corone from land and sea. A wart on the little finger of the Morea, Corone used to be a Venetian colony, an entrepot and a vantage onto the Ionian and Mediterranean seas. This state of affairs ended in 1500, when the Turks, capitalising on their triumph over Antonio Grimani at Lepanto, seized it. Now Doria wants Corone back. Not for the Serenissima. If there's one Republic a good Genoan cannot abide, it's the Venetian. No, he wants it for Christendom and Charles.

Five days after Doria's cannons open up, the castle is his and Imperial and Papal banners fly from the battlements. Leaving behind a garrison, he sails north again, seizing the port of Patras and two Turkish forts that command the narrow entrance to the Gulf of Corinth. Not once in the course of these actions is he engaged by the admiral of the Turkish fleet, another Ahmet Pasha, whose two dozen galleys only reach Corone after the city has fallen. Later on, Doria breaks through the blockade that Ahmet has set up and provisions the town's inhabitants. Then he goes on a razzia up the coast. The booty he brings back to Genoa includes Turkish cannons which he puts in a church that was built using prize money from an earlier campaign.

News of the fall of Corone and Doria's subsequent raids

causes unease at the Porte. It is feared that the Spanish will use Corone as a bridgehead to threaten the Empire's possessions in Rumelia. Much criticism is aired of Ahmet Pasha, who is known to be a frequenter of taverns and a drinker of wine. And the speed with which Corone capitulated smacked of cowardice and lack of backbone.

~

The problem isn't one of resources. There is no want of Bithynian oak for timber, Thracian bitumen for caulkage or Nile flax from which to make lateen sails. Anatolia produces iron for anchors and chains; Russia sends hemp for ropes. And although fitting a fleet is costly, the Sultan's wealth is so vast that even expenditure on this scale isn't really significant.

It's a question of prestige. Each spring the palace page watches the Sultan and his Pashas march off to fight wars on land. The martial training he receives is heavy on scimitars and sieges, light on northerlies and navigation. He naturally dreams of becoming Chief of the Janissaries, not Captain of the Fleet. While for a well-born Genoan like Andrea Doria it is a matter of pride to take up a vocation at sea – half a dozen Dorias have done so over the centuries – the Ottomans must strongarm their captains off the land. The Governor of Gallipoli doubles up as Captain Pasha, or head of the navy, simply because Gallipoli is site of a big naval base, and regardless of whether he has marine expertise or not.

The more established navies take measures to ensure that skills and insights are preserved and improved upon in the lulls between fighting. The craftsmen of the Venice yard are kept in continuous employment, refitting old ships and building new ones, which in turn fosters innovation and team spirit. Their equivalents on the Horn, by contrast, are hired and fired according to the immediate demands of war and peace. Whenever new ships aren't urgently needed, the shipwrights and caulkers go home to their lemon boats. And when the order comes in for new galleys, the yard sends off to the Greek islands for craftsmen who dribble into town weeks later.

In the lulls between panic-building, if you duck into the yard – it isn't hard, security is deplorable – you'll find a few dozen wide-hull galleys in varying states of disrepair, lacking either rowing boats or cannons. You'll find a score of workers banging away amid the cormorants and herring gulls, among them Francesco Giustiniano, a homesick Venetian who is sawing planks for dispatch to the Red Sea, where they will be assembled into galleys for service against the Portuguese. What you won't find is a sense of purpose, urgency or pride.

In the European maritime states, expertise tends to flow to the navy from the merchant marine, men going from the latter to the former as war approaches and with it the promise of pillage, rapine and suchlike entertainments. Spanish naval captains have thousands of commercial sailors to draw on. The same is true of the Republic of Venice. But Ottoman maritime trade is conducted by the Empire's Greek subjects and one can hardly ask Greeks to take to sea against their fellow Christians. To compensate for the shortfall, the naval authorities plunder the hillsides. The deck of a Turkish galley is full of shepherds who can't stand upright in a gale.

Now that the Turks and the Austrians are at peace and the Empire's northern border is relatively stable, the crucible of conflict is indeed shifting, as Ludovisi predicted it would. At issue is anything solid in the greater White Sea: the Morea; Minorca; North Africa; you name it. Without revamping the navy, the Sultan will be unable to fight this big new war against Charles V. He will be unable to cover the ground. The good news for him is that while none of the structural weaknesses of the Ottoman navy can be dealt with overnight, they can be substantially mitigated and steps taken to rectify them permanently. The cash is there. All that's missing is a leader.

~

Being so close to the Turkish mainland, and a base for Christian pirates, the Greek isle of Lesbos was an inevitable casualty of the Conqueror's acquisition drive of the 1460s. A Sipahi, or household cavalryman, from the vicinity of Salonika, Yakub by name, took part in that invasion, was rewarded with land, and stayed on. Yakub had four sons from his marriage with the widow of an Orthodox priest from Mytiline, the island's capital. He called them Ishak, Oruc, Ilyas and Hizir. Ilyas was killed while fighting the Hospitallers. Oruc was captured in the same engagement and, after a period as a galley slave, was ransomed. But opportunities grew scarcer in the Ottoman lake that the eastern White Sea went on to become; Turks can hardly ravage Turks. In 1504 Oruc and Hizir shifted operations to Tunis on the North African coast, entrance to the sea's western basin, where in due course Ishak joined them.

When Ferdinand and Isabella completed the reconquest of Spain in 1492, many Spanish Muslims, rather than submit to baptism, left their homes and established themselves in North Africa. From here they launched raids on the Iberian coasts with which they were so familiar. News of their success attracted adventurers from the eastern Mediterranean, who, with their faster craft and experienced crews, pushed aside the exiles and expanded the range of targets to include Christian ships on the open sea. The Spanish set up fortresses and protectorates along the same coast, but were unable to eradicate the problem of piracy.

North Africa is notably welcoming to the shallow-draught pirate galleot. The inlets and lagoons of this marvellously varied coastline offer protection from storms, and bolt-holes inaccessible to the heavier Spanish ships. And the White Sea is a giving sea. One sweep yields a vessel fraught with copper goods and Flanders cloth. The return from a landing on Calabria is measured in silver and slaves. Markets for the contraband spring up along the African coast. The local rulers who vie for these roadsteads can usually be persuaded to billet an international force in return for a cut and protection from Spain.

Oruc of Lesbos heads such a force. His hair and beard are bold red. Barbarossa, as the Christians call him, scratches out a fiefdom along the coast. He is helped by his younger brother,

Hizir. In 1516 he receives a request from the Muslims of Algiers to help them against the Spanish. Algiers sits just off the sea lanes linking Spain, the Kingdom of Naples and Genoa. A short distance to the east lie Sardinia, Corsica and Sicily. Oruc doesn't wait to be asked twice. After gaining entry to Algiers, he takes control of the town, massacres his hosts and mints money in his own name. His death in 1517 is from a Spanish pike thrust.

This is also the year in which Sultan Selim invades Egypt, which makes him a near neighbour of Hizir, who has inherited his older brother's empire as well as his nickname – not very accurately as Hizir's beard tends to auburn. Ishak has been lost by now, killed by the Spanish. Understanding the benefits of having a client in North Africa, Selim awards Hizir the title of High Governor of the rather theoretical Ottoman province of Algeria. Hizir gets to keep his autonomy while gaining two thousand Janissaries and a conveniently hands-off patron. Over the ensuing decade the new Barbarossa eclipses the old, absorbing rival pirates, fending off Spanish attacks and expanding his possessions along the coast. His ports are efficiently run and his ships are as well maintained as those of any national fleet. And Algiers, his on–off capital, is North Africa's most opulent city.

First the approaching privateer fires its cannon to denote the value of its human cargo. The harbourmaster comes aboard for a preliminary appraisal. Once ashore, likely candidates for ransom have their particulars taken down. For the unlettered, a scribe is on hand to write to the family. The remainder defile to market, runners going on ahead and shouting out their age and value. In case of a glut, rich Tuaregs or Jews step in loyally to support the market, the Porte and Hayreddin having already reserved their share of the proceeds.

For Hayreddin – not Hizir; not Barbarossa – is the name by which his men know him. It means 'boon of the faith'. He loves Christians as Sari Saltik did, with a sword, the difference being that his golden apple isn't in Germany but all around the White Sea. His sailors chase Christian prizes, his sea walls are built by Christian slaves, his caskets are filled with Christian ransoms.

And Hayreddin is the reason the towns have emptied along the coast of eastern Spain. The people, priests and soldiers have withdrawn into the mountains or to the top of cliffs which are accessible only by windlass.

Back in 1512 his brother Oruc lost an arm. It was shot off by a cannonball fired from a Spanish fort whose walls had already been weakened by Oruc's artillery. He was too impatient to wait for his own guns to finish the job. This is the kind of error that Hayreddin wouldn't make. Once Oruc reproached him for seizing only the laggard in a flotilla of ten Christian ships. Overlooking the insinuation of cowardice, Hayreddin replied, 'As our forefathers in the sea lanes used to say, don't over-chase, or you'll regret it.' Even then he was the less impulsive, the more calculating of the two.

A certain anti-Christian feeling can be expected from someone whose one brother fell to the Hospitallers and two more to the Spanish. A certain robustness in the waging of holy war. And both Charles V, by treating the Muslims who have stayed on in Spain abominably, and those same Muslims, by looking to their brethren across the straits, dance the same dance of violence and revenge. None of which is to the detriment of the interests of Hayreddin Barbarossa. As the kinsmen of Muhammad discovered when first they first touched on Spanish shores a few decades after the Prophet's death, the best jihad is a profitable one.

~

Hayreddin's shipmate, Seyyid Murat, has pen and paper and a literary style. Murat writes that from the moment Charles's priests made it illegal in Spain to worship according to the rite of Muhammad, great woe befell anyone who issued the call to prayer or knelt to Mecca or so much as remembered Allah in an invocation. And when the Spanish Muslims heard that whoever was a Muslim was to be burned, they gathered in their thousands and went to a high mountain and the infidels sent soldiers after them and with great excess made terrible war against them. And the Muslims sent word by fast ship to Hayreddin. When the courier landed at Algiers and coming into Hayreddin's presence gave him a full account of the situation, his heart bled and he ordered thirty-six ships to be rigged for the rescue.

Coming ashore on the Spanish coast, the pious ones climbed the high mountain and defeated their foes and enslaved them and seized their possessions. Then they brought all the Muslim women and children they had rescued down to the beach, embarked as many as they could, and took them over to Algiers, leaving behind a thousand brave and capable companions to protect the rest and guard the captives. Seven times Hayreddin's fleet made the trip from Algiers to Andalusia and back again, and a total of 70,000 people were taken away from the infidel and brought to the Muslim lands and mixed up amongst the Muslims there.

The pious ones are holy warriors and *Allahu Akbar* is their cry. They observe the fast even on the oar bench in midsummer. They keep the Virgin Mary in reserve, however, and call on her if Allah is busy when they are in peril. To ward off storms they turn to starboard to imprecate the good angel, then to port to deprecate the bad, then the ship's imam fills a beaker with olive oil which he throws into the wind to calm it. On shore, in taverns attached to the prisons where the slaves are kept at night, they cavort to the double-reed zurna and slur their pidgin which is drawn from a dozen languages. At Easter they rampage through the ghetto shouting, 'Jews! You killed Jesus!' and celebrate the Resurrection to the accompaniment of guitars and a lute shaped like a pear. No, their conduct cannot be described as strictly Islamic.

~

The Spanish soldiers on the Peñon of Algiers, a fortress on a rock at the entrance to the bay, resisted Oruc and now they defy his brother. The Peñon is provisioned from the sea. With a following wind, abuse hurled from its ramparts carries ashore and disturbs the faithful at prayer. For fear of the Peñon's cannons, Hayreddin's captains must go up the coast whenever they want to put to sea.

First Hayreddin's ships relieve a Venetian galley of her cargo of gunpowder. Then they impose a blockade on the Peñon. When the garrison is close to starvation, Barbarossa offers terms. The rock's commander, Martin de Vargas, confesses surprise that the great pirate King is ignorant of Spanish resolve. One May morning Hayreddin orders his gunners to start using up their Venetian powder. For ten days they and the Spanish gunners lash each other with meteors of fire. Algiers is ablaze, minarets topple and on the disputed islet the walls of the fortress are breached. And only now do Hayreddin and his force of 13,000 men, armed with guns and crossbows, cross the bay in fourteen galleots to finish the job.

Martin de Vargas is on the ramparts, fighting off a dozen assailants, but Hayreddin orders that he be taken alive. After an exchange of amenities, Hayreddin voices – in plausible Spanish, complete with Castilian lisp – his desire for Martin de Vargas to cap an illustrious career by crossing the theshold into Islam. Vargas replies coldly to this suggestion, contemptuously even. The exchange sours, esteem turns to fury, and in no time Vargas is a lifeless pulp.

~

Piracy isn't about sinking ships or winning battles. Piracy is burglary when the owner is out. In 1529, when Andrea Doria and the Spanish fleet are taking Charles to Italy for his coronation, Hayreddin sends Aydin Reis, one of his lieutenants, to ransack the Balearics. After seizing a big treasure and liberating many Spanish Muslims, Aydin's galleots come across eight galleys that are commanded by the Captain-General of the Spanish fleet, Rodrigo de Portuondo, off the island of Formentera. Disregarding the grotesque disparity in firepower between the two sides, Aydin engages the superior Spanish force and, using a combination of cunning and ferocity, captures seven of the eight galleys with their crews. Portuondo himself is killed, shot in the chest by a Turkish arquebusier.

The following year, Doria returns the compliment while

Hayreddin is besieging Cadiz, pillaging the Algerian port of Cherchell and snapping the chains of the Christian slaves who are building Barbarossa's fortress there. Hayreddin sails to Cherchell as soon as he learns of the outrage but he is too late to stop the Genoan disappearing over the horizon. And that is perhaps fortuitous.

For if there's one thing the two mariners know as well as this tideless sea, it's each other's worth. Given their parity as sailors and their similarity in age and experience, the outcome of any confrontation between them will likely be decided by divine intervention: a sudden calm, a drop in visibility caused by dust off the Sahara. Like the Sultan and the Emperor, circling nervously in southern Austria, or the Emperor and the Most Christian King, somehow not quite contriving the logistics of a duel, Hayreddin and Doria seek each other but not too hard.

And why would Hayreddin Barbarossa, who stomps through the nightmares of Christian children from Valencia to Otranto, whose haul of hostages from Formentera includes twenty men of quality, knights and captains – why would Europe's bugaboo risk his achievements to satisfy a private vendetta? No Imperial force, Castilian or Genoan, dares impede his fleet, which boasts such advanced rogues as Sinan the Jew, so-called because of his positively rabbinical understanding of the stars, and Anatolian Turgut, who sows terror in the Tyrhennian Sea. Pope Clement himself is too terrified to leave shore for fear of Hayreddin and his merry band!

Apart from Suleyman himself, Barbarossa is now the most famous Turk. No amount of information about him is too much for Europe's titillated opinion-formers. From Rome, Francois Rabelais, who is working as secretary of the French ambassador while putting the finishing touches to *Pantagruel*, sends Barbarossa's portrait to the abbot of his former monastery in France, along with a map of Tunis. Everyone wants to know where Barbarossa will obliterate next and whose maidens he will ravish.

He doesn't neglect his master, bringing cadavers and dropping them at his feet. The coverlet of General Portuondo is delivered to the Sultan with Hayreddin's compliments. One summer a Spanish barge of seven hundred barrels is towed into Istanbul, full of captured ship's biscuit. Then it's a Flemish vessel, the pennant of Charles V trailing ignominiously in its wake. The passengers include two lions in a cage.

He is robust and well-set, with a rounded, commodious chest, a black kaftan and a muslin cummerbund. What people find most arresting about his appearance is his thick brows and lashes which overhang his eyes like a vine. While he rarely shows pity to anyone he suspects of disloyalty, to favoured subordinates he is notably unselfish. After a raid by one of his captains, Mad Mehmet, Hayreddin waives his share of captives, among them an adorable Genoan boy. When he realises that the boy is to be his, Mad Mehmet drops to his knees and kisses Hayreddin's hand and feet. 'My son,' Hayreddin says indulgently, 'I've given you my share of booty in the past, and you never kissed my hand and feet in this way. What's so special now that you cover me in kisses?'

Every prize he takes is part of his plan to become master of North Africa and leave it to his protege, a boy called Hassan. And by the time that Doria takes Corone in 1532, humiliating Ahmet Pasha in the process, Hayreddin's empire is growing strongly, replenished by 70,000 grateful and industrious Spanish Muslims, while his Christians toil away in the galleys, quarries and fields.

'His Excellency Hayreddin Bey's ships were prowling in the direction of Spain,' Seyyid Murat relates, 'when they heard that the accursed and soulless Spanish King had taken his accursed army and gone by land to do battle with his Excellency the World-Protecting King as well as sending Andrea Doria and his obliteration-meriting fleet to the castle of Corone, which is part of the royal and protected domains, and they immediately communicated this news to the honourable hearing of his Excellency Hayreddin Bey, and he, judging this news to be correct, immediately rigged fifteen warships and sent them to Spain. And the captains, upon reaching Spain, captured many ships and prisoners and burned and destroyed castles and waged holy war in the provinces and caused immense damage. And from there they went to Andalusia and took off as many Andalusian Muslims as they could. They caused great damage to the Spanish provinces, so much so that along the coast no castle or town was untouched. For two months in this manner at sea and on land they went around pillaging and plundering.'

~

It is accepted practice to cut off the ears and noses of prisoners who are badly behaved or try to escape, but the Spanish have extended this to include quite innocent prisoners. The Spanish, Seyyid Murat writes, cut off the ears and noses of all the Muslims who fall into their hands. They even sever their nerves and maim them so that they can't run away. The White Sea is as small as the market place at Mytiline, and everyone is family, so to speak, so whenever an outrage of this kind is committed Hayreddin hears about it. His solution is decimalisation. For each Muslim the Spanish maim, Hayreddin maims ten Christians.

The effectiveness of Hayreddin's new policy is demonstrated after the Christians capture Salih Reis, who served at Formentera and is much despised by the Christians. When Salih is brought in chains to Jijel, a Spanish port on the Algerian coast, the local Spaniards gather on the quayside and offer to buy him. Their intention is to kill him slowly. But the captain of the vessel refuses their offer, saying, 'If you kill him, do you know how many captives Barbarossa will kill?' And nowadays, writes Seyyid Murat, if a Christian infidel beats an innocent captive excessively, the other infidels complain to their lords, saying, 'Barbarossa has so many of our people in his gizzard and there is no doubt that Barbarossa is a real demon, and whatever we do here he will know about it by this evening and kill our prisoners.'

In due course the families of the Spanish knights and captains who were captured at Formentera send the 20,000 gold pieces

Hayreddin demanded in ransom to Algiers. But he is troubled by the thought of liberating so large a number of vengeful enemies. 'These people,' he reasons, 'still have all their strength and if I sell them they will find a good number of ships and go about doing harm to the people of Islam.' So he rejects the money and keeps the prisoners.

At his side he has a young compatriot from Lesbos. Seljuk is his name. Hayreddin welcomed Seljuk to Algiers and gave him a small fiefdom and responsibility for guarding the knights and captains. One night Hayreddin dreams that he and Seljuk are back home in Mytiline and the central pillar of Seljuk's house is about to collapse, and Hayreddin has to shore it up with his own hands. The following morning, pondering the meaning of this, Hayreddin summons Seljuk and says, 'These infidel knights must be up to something. Now you must pretend to be in league with them and draw out the truth.'

Seljuk goes to the captive captains and tells them how much he hates Hayreddin for giving him a prison to look after rather than an honoured position, and the captains, thinking that he is in sympathy with their aims, tell him that they are planning to escape and liberate all the Christian slaves in Algiers.

When Seljuk comes back with this intelligence, Hayreddin does not rush. He cannot execute the Christian rebels without showing evidence of their treachery. Otherwise the Spanish will say that he killed them out of cruelty and will avenge themselves on Salih Reis. After giving the matter some thought, he sends Seljuk back to the captains with the suggestion that he, Seljuk, take a letter from them to the Spanish commander of Bejaia, up the coast. And the captains give Seljuk a letter asking the Spanish for a ship and some men to help them carry out their plan. Seljuk keeps the letter but makes a copy, which he takes to the commander of Bejaia, who replies with a letter of his own which says that he will send a ship and soldiers. It is not difficult for Hayreddin's men to intercept the ship and seize the soldiers. In Algiers Hayreddin has the captains brought to him and he shows them their letter, which they cannot deny, and he has them executed. He sends the commander's letter to the place where they are holding Salih Reis, to show that the captains were not executed for pleasure or out of cruelty, and not a hair on Salih Reis's head is touched.

Barbarossa can now set out for Istanbul.

~

The Turks have a new ally, better than Venice in every respect: committed, powerful and unafraid. The relationship took root after the French were defeated at Pavia. When the Most Christian King was in captivity and before he agreed to the extortionate ransom that secured his freedom, the Sultan sent him a morale-boosting letter. Take courage, the letter said, kings must expect to lose battles and be imprisoned from time to time. The important thing is not to let it get you down! And don't forget that I – and here the Sultan listed his various titles, King of Kings, Shadow of God on Earth, Emperor and sovereign lord over the White Sea and the Black Sea, Rumelia and Anatolia, the province of Sulkadr, Diyarbakir, Kurdistan, Azerbaijan, Iran, Damascus, Aleppo, Egypt, Mecca, Medina and Jerusalem (the list went on for a little while longer) . . . , don't forget that I have your back.

In 1528 came another affectionate letter in which Suleyman apologised to Francis that he could not comply with his request that a certain mosque in Jerusalem be turned back into a church. But the Sultan very earnestly promised to guarantee freedom of worship for Christians everywhere in the Empire, not just in Jerusalem, so that 'it is impossible for anyone at all to torment . . . them in the slightest.'

The Sultan's words seem all the more generous if one recalls the scenes of butchery that attended the Crusaders' capture of the same city, in 1099, when Francis's ancestors were up to their ankles in Muslim blood.

The upside of the French investment in the new alliance is Hayreddin Barbarossa. Francis wants the help of the King of Algiers – this is the title by which Hayreddin styles himself in foreign affairs – in taking Genoa from Andrea Doria. In return, Hayreddin wants money and the use of French ports for his galleys. But before any of this can happen Hayreddin must release the distinguished French gentlemen, including associates of the Dauphin, who are among the captains he seized at Formentera.

In the summer of 1533, Serif Reis, gentleman at Hayreddin's court, steps onto French soil with the captains in question. The Admiral of France's Levantine fleet escorts him, his prisoners and some caged gifts of the maned, four-legged variety across the mountains to Puy-en-Velay, near the Loire where the great river rises. The Most Christian King has come to Puy to hold intercourse with the Black Virgin, an ebony depiction of Our Lady.

On 19 July, in the presence of Francis and Serif, the prisoners' fetters are solemnly snapped. And when Serif goes back across the mountains, he has in his possession a signed declaration of friendship between the two kingdoms and a trade agreement.

The following month, leaving Algiers in the hands of Hassan and some Janissaries, Hayreddin sets out with seventeen of his own captains to terrorise the Tyrhennian Sea. Messina, Sicily's northeastern tip, is sacked. Taking Elba by surprise after nightfall, he hustles almost the entire population under the age of twenty-five onto his ships. Sinan the Jew bags an enormous Venetian galley that alone yields four hundred captives.

The panic that Barbarossa and his captains cause along the coasts of southern Europe is unprecedented. When Philippe de Villiers de L'Isle-Adam, the Hospitallers' frail Grand Master, is informed that Barbarossa is making for Malta, the knights' new base, the veteran of Rhodes drops dead without ado. The information turns out to be erroneous. Pope Clement refuses to step off dry land to go to the wedding of his niece and the son of the Most Christian King. As Hayreddin's fleet, loaded with plunder, sails on calmly towards Greece, Andrea Doria, wrong-footed, heads towards Sicilian waters.

After stopping to buy the freedom of some Turkish prisoners at Corone, Hayreddin continues up the Aegean and drops anchor at the entrance to the Dardanelles. His crews spend the next few days mending, scrubbing and painting their vessels. When the state messenger delivers the Sultan's mandate to proceed, Hayreddin brings it over his face and eyes before kissing it as one might an object of great sanctity. On 21 November, at an hour considered auspicious by the astrologers, his forty galleys, galleots and smaller craft come around Palace Point and enter the Golden Horn, their decks waxed, their guns booming, their flags aflutter.

~

If Hayreddin is the sea captain who strikes most fear into Andrea Doria, it is to Hayreddin that the Ottoman Navy must be confided. This is the Porte's logic. But the Porte is a behemoth whose limbs don't always agree with its brain.

Although Sultan Suleyman receives Hayreddin well enough in the New Palace, behind the courtesies there is an irresolution, or perhaps a weakness. Of the Pashalik that the pirate King has been led to believe will be his, the lucrative fiefdoms and the immense budget: no sign. The second and third Pashas, Ayas and Kasim, and the captains of the fleet, are all hostile.

It's a question of upbringing. Hayreddin was not educated in Istanbul or weaned in the ways of obedience to the Sultan. His morals are dubious, his grasp of Islamic practice vague. And his interests lie at the other end of the Mediterranean. How, they are wondering, can the Frank be so sure that, once Hayreddin has taken control of the fleet and entrusted the key captaincies to his own men, he won't simply commandeer it for his own ends?

For it was Ibrahim who urged the Sultan to bring in Barbarossa, and Ibrahim is an inconvenient 250 farsakhs away. Having crossed Anatolia and entered Syria with 50,000 men, the Grand Vizier is wintering in Aleppo before he marches on Baghdad, whose people have asked to be liberated from the tyranny of Iran's Shah Tahmasp. It will be a year before he returns to Istanbul. Perhaps more.

~

Ibrahim's absence is an obstacle to Hayreddin's plans, but not an insuperable one. Taking the initiative comes more naturally to him than it does to the complacent Pashas. So, after disarming his ships and locking up his Christian captives in the city's prisons, Hayreddin takes a detachment of Sipahis and sets off through the snow. Before the winter is out, he is on Aleppo's crouched acropolis.

Ibrahim Pasha has convened the city's Council, a body made up of senior divines, merchants, judges and so on. When Hayreddin is invited to join their deliberations, these proud gentlemen show him to the inferior end of the room, the one farthest from the Grand Vizier. But after the meeting, Ibrahim summons Hayreddin to talk with him and the Frank likes what he hears. He invests Hayreddin with the office of Captain Pasha, or Admiral of the Fleet, also giving him the bulbous white turban and caparisoned horse that are his trappings of office. And when the Council next sits, the Captain Pasha is at Ibrahim's side.

It's an emboldened Hayreddin who rides back from Aleppo in the thaw of 1534, no longer an incomer of uncertain status but a member of the charmed circle whom the court artists will be delighted to paint in profile sniffing thoughtfully at a rose. He sprays gold pieces at every pious foundation he passes, also stopping at the earliest Ottoman capital, Bursa, to kneel at the grave of Emir Sultan Buhari, the dervish who married a Sultan's daughter. In his suite is a Syrian eunuch, a gift that the Grand Vizier has asked him to convey to his and Muhsine's son Mehmet Shah.

Just one thing spoils Hayreddin's mood. While he was away in Syria, many of the captives he left behind in Istanbul's prisons died from cold and neglect, and others escaped and took refuge among the Christians of the city. He is upset to learn that the son of the Doge of Venice, Alvise Gritti, helped the fugitives, showing particular favour to the Venetians among them.

Hayreddin has no love of Venice. He cannot understand the Porte's attachment to a fading power that pledges herself to the

Sultan but signs the Bologna accords, that gifts alicorns to one side and indemnities to the other. His disciple Murat does not refer to the Venetians in his writings without attaching an epithet like 'godless' or 'treacherous'.

And the Captain Pasha knows theft when he sees it. He sends men to Pera to recover his slaves, and they also arrest people who organised the sedition, including certain friends of Gritti. The Beyoglu is powerless to prevent this violation of his territory.

~

In the New Palace Suleyman is reassured by Ibrahim's letters of commendation and he gives Hayreddin a rod of justice to signify his absolute authority over the Empire's ports. And Hayreddin explains to the Sultan how he has been fighting at sea all his life, about his brother Oruc, and everything he knows about the European coastline and the acute vulnerability of the Spanish vassalate of Tunis. From Tunis's Cape Bon, he tells the sovereign, it is less than a hundred miles to the Sicilian ports of Trapani and Marsala. Our galleys can be across the strait, raid and devastate those places, and get back to Tunis before Palermo knows what is happening.

Hayreddin's retinue also contains Rashid, brother of Muley Hassan, the current ruler of Tunis and Charles's client. To get where he is, Hayreddin goes on, Muley Hassan has waded through blood and the people long for Rashid. We'll invade and make Rashid King but in reality Tunis will be yours. The coasts of Italy will be impossible to defend. And our French friend is building galleys apace so he can attack Genoa. That will tie Andrea Doria down.

The Sultan sets Hayreddin's budget at 600,000 ducats a year. His annual allowance is to include 14,000 ducats from his new fiefs of Rhodes, Euboea and – a nice touch – his birthplace of Lesbos. At the yard on the Horn, never less than aware of their new boss glaring at them from his site office, two hundred master craftsmen, fifty foremen and countless other workmen labour incessantly.

Under Barbarossa's energetic leadership the Ottoman Navy gains two hundred new galleys, each one manned by two hundred and fifty oarsmen, sailors and combatants and equipped with the best munitions. In May he sails westwards from Constantinople and spends the summer ravaging the coast of western Italy, looking, all the while, for something special.

~

A cousin of the Mantuan Gonzagas to whom Alvise Gritti sends horses, young Giulia Gonzaga, Countess of Fondi, is celebrated for her intelligence and vivacity, her fair curly hair, her lips surpassing rubies in colour and beauty and her neck as white as snow. Widowed in her teens, she settles at her late husband's castle at Fondi, on the Via Appia which links Rome and the South, and eight miles inland from the port of Sperlonga. Here she holds a famous court, frequented by artists, poets and ecclesiastics – the historian Paolo Giovio, now Bishop of Nocera, is a guest – who consistently situate her near the peak of human perfection. Of the day which he spends with her at Fondi, the religious reformer Juan Valdes writes, 'it is a great pity that she should not be Queen of all the world, although I believe that God has thus provided, in order that we poor creatures should enjoy her divine conversation and courtesy, which is not inferior to her beauty.'

Giulia would please the Sultan better than ship's biscuit or a wet flag. This insight suggests itself to Hayreddin and, after some pleasant weeks spent attacking Messina, sacking San Lucido and passing boldly in sight of Naples, one night he comes ashore at Sperlonga. A stealthy nocturnal march brings him and his men unopposed to Fondi and they gain entry without difficulty to Giulia's castle. Giulia is minutes away from being kidnapped by the most feared man in the Mediterranean in order to adorn his master's harem. Roused by a servant, wearing only her nightdress, she escapes through a window, over a secret drawbridge and into a moonlit courtyard, from where she gallops into the night and to safety. Angered by this reverse, Barbarossa lets his men loose on Fondi, which they sack, and on a nearby convent, whose sisters they slaughter. By the time the news of the outrage reaches Rome, and the Cardinals are stirred from their vigil around Pope Clement's deathbed and into belated action, Hayreddin and his men are halfway to North Africa.

~

Tunis is the size of Rome. Its merchants, and the pirates who have for generations been paying its Hafsid rulers a fifth of their spoils, have embellished it. It has more than a hundred mosques held up by pillars of jasper and porphyry and walls so finely polished you can see your face in them. There are also splendid churches and a monastery that Hayreddin intends to silence because he doesn't like the sound of Christian bells.

Tunis is rich in olives, lemons, limes and oranges. It is also rich in linens and Christian slaves. But it is poor in water. The great aqueduct that used to supply Roman Carthage runs nearby but no recent ruler has deigned to maintain it, let alone divert it to where it would be of most use. The aqueduct's ruined arches stand in a plain that is covered in orchards irrigated by wells, while the city itself, three miles away, has just one well and its inhabitants rely on cisterns. And the Bay itself isn't much of a bay, rather a basin that collects filth and run-off from the city, wadeable for much of the year.

Landing at the Goletta, the fort that sits astride the spit of land that divides the Bay from the sea, Hayreddin wins over the garrison by announcing that he has Muley Rashid, Muley Hassan's infinitely preferable brother, on board. Only an unfortunate illness, he explains, prevents the Kingdom's rightful ruler from showing himself to his subjects. By the time the people realise that Rashid is actually in jail in Istanbul, they have unwisely let Barbarossa and his force of 5,000 into the citadel of Tunis and Muley Hassan has fled to the desert with his mother and son. Whatever Hassan's unpopularity, there is a general anger against the deceitful newcomer and only with great difficulty, and much bloodshed, does Hayreddin impose a sullen peace.

Hayreddin spends that winter looking for Muley Hassan. He puts a bounty of 30,000 gold pieces on the fugitive's head and seizes a son apiece from sixty influential men of religion as an incentive to behave. He sends sail-powered artillery pieces scudding across the desert to impress the herdsmen and their families. But the sheikhs and seers are anything but pliant and their acolytes do not hesitate to murder Hayreddin's men while they are at prayer in the great mosque of Tunis. The city is full of Hassan's agents, warning of retribution for collaborators. No, the life of a coloniser isn't an easy one, particularly if a rival has designs on the colony in question.

XIII

Titian's portrait of Charles is a celebrated likeness. It shows the Emperor's big beautiful eyes to best effect, their expression of curiosity or gentle surprise prompting the thought that his mouth is open because he wants to say something, not because he is incapable of closing it. A smear of beard and shadow hides his atrocity of a chin. But anyone seeing this picture is soon distracted from the Emperor's face, from his costly jerkin and hose, and is drawn to the dog at his feet. A powerful animal sniffing a little too familiarly at the emperor's codpiece which hangs, like a ripe jackfruit from Taprobana, inches from its muzzle.

The Empress Isabella is pregnant again and the new Pope, Paul III, is thinking of alternative uses for Charles's manhood. The Turks are busy in Persia and Mesopotamia, a state of affairs which, according to the pontiff, represents 'a great opportunity for the Emperor to attend not only to everything required for Africa but also for a greater and more honourable enterprise,' and he urges him 'not to waste this wonderful opportunity given by God.' By 'everything required for Africa', Paul means expelling Barbarossa from Tunis. By 'a greater and more honourable enterprise', he means the reconquest of Constantinople.

It is one of the oddities of contemporary politics that the infidel King of Spain, who is obsessed with his crusading heritage and knows exactly which of his ancestors fought at Acre, Jerusalem and so on, will be welcomed by Muley Hassan when he lands on North African soil, while Hayreddin, trusted representative of the Caliph of Islam, is the Muley's enemy. But then, as Hayreddin's brother-in-arms Murat points out with his customary frankness, while Muley Hassan 'is called a Muslim, and presents the face of one, he is responsible for misdeeds not even an infidel would commit'.

A Crusade led by the Emperor himself attracts a better class of volunteer. In April 1535, Charles's brother-in-law, the Infante Luis of Portugal, puts into Barcelona with a fleet. He is joined by Ferrante Gonzaga, brother of the Duke of Mantua, who is fired up by his kinswoman's recent narrow escape from the predations of Hayreddin, and Fernando Alvarez de Toledo, third Duke of Alba, fourth Marquess of Coria, third Count of Salvatierra de Tormes, etc. The poet Garcilaso de la Vega, the chronicler Jean de Vandenesse and the artist Jan Cornelisz Vermeyen will take care of publicity. Not for them the stay-at-home approach that was adopted by Kemalpashazade, the Ottoman panegyrist, for the Mohacs campaign of '26; they are being measured for cuirasses and putting their horses through their paces. On 21 May, Andrea Doria arrives with 22 ships. The poop of his galley, the *Reale*, is covered with crimson velvet with gold brocade and is forested with banners showing the saints. The Viceroy of Genoa comes ashore and he and the Emperor huddle over maps and plans.

Back in Madrid the Empress is readying herself to give birth, as ever, without her husband. She is, according to one of her ladies-in-waiting, 'as lonely as can be, may God have pity on her'.

On 11 June the fleet puts into Cagliari, on Sardinia's southern coast. After taking in more recruits from Italy, Germany and Spain, his combined strength exceeds 50,000 men on 400 ships. The armada includes the famous carrack of Malta, belonging to the Hospitallers, eight floors of the hardest oak and impenetrable metal sheathings fashioned into a vessel of faun-like speed and agility. At Cagliari the Emperor is told by Christian slaves who have escaped from Tunis that Barbarossa is fortifying the Goletta. After Charles makes landfall it should be possible to skirt the Bay and approach the city from the west; possible but inadvisable, for that would leave the now bristling enemy fortress between the Emperor's army and his means of escape.

~

The pirate King knows what the Emperor is up to. His French friends have told him. So he builds up the city walls, expels the infirm and locks up thousands of Christian slaves in the citadel to prevent them becoming a fifth column. But he cannot raze the outskirts to create clear fields of fire, as, for example, Nicholas von Salm did at Vienna. That would risk igniting a massive rebellion among people who already hate him. Nor can he expect reinforcements from Istanbul. The Sultan is far away in the east and the ships coming off the stocks at Gallipoli are intended for the defence of Istanbul against the Pope's 'greater and more honourable enterprise'.

On 16 June Charles makes landfall. Over the coming days his coalition – princes, pikemen, ecstatic priests, human centipedes dragging heavy guns, women selling animals for food and boys on dromedaries brandishing palm stumps – advances on the Goletta. Arab and Berber lancers on fleet horses and sharp-shooting foot soldiers harry them as they come through the sand and ruined arches of Roman Carthage. Frequently it is the Emperor himself who leads sorties to confront them.

The Goletta is a modern brick castle, thickly made on sandy ground, with one decent-sized cistern. Sinan the Jew is responsible for its defence which leaves Hayreddin free to hold the fort in Tunis – watching for signs of rebellion, provisioning his lieutenant and making sorties to harass the advancing Imperial army. And so effectively do the defenders impede Charles's progress that, in Murat's words, the Imperial forces are obliged to 'go to ground, building tunnels like blind moles and swarming along them'.

For thirty days the Christians burrow and the Muslims pull

them out by their tails. As Murat records, 'the people of Islam . . .
cut to pieces the ill-fated treacherous ones and when the pious
ones joyfully and ardently plunged their swords into the death-
meriting infidels, the infidel host . . . turned and fled, and the
Muslims repulsed three or four thousand of them and and threw
the King of Spain from his horse.'

The going is undeniably heavy. The ship's biscuit that the
Imperial soldiers have brought ashore is breeding maggots and
the market for food turns sharply inflationary. For a hen the
tradeswomen demand the scandalous price of a whole ducat,
while a small cow costs fully ten ducats and a starving sheep,
four. And there is never enough water, only wine. When discipline suffers it is predictably the Germans who are the worst
behaved, and Charles himself has occasion to strike a disobedi-
ent Landsknecht with his lance. The German rashly shows His
Majesty his own weapon, for which he pays with his life. The
men cheer feebly at the news that the Empress has been delivered of a daughter.

But for all the wavering spirit among the Christians, they
have one priceless asset, and that is continuity of supply. Each
time Sinan launches another attack that obliterates a trench or
leaves enough Christian bodies in the sun to infect the very air,
a ship arrives from Sicily, Biscay or Genoa containing fresh men
and cannonballs and faggots for the Imperial earthworks. The
trenches and tunnels get closer and closer to the walls of the
castle.

On 14 July, after Charles hears Mass, he gives the order for a
tremendous bombardment of the Goletta from land and sea.
Sinan's heavy guns shoot out iron chains like the nets thrown by
the gladiators at the Carthage amphitheatre, with the difference
that these ones clench and snap with diabolical force, cutting
men's bodies in two or their heads from their shoulders. After
seven hours of combat, the Imperial galleys make a breach in
the walls near the shore and Charles's troops pour through,
encouraged by a friar carrying a crucifix. Their ammunition
exhausted, their spirit broken, Sinan's men stream backwards

and into the Bay, running into the water up to their armpits while the Christians pursue them. That same afternoon Charles and his new client, Muley Hassan, take possession of the Goletta. Two thousand defenders lie dead at their feet. Some four hundred pieces of cannon have been captured, many of them emblazoned with the French fleur-de-lys. Scores of Barbarossa's vessels have been captured or destroyed.

Summoning the leaders of the city's various districts, Hayreddin warns them not to trust the assurances of the King of Spain that they will come to no harm if they throw down their weapons. Then he leads thousands of Turks, Arabs and Berbers to the orchards among the ruins of Carthage. The Imperial troops are out of water and the sun is pitiless; if they do not secure the wells, they die. It is beyond Charles's capability to demand more effort from his men, so caked is his mouth with salt and grime, but after furious fighting, when both sides are almost spent from the heat, an Imperial force led by the Duke of Alba make a breakthrough and Hayreddin's men take to their heels while the Imperial troops drop to their knees at the wells and just drink and drink.

Returning to the city from his abortive rearguard, Hayreddin discovers that many of its inhabitants have run for their lives and that the Christians have broken out of their dungeons. 'And seeing,' as Murat writes, 'that there was no way back,' Hayreddin flees the city and 'after going a long distance he came across more than 50,000 people, women and children, and others, young and old, all fleeing the city . . . and when he saw the degradation of every one them, and their weakness, afflictions and hardships, and misery, his heart bled for them and he began to cry and he cried so much he almost expired.'

The 50,000 are the lucky ones. Charles does not deny his troops the customary three days' looting after the reduction of an enemy city. They go to work with a vim that is remarkable in men so weakened by the ardours of a military campaign. It is perhaps the wine. When they have had enough of killing and raping and ripping apart houses and shops in their search for treasure, they enslave, and by the time they are done some 18,000 Muslims are in chains and the market price has come down to 10 ducats, the cost of a cow. The liberated Christian slaves will be repatriated to their homes in the Balearics, Italy and elsewhere.

~

Retreating westwards, hearing about the suffering of his fellow Muslims, Barbarossa feels no pity for these traitors who trusted the assurances of the infidels and gave them intelligence and encouragement, even coming out of the city to assure them, 'Barbarossa has gone out and away!' and, when the invaders hesitated, urged them, 'Come into the castle!' Murat, as ever, is his master's voice. 'Almighty God, on whom be glory, has once again brought catastrophe swiftly onto the heads of those who betray Islam, for they unjustly hated and resented and were hostile to the people of Islam and I pray that Almighty God, on whom be glory, send disaster and punishment, in this world and in the afterlife, on anyone intending such a thing.'

It is Islam that Hayreddin Barbarossa grieves for, a most perfect artefact of God that can be so heinously betrayed by those who claim adherence to it. But Hayreddin never lets his emotions impair his judgement. There is nothing attractive about a lost cause, nothing romantic about incompetence, and while he strives for the best he never fails to prepare for the worst.

He has fifteen galleys which he sank as a precaution in the mouth of a river flowing into the sea at Bona, two hundred miles up the coast. After a forced march of five days and five nights, in which he shows more physical strength and mental endurance than many of his younger comrades, he reaches Bona, retrieves and refloats his boats under cover of night, and bursts through Andrea Doria's feeble blockade and into the open sea. A day later he reaches Algiers, where the people have heard about the catastrophe at Tunis and explain his miraculous deliverance with the words, 'it is clear that Almighty God has created you for a purpose.' Within fifteen days of his return to his fief, this white-beard in his early sixties, who has just experienced a crushing military defeat, and who might be forgiven a period of reflection among his marrows, is at sea again.

What, he is thinking to himself as he sets sail with thirty-two ships, would take the shine off Charles's triumph at Tunis, what would tarnish his liberation of the Christian slaves and interrupt the tsunami of propaganda – the victory odes, the paeans to chivalry and derring-do, the tapestries that will hang on the walls of palaces – that is being whiffled up by his publicists? And even Hayreddin's captains do not know where he is taking them until they come into Port Mahon, the great harbour on the Balearic Island of Minorca, sack it without mercy and carry off to Algiers thousands of Christians who were liberated from Tunis only days ago.

From Madrid the recently disburdened Empress writes to her husband, telling him that, coming so soon after Tunis, whose benefits will be felt mainly by Italians, the sack of Mahon has hurt the Spanish 'more than it would at some other time. They talk here of nothing else.'

The point that Barbarossa is making is that ownership of a fixed location is less important than intelligent use of the wind. His assets cannot be counted in tax revenues, fields and cities, but impunity on the sea, and who would argue that this isn't his? In evading death and racing across the White Sea to impale and rape the very Spaniards who left him for dead under the arches of Carthage, he has raised his status above that of a mere sailor. He is a shape-shifter, a djinn, a mythical creature of the deep whom Andrea Doria, that most tentative of High Admirals, let slip at Bona. As the saying goes, crows don't take each other's eyes out.

An Italian who took part in the capture of Tunis is sceptical of the Emperor's claims to have changed the course of history. 'Barbarossa got away with a great treasure and 4,000 Turks,' he writes, 'and it is said for certain that he still has in place and in good order fifty ships even after losing forty galleys and an infinite number of galleots and fustas at the Goletta. And up to 3,000 slaves were saved which is a great number. And when we weigh the fact of Tunis's loss, it amounts to little or nothing. It is more smoke than grilled meat because Barbarossa, having so many galleys, slaves and Turks, will recover easily. In sum, the sack of Tunisia is a very thin affair and of little importance . . . and by going to Tunis with the army His Majesty put himself in grave peril; had Barbarossa restrained himself for two or three days from fighting the army, His Majesty would certainly have been defeated, and all would have been cut down by the great and uncomfortable thirst, and in our company there is not a man who has not fallen ill, and our standard-bearer, Cicero of Arpino, succumbed and died from thirst.'

XIV

It is the spring of 1534: before Fondi, before Tunis.

The Queen Mother is dead.

The eulogists proclaim her another Aisha (wife of the Prophet), another Fatima (his daughter). Not even Hafsa could cheat her appointed term. In this the Queen Mother and the beggar are the same.

While she was living in Manisa she was allowed to build a mosque with not the usual one minaret but two, the first female member of the royal family to be favoured in this way. Mother of the Sultan, Refuge of the World, whose whole work was piety, whose every thought was good. She showed compassion in victory and gave money to former concubines who had fallen on hard times.

It is some years since the last rumour of a baby for Hurrem, the last cannon report. Her litter: three sons of healthy mind and body. The fourth, Cihangir, is a hunchback and out of the running.

She is still of child-bearing age. One must assume that before the Sultan lies with her she avails herself of the cornucopia of intravaginal suppositories (peppermint juice, pennyroyal leaves, dill, cabbage petal oil) that are available to the careful homemaker.

The Sultan's eldest son Mustafa has gone to Manisa to take up the Governorship. Just like his father before him. The Pashas saw him off in the March squalls, Ayas holding his stirrup, Kasim his sword and Ibrahim the hem of his robe. He is pale, swan-necked (like his father) and dignified, his white turban decked with gems. His stipend has been set at 40,000. He is accompanied by a secretary, who will spy on him and report back to the Sultan, and his mother, Mahidevran, who plays Hafsa to his Suleyman as they establish their court-in-miniature.

So, counting Mustafa, the contenders for the Sultanate are set at four. And with Hafsa gone there will be no one to stop the killing and blinding once it all starts, no one to beg clemency or urge moderation from her pulpit of long years.

Within a few weeks of the Queen Mother's death – her shrouded body buried next to Selim in his complex on the Sixth Hill, Quran-reciters ushering her to heaven – the news spreads that Suleyman has wed Hurrem. The Pera agent of the Bank of St George, the institution that got Andrea Gritti out of the Seven Towers all those years ago, declares in perplexity, 'None can say what it means.'

It means that the Russian is making her move.

Ottoman Sultans used to marry foreign princesses and the daughters of vassals. But the brides' male relations would use these alliances as an excuse to invade, so the practice was stopped, the foreign wife being replaced as a secure womb by the foreign slave concubine without attachments. For as long as his mother was alive it was impossible for Suleyman to honour Hurrem with matrimony. He could not raise her above the status his own mother enjoyed. But Hafsa's death has removed the need for such delicacy.

In one gigantic leap, Hurrem has got herself both married and manumitted. Her next significant act is to take up residence in the New Palace.

No royal wife or concubine has lived in the New Palace since it was built following the Conquest. But when Ibrahim renovated it a few years ago, he had the foresight to embellish and extend its rather subfusc harem. So the accommodation that Hurrem and her suite of ladies and eunuchs will now occupy, its bathhouses and private chambers, corridors, courtyards and prayer rooms, are gilded, tiled, and gem-studded to the same exacting standards as those of her husband.

The most significant thing about Hurrem's new home is its location. No longer is she separated from Suleyman by the length of the Council Road and a purgatory of protocols. From her rooms she has access to a small walled garden, from which a gate leads into the Sultan's hanging garden and to the door to his Privy Chamber. To see her husband, to consult, influence or enjoy him, requires walking a few paces.

By moving into the New Palace, Hurrem has united the political and the procreative components of her power. To put it another way, she has grafted herself onto the trunk of the Sultanate, inserted herself into its bark. She is in the place that Ibrahim of Parga used to occupy, it is she who eats with the Sultan using a wooden spoon.

Over the doors of their houses the Turks put the skull of a donkey or a horse to defend against the evil eye. Suleyman has a specialist of divination in his retinue. The astrologers give a view before any decision of consequence is taken. The Sultan, in short, is well equipped to foresee the future and protect himself against its ill effects. But all these safeguards have been shown to be inadequate in the face of a single determined female. That she has monopolised the Sultan and established herself in the New Palace can have but one explanation. The Russian has bewitched him, certainly she is a witch, a *ziadi*, and as a consequence the whole court, in particular the Janissaries, hold her in much hatred, her and all her children.

~

Since last summer's peak, when fifteen hundred people were dying every week, the plague has fallen back. It will return; the question is when. The people complain of a sense of peril that is made more acute by the long absence of the Grand Vizier, who, for all his disagreeable qualities, is at least competent, and the imminent departure of the Sultan to join him.

The Sultan is all amiability one moment; then something irritates him, his voice harshens and the colour rises from his neck like smoke up a candle jar. A servitor of one of the Pashas was recently overheard saying that this regime isn't long for the world. And a prophecy is circulating which says that the Empire of the Turks will be extirpated thanks to a bastard, the son of a prince, who will urge them to some exploit that brings about their ruin.

It's in part down to Ibrahim's protection that Alvise Gritti has survived this long. The Beyoglu gave himself an extra layer of armour when he convinced the Christians that his buy-in was essential to any diplomatic initiative involving the Grand Turk. And for some years this was correct. The Beyoglu was critical to the smooth functioning of relations between his father and the Sultan. The truce with Ferdinand was his achievement. Even now, when he sends a letter to Charles V, the Emperor forces himself to focus his beautiful pale blue eyes on Gritti's words, no matter how nauseating the sentences they form.

But the world is changing and the base of Alvise's supremacy is as vulnerable as the piles of alder and larch that keep Venice above the waves. Ibrahim, a titan of Europe, no longer needs Alvise to hold his hand. And the bilateral relationship between Venice and Istanbul is going sour. The irritants and misunderstandings that arise with growing frequency between the Porte and the Serenissima attest to Doge Gritti's desire to be a friend both of Turkey and Spain. The Porte will never accept such equidistance. The Sultan's attitude is: you're either with us or against us.

Last year Venetian warships attacked a squadron of Turkish navy vessels, sinking two and capturing five. The Venetians frantically excused themself, their commander, Girolamo da Canal, insisting that he mistook the Turks for pirates in the gloaming. But when da Canal returned home and came ashore at the Molo, the waiting crowd cheered him wildly. Are these the actions of a friend?

There are no such points of friction with Francis. But the

Beyoglu's prestige with the French doesn't approach that of the King of Algiers. The irony is that it was Gritti's idea to bring in Barbarossa in the first place. And now Hayreddin has given him a nasty surprise, exacting more money and power from the Sultan than anyone thought possible. The shocking truth is that the Sultan has adopted the very expensive naval strategy of a newcomer.

The slights and insults are mounting up. Barbarossa refuses to pay back Gritti the money he borrowed all those years ago when the Beyoglu was offering credit to every chancer in the White Sea. Compensation, as Hayreddin sees it, for the loss of his slaves while he was in Aleppo. He and Iskender Celebi have struck up a barely concealed alliance against the Beyoglu. Until recently, Iskender would allow Alvise to pay the taxes he collects from the Thracian ports in the form of gems, cloths, or anything else he happened to have a lot of. But now Iskender is telling him to hand over his dues in coin. Suddenly Gritti has a liquidity problem. That's right: the Beyoglu has a liquidity problem. Two hundred thousand ducats in arrears, he is obliged to pawn some of the gold and silver furnishings from his own house. Iskender issued his directive at Barbarossa's urging.

At least he has Hungary. They haven't taken that away from him. But they might. The regime he has set up there, with himself as absentee landlord and Janos as estate manager, benefits him more than Janos and the Sultan least of all. Suleyman is said to be warming to the idea that the Kingdom should be formally annexed and turned into a province like Cairo or Aleppo, with a salaried Governor and an army funded by local taxes. As things stand, Suleyman is maintaining 6,000 Turkish troops there at his own expense. He is tired of paying an annual subsidy of 200,000 ducats to a land-locked kingdom that brings him nothing but trouble. If it is incorporated, Hungary can contribute to the Ottoman exchequer instead of Gritti's empire.

~

A native of Nieuwpoort, in Flanders, a denizen of the Holy Roman Empire's northern wing, Cornelius de Schepper negotiated last year's truce for Ferdinand. Now he is back in Istanbul, this time for Charles, who has asked him to take soundings on a wider peace. Schepper knocks at the Beyoglu's door but he soon grasps that his old negotiating partner has suffered a drop in status. When Gritti boasts that he has secret intelligence with the Sultan and that he has been authorised to negotiate a treaty between the Ottoman and Holy Roman empires, his words have all the resonance of a nail striking tin.

Testing his hunch, Schepper tells the Sultan that he is expecting to negotiate a peace treaty with the Beyoglu. 'Beyoglu? Beyoglu?' Suleyman replies angrily. 'He has received no authorisation from me to negotiate on these subjects!' But Cornelius ploughs on, insisting that his impression has been that the Beyoglu enjoys such an authorisation. And this agitates the Sultan even more. 'No, no! These matters must be discussed at my Porte!' Coming out of the audience, Schepper runs the gauntlet of a troop of Janissaries who howl and bark like dogs and run their fingers over their throats.

The cohesion of any regime can be gauged by the manner in which its officials speak to an outsider. If they play down internal differences, or speak highly of colleagues they are known to detest, it means that there is an agreement to fight battles in private and not let foreigners exploit the situation.

Whenever he would go on a mission to Venice, Yunus Bey, the Sultan's translator and envoy, would be put up by Alvise's holy brother Lorenzo, at the priory. Yunus and Alvise were good enough friends to co-author a pamphlet explaining the workings of the Ottoman Empire for foreigners. But since then Alvise has eclipsed Yunus in wealth and influence, and a good working relationship has been destroyed by jealousy and mistrust.

When Alvise meets Schepper in Istanbul, he advises the Fleming not to reveal anything to Yunus about his mission. And when Yunus calls on Cornelius to welcome him and ask about his aims, Schepper is studiously uninformative.

Yunus guesses the cause of Schepper's evasions and becomes angry, intimating that Alvise's mother was in the personal service sector. 'Every one of us,' he goes on, 'ought to weep over Alvise Gritti, may God destroy him, he who is the founder and source of all disorders. For he is neither a good Turk nor a Christian, and his words are lies and flattery. Oh, what a work of kindness to God and the whole of Europe and Asia if this dog were to be killed.'

~

On 11 June 1534, in the interval between the Sultan's departure for the east and his own for Hungary, Gritti calls on Schepper to tell him what will happen next.

Once the Shah has been defeated, he starts, Ibrahim will be sent to occupy an Italian port near Rome. The Sultan will cross from Greece and invade Rome.

And he warns Cornelius: if you don't get ahead of events, they will end badly for you.

Happily, the Beyoglu goes on, there is another way of looking at the situation. Barbarossa is halfway to Tunis. Ottoman Greece is defended by irregulars. And now Constantinople has been abandoned by the Sultan and his Captain-General. Your masters Charles and Ferdinand will never have an opportunity such as they have at present.

Now listen.

From here I will go to Transylvania and from there to Buda, and from Buda I will covertly send men to your master, the King of the Romans, and then follow myself. And you, Cornelius, must tell Ferdinand not to be surprised if I carry out certain actions that appear hostile to his interests. I need to allay suspicions that have arisen, suspicions that I am favourable to the King of the Romans. It would be dangerous for me to act in any other way lest King Janos send complaints about me to the Porte. Dissimulation at all times!

In the meantime, the Emperor Charles must increase the size of his fleet so he can oppose Barbarossa. If Barbarossa enjoys success, the Sultan will have more confidence in him and give him more ships, more money, more fighting men. And with these advantages he will be able to strike at the heart of Spain.

The Emperor Charles should know that defending himself against Barbarossa will be more costly than attacking Constantinople, because there isn't a single galley left to defend the city. The Emperor's fleet will find untold riches here and will encounter no resistance. But he must hurry. If he leaves things until after the Turk returns from the east, the war will be difficult to win. One shouldn't always think of defence, but sometimes also of attack.

As for myself, I need to cut the proud Hungarian chiefs down to size and put that country in order. I have already threatened bitter measures if soft ones don't work. And that's how I will behave now. Whoever intends to reign must not fear to let blood flow.

In this way, on 11 June 1534, after eleven years in the service of the Ottoman Empire, Alvise Gritti changes sides. He will have Hungary and this time it is Ferdinand who will give it to him. And Constantinople will fall, and Barbarossa will fail. He will yet be brother-in-law of the King of Poland!

~

A week later he quits Istanbul. His escort is made up of Turks and Greeks: a thousand infantry and a similar number of cavalry. Servants and attendants. Scribes, musicians and cooks. Twelve-year-old Pietro, his son, has his own cart with three servants and a preceptor. This is without even mentioning the merchants, pilgrims, dervishes and prostitutes who attach themselves to every caravan for business and protection.

The Beyoglu's carpets, silks and brocades have been strapped to mules and loaded onto carts that are pulled by camels. His secretary, Tranquillus Andronicus, and his Venetian chamberlain, Francesco Della Valle, have charged their carts with vases, books, hangings and other valuables. All told, the chattels that the Beyoglu and his companions bring with them are worth in the region of one and a quarter million ducats. That includes 10,000 florins in gold and silver from his own treasury and the choicest items from the gemstore.

The palazzo in the vines of Pera wears a forsaken air, the state rooms emptied of the best pieces, the stables, dormitories and gardens deserted and bereft. A visitor might wonder if its owner intends to return.

The road westwards from Istanbul in the livid month of June. Gritti's caravan follows the gentle contours of golden, poplar-avenued Thrace. Everywhere there is evidence of Ottoman good sense: hospitals, mosques, caravansarays. And at each stop the best rooms are put at Gritti's disposal, even if the fief-holder in question is away on the eastern campaign.

At Sofia, the caravan turns in a northerly direction, towards the voivodates of the eastern Balkans. The Sultan has instructed Gritti to collect tribute from Vlad Vintila, Voivode of Wallachia. He is then to cross the southern Carpathians and do Janos's job for him by quieting the principality of Transylvania. Finally, he must continue northwards to Vienna to set the borders between Ferdinand's territory and that of Janos. He is also to negotiate the restoration of the dowry that Queen Maria, Louis's widow and sister of the Hapsburg brothers, was forced to abandon when she fled Hungary after Mohacs. Resolution of this question would greatly advance the cause of peace between the Ottomans and the King of Rome.

But the bond that ties Alvise to the Ottoman State has thinned to a hair's width. The Porte has taken note of the manner of his departure. Rumours of his conversation with Schepper have leaked. Or they will. It is inevitable.

The local Balkan chiefs are good at sniffing out yesterday's men. As Gritti approaches Wallachia, a bad-tempered vassalate at the best of times, his private army seems a lot less formidable than it did in Thrace, less an army than a provocation. The wisdom of bringing one of the Empire's biggest treasures to one of its most rebellious regions is also open to question.

But Gritti's true vulnerability does not stem from the number of his troops or the size of his treasure. If you have the greatest empire in the world at your back, you can have asses for guards and pearls hanging from your hair: no one will touch you. But Alvise Gritti's back is exposed. Quite how exposed, he perhaps doesn't realise.

On the banks of the Danube, Wallachia's southern border, he leaves the corpse of a local lord hanging from a gibbet, punishment for failing to provide barges to carry his men across the river. From now on everything depends on his ability to strike terror.

But he is being undermined by the Porte itself. Vlad Vintila receives a letter from Iskender Celebi telling him to refuse any demands Gritti makes for extra troops. Troops he is sure to need in Transylvania. It is impossible to imagine the Treasurer issuing such an order, effectively an incitement to sabotage Gritti's mission and place him in mortal danger, even a few months ago.

Shortly after Gritti crosses the Danube into Wallachia, some 180 Wallachian nobles approach with 9,000 cavalry and demand his help in unseating Vlad. Two days later, Gritti and the rebels are surrounded by the Voivode himself and a huge army of horsemen. Alvise has no choice but to hand the rebels over to their master. Then he is escorted by Vlad to his capital and invited to watch as the ears and noses of the rebel lords are cut off and their eyes are shucked from their sockets. The limits of his tolerance thus demonstrated, Vlad pays his tribute and sends the Beyoglu across the Carpathians with 800 men as a farewell gesture. Officially, at least, the Beyoglu is still the Sultan's representative, and Vlad wants him off his patch.

~

Transylvania is in chaos. Arbitrary taxes, savage methods of collection and hunger have come together to generate intense resentment against Gritti. And the *Gubernator Regius* has a notoriety in this region. The last time he was here, in March 1533, careering back to Istanbul for urgent 'consultations', his men made time only to stop and rape the women who were living in the towns and villages in their path, conduct that merited, in the words of King Janos's chaplain, 'the vengeance of God'.

Now the same crew are back again and the people of one town send messages to Archduke Ferdinand imploring him to deliver them from those rapacious wolves, the Grittiani. Imre Czibak, Bishop of Oradea, pained by the memory of bowing and scraping to the Beyoglu in '32, is inciting the people to rebel. The Beyoglu, he tells his flock, has impoverished the lords, kidnapped members of the Diet and killed innocents; he has usurped rights, acquired honours and reduced the King to penury. And now this uncircumcised Turk is coming north to add the crown of Hungary to his extensive list of stolen titles.

Like sound, anarchy is susceptible to orchestration. As Gritti's caravan comes north, guns are being given out from Czibak's seat of Oradea. Carts are trundling along the tracks, bringing lances to those who have none. So imminent is the coming storm, a farmer's wife, taking pity on one of Gritti's companions, urges him to abandon the Beyoglu or face inevitable death.

Brasov is a town in southern Transylvania, walled by mountains. Alvise arrives there in early August, pitching his 250 tents outside the city, whose gates are firmly shut. From Buda he is joined by his elder son, Antonio, just down from Padua, and two of the most stalwart Grittiani, Orban Batthyany and a former regional treasurer called Janos Doczy, with 4,000 Hungarian cavalry. 'Well, son,' Gritti tells Antonio, 'what you see is me and your brother, and we are having a lot of trouble with the Hungarians. But, with God's help, I want to punish those same rebels who stand against me.'

Bolstered by the new arrivals, Gritti proclaims a Diet that will meet on August 26 at Medias. It's at Medias that he will bend the knee of intractable Transylvania. It's at Medias that he will take control.

~

Istvan Bathory is to attend the Diet, representing King Janos. As Voivode of Transylvania, it is his prerogative. But suddenly Bathory dies, probably poisoned, and the King asks Imre Czibak to represent him instead. Bathory's convenient elimination might even open Czibak's path to becoming Voivode, a long-standing ambition of the Bishop.

When Czibak sets out for Medias with his squad of cavalry, he carries with him a gold cup, encrusted with precious stones, which he ordered specially for the Beyoglu. Czibak's intention may be to reconcile his interests with those of Gritti and win the Governor's approval for his ascent to the Voivodeship. Or it may be to undermine Gritti's authority within the Diet. Or it may be to put off the rebellion until he sees how strong Gritti really is.

But if the Bishop thinks he can distract Gritti with a pretty cup, he hasn't reckoned with the Grittiani. These include Orban Batthyany, passed over for the senior jobs by King Janos on his accession but saved from irrelevance by Gritti when, early in his Hungarian career, the Beyoglu needed local supporters; now, at Brasov, he gives Batthyany command of the private army. Likewise Janos Doczy, viewed by King Janos with disfavour, but appointed by Gritti as his Deputy Governor anyway.

The Grittiani are so called because they owe everything to Gritti and their survival depends on him. So Czibak is a threat to them all. Batthyany suspects that the rebellious prelate was responsible for the despicable rumour that Gritti had been hanged and stuffed with straw. Doczy, too, has been bad-mouthed by him. Now the object of their loathing is camped barely a day's ride from Brasov. And he has a tidy 50,000 florins in his tent.

The Beyoglu's attitude to rivals is defined by pride. By bringing with him a mounted bodyguard, armed as if for war, Czibak is challenging the monopoly of force that can only belong to the Governor. When he hears that Czibak has arrived in the neighbourhood, the Beyoglu rises from the table he is sitting at, removes his sable beret and shows it to his companions. 'This cannot cover two heads,' he says, his voice trembling with anger. 'It can only be worn by one.' And he places it firmly back on his own head. Then Czibak's cup is delivered to him, filled with gold coins. Gritti likes the gift more than the gift-giver. 'I will certainly punish him!' Doczy persuades Czibak's courier not to reveal Gritti's displeasure to the Bishop. And in this way when he hears what transpired in the Beyoglu's tent, Czibak is lulled into believing that Gritti is satisfied with him.

The commander of Czibak's squad of cavalry is a local notable called Gotthard Kun. His men deployed around an undefended village, Kun feels exposed. But when he urges his master to shift camp into a nearby bastion, Czibak rejects the suggestion.

The Beyoglu may never have a better opportunity to deal with Czibak. This is what Doczy and Batthyany tell him. 'Truly,' Batthyany says, 'if today with steadfast and virile resolve you do not defend your honour and that of Suleyman, you will never freely have your authority and your empire. And you do not know Imre, that proud and cruel beast, whose pride and insolence I will immediately quash, if you so desire.'

On the night of 11 August, Batthyany leaves Brasov with a hundred horsemen. They are going to the relief of Antonio Gritti's Bishopric of Eger, which has been besieged by pro-Hapsburg forces. Or so they say. Instead, they ford the River Olt and fall on Czibak's camp at dawn, taking Kun's men, who are in any case at a numerical disadvantage, by surprise. Czibak resists bravely, killing several assailants at the entrance to his tent before one of Batthyany's men has the bright idea of cutting the guy-ropes that are holding it up. Then it's pig-sticking in a blanket.

When Batthyany brings Czibak's head back to Brasov, Doczy speaks to it. 'I told you that your maleficent tongue would be the death of you!' And he reaches into Czibak's mouth with a whittled stick, skewers the offending organ and draws it out, murmuring, 'Oh, wicked tongue that defamed me! Now your only hope is the mercy of God!'

The Beyoglu himself behaves more nobly, like Julius Caesar when they brought him the head of Pompey. He shows remorse at the demise of a great man whose death he never desired – only his capture. The Franciscans of Brasov receive the head and Gritti orders them to bury it honourably in their big church, donating a fresh linen sheet from his own stores to wrap it in. The following day, Gritti visits the scene of the murder and has the body, with its sixteen stab wounds and one gaping tear, placed in a nearby chapel, from where it will be taken to Brasov to be reunited with its head. And still the Beyoglu wipes his eyes. And still there is no sign of Czibak's 50,000 florins.

~

After the death of Imre Czibak, Transylvania explodes. The divisions between Magyar, Saxon, Vlach and Szekler, between Lutheran and Catholic, are sealed by the hatred that everyone feels for the outsider. Regardless of whether they are in the camp of Ferdinand or Janos, men rush to join the army that is being raised by Istvan Maylad, lord of the bastion of Fagaras, and Gotthard Kun, bystander on the day Czibak died. In the words of Paolo Giovio, Bishop of Nocera, following events with his usual assiduousness in Italy, 'no nation ever ran to arms more diligently'.

'Listen to me, my brothers,' Kun declares, in a proclamation that he sends around the Principality, 'we have a powerful opponent, and just as a viper enters the nests of birds, and there lays waste and consumes in many places, the same is true of the Governor, Gritti, a Turkish Italian. We elected him without our knowledge. He has similarly entered us and now kills and consumes Imre Czibak, one of our brothers.' Bloodied swords are sent out as a signal to rise.

News that the possessions of the richest private citizen in the Ottoman Empire are adrift on the Transylvanian plateau is attracting understandable interest. If the Beyoglu comes to grief, it stands to reason that his treasure, and those of the members of his suite, will need homes. Each of Gritti's 8,000 troops may

be assumed to have an average of fifteen florins in his possession, meaning an additional 120,000 florins up for grabs. The
Beyoglu is said to be unusually attached to his stockings, which
suggests they contain more than his legs. The dead Bishop's
nephew, Miklos Patocsy, is stirring the people to a frenzy with
his demands for justice for his uncle. From the perspective of
the hard-pressed citizen of Transylvania, it is hard to imagine a
neater dovetailing of principle and profit.

Alvise is now vulnerable to sheer weight of numbers. He
sends an order to Jerome Laski in Buda to bring him the Turkish troops that are stationed there. The Danube flotilla must
also sail to his aid. A similar message goes to the Ottoman Governor of Nicopolis. And to Mehmet Bey of Smederovo, who put
the Austrians to flight when they were besieging Buda in 1530.

But the Gritti of that siege was unsurpassed as a warrior and
kingmaker. Four years on, he is indelibly associated with deprav-
ity and corruption. Even Jerome Laski was sickened by the
murder of Imre Czibak, and Jerome is a man with a strong
constitution.

It is possible that Gritti cares little about this. He stopped
wanting to be loved the moment he decided to be great. But to
kill the King's ally suggests someone with designs on the throne,
and this is a question of judgement, not ethics. There is no gloss-
ing the premature exposure of the Beyoglu's intentions. The
slaying of Czibak was not the master-stroke of a political genius.
It was the blunder of an amateur.

Buda, where until recently the King lived in terror of his own
Governor, where he would confess himself powerless to curb
the Venetian's excesses and would meet him with tears streaming down his cheeks, now radiates cautious optimism that Gritti
can be removed. Janos is urging Istanbul to recall this person
who has become a menace to his throne and his life. He summons the courage to start shutting down the Beyoglu's network.
Laski is arrested. So are Doczy's wife and children.

When he receives a letter from the Beyoglu, appealing for
help, Janos sighs blissfully. 'How can I help him if I have no

soldiers? Those I had he took with him!' After a meeting with a Transylvanian delegation in which Janos is told in no uncertain terms not to interfere in the crisis, a course of abstinence he was intending to follow in any case, the King leaves the capital, meanders eastwards with the urgency of a funeral cortege, and shuts himself up at Oradea, Imre Czibak's old castle, to wait on events. All the while, the Danube barges continue to bob placidly at their moorings.

~

Medias is a town set in orchards with a river running through. Its citizens are concerned at the news that 8,000 armed men are bearing down on them with every intention of using their walls, their homes, to resist a huge rebellion. Whatever follows, the name 'Diet' is unlikely to do it justice.

When Gritti and his men arrive on 23 August, they find the gates to the town shut. They threaten the inhabitants with annihilation, take the Governor's son hostage and, when none of this works, use heavy carts to force their way in, slashing and clubbing as they go. The bloodied townsfolk take refuge in a fortified church on a mound inside the walls, where, Gritti assures them, they will not be molested provided they do not help the enemy. Then, under the direction of Orban Batthyany, the invaders take over every dwelling and get to work strengthening the walls.

A few days later, Istvan Maylad's army starts arriving from all directions. A horde of agricultural appearance, carrying hooks, scythes, hammers and staves, along with the guns and lances they received from Czibak. They pitch their tents and light their fires next to the Brasov road. And they keep on coming.

When he was in Wallachia on his way north, the Beyoglu received envoys from Petru Rares, Voivode of Moldavia, the Sultan's tributary on Transylvania's eastern border. The envoys promised him men, money and whatever else he might need for the campaign, and he, magnificent as ever, showed his appreciation by giving the envoys horses and fine clothes to take for their master. Now that Medias is surrounded by hostile forces, Gritti is relieved to learn that Petru is a man of his word and that a relief force, 12,000 strong, is on its way.

The siege starts sluggishly, with the feel of an unruly open air Mass and little in the way of proper fighting. Whenever the besiegers get too close for comfort, Gritti leads sorties to repel them and, with the help of his arquebusiers, sends them surging away from the walls as one might a herd of pigs.

~

As September goes on, Medias ripens like one of the succulent cherries after which the town is named, just before it falls into the picker's basket.

Gritti lies prone on the bed in the house he has seized, hosting an old friend. His body is a sack of bile, his forehead an oven plate, his legs are stovepipes.

Up on the battlements his men are trying to repel the enemy while also conserving ammunition. In the respite between assaults, they eat salted horsemeat or curl up for an hour or two.

One morning a trumpet blares out from the ramparts. Hostages enter the city and Doczy comes out. Doczy goes to the enemy camp to speak with Maylad on the Beyoglu's behalf. But it is hard to imagine a negotiating partner less acceptable to the other side than Doczy. It is he that the whole of Transylvania blames for Czibak's death. Everyone has heard what he did to the Bishop's tongue. For years now, Doczy's collaboration with the Turks has gone beyond anything justifiable on grounds of national interest.

Maylad informs him that he, Doczy, will be central to any deal that allows the Beyoglu to walk away. Doczy must surrender himself to Transylvanian justice and answer for the Bishop's death. That is the condition before the other conditions can even be discussed.

Returning to the besieged city, Doczy reports the failure of the negotiations without mentioning Maylad's proposal. And, to be fair, it is hard to know whether to trust an opponent who enjoys a numerical advantage of five to one, who knows that you are on your last quintal of gunpowder, and whose eyes are full of gold.

~

Alvise's secretary Tranquillus Andronicus was asked by his previous employer, King Janos, to spy on the Beyoglu. Now this scribe of questionable loyalty has a scheme. Load up your treasure, he urges Gritti. Take the besiegers by surprise and make a break for it. Eight days from now, you'll be in Constantinople or Belgrade.

Doczy and Batthyany hear this and shake their heads: you won't stand a chance, best await the Moldavians.

That's what they would say, Tranquillus whispers in Gritti's ear. You can expect them to reject any plan that separates them from your gold. Doczy's legendary avarice, Tranquillus goes on, makes him impossible to trust, while Batthyany's worth as a military leader is a measure of his worth as a man. And they are playing the race card, turning your Hungarian soldiers against you.

One day the eight hundred Vlach horsemen who were supplied to Gritti by Vlad Vintilla are nowhere to be seen. They have slipped out of the city. The defenders' anxiety turns to delirious relief when thousands of Moldavians arrive under their captain, one Hurul, and then to fury when Hurul and his men take their place among the besiegers. Thus Petru of Moldavia declares his interest in the Gritti treasure. Another, smaller contingent arrives, this one made up of King Janos's men. They also attach themselves to the Transylvanians.

All the while, from the Governor of Nicopolis; from Mehmet Bey in Serbia; in fact, from the whole of the Ottoman Empire whose palaces he has adorned, whose soldiers he has fed, whose wheels he has oiled, no help arrives for this man who used to declare with pride, 'I am the servant of the Turkish Sultan.'

The Beyoglu is alone.

~

Now that it is certain that there will be no relief, only the heroic hearts of the defenders stand between Gritti and oblivion, just as the resolve of Nicholas Jurisic's followers kept the Turks out of Guns.

Such a comparison flatters the defenders of Medias. The men and women of Guns became indestructible giants when uniting in defence of their turf and their God. Diversity is all very well while the sun shines, but what are the Grittiani fighting for now? Not for the man himself, who has been abandoned by both his patrons and is execrated from Istanbul to Vienna. Nor for his treasure, which will be lost come what may. The Grittiani are a tribe on the verge of extinction. They are becoming Turks, Hungarians and Greeks again, each seeking his own path to salvation.

On 28 September, a Janissary ignites his remaining powder and the last lead ball arcs out from the city. In the vacancy left by the silenced guns, Hurul's Moldavians wander right up to the walls, marvellously insolent, and inspect the defences while scratching their testicles thoughtfully.

That night they empty their eight cannons at the weakest point, a bombardment that lasts until dawn and makes a breach forty feet wide. Indomitable, magnified by fever, Gritti supervises emergency repairs: earth and wood. He is once again the Gritti of the siege of Buda and the new wall is stronger than the one it replaced. The sun is high in the sky by the time he staggers to his sons' lodgings and falls into bed.

He is woken at noon by bells pealing insanely. Pietro's tutor rushes to the window and sees that the people of Medias are waving a white flag from the fortified church they have been living in, and shouting, 'Come in! Come into the city! Now is the time!' Then they bring out guns which they have kept hidden and start firing at the defenders, who have their backs to them and nothing to return fire with.

Pietro stands over the bed, his eyes fearful. Pietro, to whom the Beyoglu intends to pass on the title of Count of Maramures, and with it the Royal Hungarian mines. Pietro's tutor was sent by his grandfather the Doge, who was concerned for the quality of the religious instruction he was getting. Is there not something of Andrea Gritti in the set of the boy's jaw?

Next to him is a fast young man, slight of stature. Antonio, Bishop of Eger, his head full of college humanism.

The Beyoglu is a father like any other.

If the boys fall into Transylvanian hands it won't be for footbaths and sweetmeats. One wonders which of their body parts will be skewered first.

He will give them to the Moldavians, the lesser of two evils.

By Gritti's side there is a Turk. He is one of those Turks who has tasted the Beyoglu's kindness. Ayat is his name. 'For the past four years of good fortune,' Ayat declares, 'I have served you and it would disagree with me to abandon you in adversity. The fate of your illustrious lordship will also be my fate.'

Ayat is put into Moldavian clothes and sent off through not-quite-liberated Medias into the countryside beyond. When he returns, he carries a letter from Hurul.

'Signor Gritti, come out in safety, with your sons, your clothes, your servants and whatever else, for we promise you in the name of God, the Virgin Mary, the four elements, bread, wine and our scimitars that you will be in safety and will be escorted wherever you wish to go. In attestation of this promise, we send you the present letter with the seal of Petru the Moldavian.'

The evacuation of the boys begins, with Ayat as their guide.

First to leave is Pietro, brave, uncomprehending.

When Ayat returns, Gritti looks at Antonio. 'Go.'

Antonio says gutturally, 'Father, since we are to die, I will die weapon in hand.'

Gritti replies, 'Don't add sorrows to those I have already. Just do as I say.'

~

Now there is one of those calms as the wind toys with a listless sail before freshening in one direction or another. A hush while the Grittiani look at the door to see who will enter next. Death or salvation. They are six now. The Beyoglu's cousin Giovanni Gritti, four loyal soldiers and the chamberlain, Francesco Della Valle. The chamberlain whose uncle is the personal doctor of the Doge. Who was sent as an act of fatherly kindness by Andrea Gritti.

A soldier rides up to the door, enters and announces gravely that the Beyoglu's lodgings are being ransacked. Alvise shakes his head in disbelief that the enemy have gained entry to the city so quickly. No, no, the soldier corrects him, your own faithless Hungarians are doing the sacking.

Batthyany. Gritti's Commander-in-Chief has gone over. And once he and his men are done ripping apart the Beyoglu's quarters in their demented quest for loot, they open the castle gate and let the besiegers in. Then, along with their new friends, they get to work slaughtering the Turkish soldiers who until an hour ago were their brothers-in-arms.

The scope of Alvise Gritti, which once covered half the world, has shrunk to a single room. And in this room, while the Grittiani wait, while horses are being sweated to exhaustion to convey the news to Venice and Vienna that a significant death is at hand, the appetites and desires of the hunted man wither. Humility trickles into his corroded soul.

At this moment of recognition, Alvise speaks lovingly to the men whose wide eyes are upon him, thanking them for their services and regretting that his intention in bringing them to these parts, which was to reward them, has not met with success. There is no alternative, he goes on quietly, but to bow to the will of God and tolerate everything in good cheer. He advises them not to be downcast, for their lives will be safe, come what may.

And with this baseless assertion the Beyoglu gives one of his superb smiles. 'I have nothing else to give you, for I have lost everything.'

~

On the left-hand side of the road as you leave the town, there is a swamp, and on the other side runs a wall, the length of an arquebus shot. Gritti, Della Valle, Ayat and the other four soldiers are coming along this road. Reaching the end of the wall, they see the enemy camp, split by a stream into its Transylvanian and Moldavian sections.

Then they whirl and look in alarm towards a horseman who is galloping towards them. Alvise asks Ayat, 'Do you know him? Is he one of us?' Ayat doesn't recognise the man. The Beyoglu says, 'Let us see who he is and what he wants.'

Charging at the Beyoglu, the stranger lands a vicious blow on his shoulder, pulls the white sable beret off his head and races away. Alvise is powerless throughout, just sits dully in his saddle, so bowed and passive, so drained.

Della Valle was with the Beyoglu at the siege of Buda and it enrages him to see his master abused in this way. He screams at the Turkish soldiers: we must give this dog his reward! Spurring his horse, the chamberlain catches up with the Beyoglu's assailant, slashes at him with his rapier and hurls him to the ground. The Beyoglu is shouting in Turkish, *incitme! incitme!* 'Don't harm him!' But Ayat and the Turkish soldiers are already standing over the prone figure with their scimitars raised. Within seconds he is in pieces.

As more Moldavians approach, Della Valle begs Alvise to return with him to Medias, where at least there is somewhere to hide. 'You go back!' Gritti orders him. 'It is I the enemy want, and nobody else.' As Della Valle turns his horse towards the fallen city, he hears Alvise, already far away. 'If you ever get back to Venice, I want you to tell the poor old man everything you have seen.'

~

Jostled, shoved and spat on. But the brain works. He fumbles for Hurul's safe-conduct. Doesn't this mean anything? And how would you like a fortune in return for my freedom? One hundred thousand ducats, here and now? Finally, from the pocket of his jacket he withdraws his letter of appointment from the Sultan. Look at the seal and be afraid. But neither his bribes nor his threats work. Why should they? Gritti isn't the Moldavians' to dispose of.

After being handed over to the Transylvanians, he is frog-marched to Maylad's tent where he swears he is innocent of Czibak's murder. He only wanted to ask the Bishop why he was arming the Transylvanian people against him. But Gritti can hardly hear his own words, so deafening is the roar of the people who have gathered outside.

'Kill the Turk! Kill the Turk!'

'Be careful what you do,' he warns the lord of Fagaras. 'You know that I represent the Sultan and was appointed Governor and Captain of the Army by his Majesty King Janos and was elected by the lords and barons of the Kingdom, and if the Sultan is insulted he will want to avenge the slight and that will bring great suffering to the Kingdom of Hungary.'

Not long ago, the name of the Sultan would have brought any uncompliant Hungarian to his senses. But things have come too far. Maylad shrugs. 'These gentlemen want you dead.' Events are out of his hands.

The Beyoglu erupts with irritation and sadness. 'May my blood fall on you and your children!' Then the son of the Doge checks himself. He is a Gritti. There is never any excuse for ceasing to think. 'If there is a little love of God in you,' he says, 'Hurry up. And let me take the sacrament of the sacred Church so I can die a Christian.'

These men, who want him dead but fear the consequences, look at the floor. Then a certain carter steps forward, a sly fellow with a sure knowledge of man's baser instincts, who says, 'If you would be so good as to give me the stockings he wears, I will do it for you.'

So the carter cuts off Gritti's head with his sword. Then he removes the Beyoglu's purple stockings and in their pockets he finds two bags full of gems of enormous value.

~

Francesco Della Valle flees Medias disguised as a Hungarian soldier. Outside the walls he sees the body of a headless, naked man. A Hungarian, mounted on his horse, is busy stabbing the body with his lance, shouting, 'Here's another one for this Turk!' Once it has been pierced enough times, the body of Alvise Gritti is sent for burial in the church of St Francis in Medias. The head goes to Petru the Moldavian.

The boys are beheaded along with their father. Or they are taken to Petru the Moldavian and finished off by him, Pietro by drowning, Antonio by decapitation. Or they die some other way. The reports disagree.

The Turkish soldiers who stayed loyal to the Beyoglu are dragged by the Moldavians to the top of a hill, stripped, impaled and decapitated.

When Maylad's men finally run Doczy to ground, they beat him to death like a dog.

Tranquillus Andronicus is captured by the Transylvanians. He is saved from certain death when one of his former servants recognises him and pleads for his life.

Jerome Laski escapes from Buda and goes over to Ferdinand.

Judging the little bags in the Beyoglu's stockings to be more trouble than they are worth, the carter sells them to Miklos Patocsy, nephew of Imre Czibak, for a horse and 38 gold florins.

When he is informed of events while campaigning in the east, the Sultan is not overjoyed with the disappearance of Gritti's treasure nor the renewed instability on his northern marches. Yunus Bey is dispatched to see if he can recover any of the lost treasure, more in hope than expectation. But now is not the time to take decisive steps in the Hungarian theatre, certainly not until matters in Persia have been brought to a satisfactory conclusion.

In the letter he writes to his vassal King Janos, the Sultan explains that the Beyoglu deserved to be killed. Even in the court of the King of Spain, that den of iniquity, no one came close to him in wickedness. He was a blackguard who hatched harmful schemes. Had the Beyoglu been bold enough to come back to Istanbul, the Sultan concludes, he would have met a similar end.

No longer must the King of Hungary live with the knowledge that his Governor has more objects of luxury than he does. Gotthard Kun retrieves a superb ivory box from the ruins of Medias, finely decorated and encrusted with precious stones, which he tactfully presents to his sovereign. And Janos sends a servant to Doczy's country seat, where a treasure so big is unearthed, twelve oxen and three carriages are needed to bring it to Buda. Also in circulation are the possessions of the Jewish, Greek and Italian merchants who were in the Venetian's retinue.

A man called Ferenc Doby used to superintend the salt mines of Transylvania for the Beyoglu and he served in the defence of Medias. He escapes from the siege 116,000 gold florins to the good. A feat of which the Beyoglu himself would have been proud. The woods outside Kormocbanya, from which gold ore has been extracted since time immemorial, are resown with gold florins from Medias that will stay underground till the fuss dies down. Anyone wandering around the countryside with a spade in their hand should expect to receive attention.

After a few weeks as the guest of Miklos Patocsy, Francesco Della Valle is allowed to go home. He arrives in Venice in mourning black and repairs to the Ducal Palace.

All those years ago, following the death of his only lawful child Francesco, Andrea Gritti appeared serene, even cheerful. Which makes his present agony, at the death of an illegitimate son he hasn't seen for decades, all the more perplexing. His friends gently remind him of the tenacity and fortitude he showed in the face of earlier hardships, but he asks them not to be surprised that he has lost his desire to live, for he never doubted that the Beyoglu was his son in all fullness, as much as any child can be.

Act Five: Suleyman Ascending

XV

In his *Epistle of Politics*, Nizam al-Mulk tells the story of the King who, while wandering in the wilderness, comes across a flock of sheep and a dog hanging from a tree.

'It was my dog,' the shepherd tells the King, 'and so well did it guard my sheep, no wolf would dare approach. I would go off to the town and come back and find that the dog had taken the sheep to pasture and that not a single one had been lost.

'Then, one day, sensing that something was wrong, I counted the sheep and found several missing. And from then on, each time I counted the sheep, I found that more were gone. And I didn't know why.

'One day I went to collect firewood and when I came back I saw a wolf approaching the flock. I got down in the under-growth and watched. The dog mounted the wolf. After they had mated, the dog lay down in the shade and went to sleep.

'While the dog was sleeping, the wolf caught a sheep and tore it to pieces and ate it. I knew then that my guard dog had been betraying me. So I hanged it.'

~

Iskender Celebi is that rare person of aptitude and means who has come far. As Treasurer, he knows what the Sultan has and what he can spend, knowledge that translates into power. Having enjoyed the patronage of others, Iskender now dispenses his own. His palaces and gardens are schools for talent. The most promising apprentices are fast-tracked to junior chancery posts that in time will lead to vizierates and pashaliks. His pages are in no way inferior to those of the Third Courtyard. And there is hardly a poet alive who doesn't call him friend and protector.

Like a horse, a slave should have expensive trappings and some meat on him. That's what the crowds expect to see when the viziers and other men of rank process to the Imperial Council. Ibrahim Pasha is typically escorted by four hundred slaves wearing tasselled bonnets, Ayas, by way of comparison, by a mere sixty. Iskender Celebi's escort is almost as big as that of Ibrahim, and his slaves all have hanging tassels and gold thread and other embellishments. Once a year the Treasurer orders an entire shipload of linens made from premium Caucasian flax for his own retinue alone.

He is that rarest of bureaucrats, a man of the heart as well as the pen. He keeps the courtiers amused with the witticisms he directs at an expatriate Iranian who has attached himself to the Sultan, asking why he doesn't love the Sunni heroes as much as the Shia ones and teasing him for his typically Persian tendency to exaggerate.

Ayas disapproves of the Treasury's patronage of poets and other certified spongers. 'What benefit does this class bring to the Sultan that they receive aspers from the public purse?' he grumbles. And the Treasurer fires back arrows from the poet's quiver:

> If there were no poets in the world,
> Who would recount the state of Kings?

Iskender used to be Ibrahim's mentor. And perhaps the memory of this former intimacy means that he sees no reason to hold his tongue whenever Ibrahim's impetuosity and arrogance harm the interests of the State. It was Sultan Selim who deprecated the power of 'good-for-nothing' slave converts in the court of his own father, asserting that 'It is never right to turn one's face away from freemen.' Iskender is such a free-born Turk. He was an expert in Treasury matters when Ibrahim was counting skins on his fingers in Parga.

At the time, Iskender made known his doubts concerning the helmet crown that Ibrahim ordered for the second Austrian campaign. Since then, Suleyman himself seems to have had second thoughts about the propriety of such a reckless and – dare one say it? – un-Islamic extravagance. The helmet has been seen only a handful of times and is now in storage awaiting dismantlement.

More recently, by instructing the Voivode of Wallachia to withhold his support from the Beyoglu, the Treasurer had the satisfaction of contributing to the downfall of an old ally of the Grand Vizier. Why did Ibrahim promote and enrich such a wicked person in the first place? Gritti's sole service to the Ottoman State was to expose Ibrahim's failings as a judge of character.

And the Treasurer remains indignant about the fate of his friend Figani, murdered, he believes, for a poem he didn't write.

~

It is customary for the Ottoman Treasurer to contribute thirty crack troops for each campaign. But when the army musters in the autumn of 1533, Ibrahim tells Iskender to supply 140. Ibrahim may have settled on that number following an assessment of the Treasurer's means. He may be testing his obedience. Either way, Iskender is offended. It's not the number, it's the presumption. The Quartermaster doesn't want to refuse the Commander-in-Chief. He doesn't want to accommodate him, either. The number of troops he eventually provides, 110, irritates them both.

Messengers have gone east to stake out bivouacs and requisition supplies. Barley, wheat, straw and oil are put in stores on the valley floors. Couriers tell the governors and fief-holders how many men to provide. The Iranian Shah, Tahmasp, has been treading all over Ottoman territory and interests in the east. It is time to do a Selim on him; time for a second Chaldiran. With the Hungarian theatre stalemated, the Ottoman Empire can afford to bring its naval resources to bear on the White Sea while opening a new front in the east. Overstretch shouldn't be a problem provided everyone plays their part.

Ibrahim sets out after the equinox. At each stop local bigwigs fall over themselves to ingratiate themselves with the 'Substitute of the Sultanate', the 'Lofty Commander-in-Chief', and the 'Warrior of States and the World'. And after the feast, against a backdrop of leaves turning, the soldiers dance to the strains of the baglama and refine their martial skills disputing carcasses on horseback.

Ibrahim is an indifferent correspondent, his wife Muhsine complains from the palace on the Hippodrome. 'What sin did I commit that you forget us and don't write to us for such a long time?' And he writes back, 'My darling one, God knows I love you more than my own life. How is it possible for you to have sinned when I am the sinner?' He has a not entirely convincing excuse for his silence. 'I am avoiding writing so as not to burden you with news of my health, whether it is good or bad.' And after kissing the eyes of little Mehmet Shah, 'fruit of my youth', as he calls him, and the eyes of the mother of Mehmet Shah, he tells her that he has reached Aleppo.

At Aleppo the soldiers disperse to their winter quarters. Officers ride out to bully and bribe the Kurdish magnates. They return with the keys to the castles of Adilcevaz, Ercis, Ahlat and Revan. The fortified bluff of Van, sentry post of the east, also surrenders. From his palace on the Aleppo acropolis, Ibrahim administers justice and resolves disputes. It is around this time that Hayreddin Barbarossa appears out of the snow and Ibrahim makes him Captain Pasha. And to each decree, each appointment, Ibrahim fixes the royal monogram as if it were his own.

A Polish diplomat is in town. Andrzej Teczynski, Voivode of Krakow, is bound for Jerusalem, a pilgrimage that is safer under the present Sultan than it was when the Crusaders held the city of King David. Expatiating in his usual manner, Ibrahim praises those small Polish falcons that fly very high and dive on other birds from great heights, and he declares that he wishes to send young King Sigismund (who is now sharing the throne of Poland with his father, old King Sigismund) some Arab horses, which are much reputed. He observes, perhaps not very originally, that young princes take much pleasure from horses, dogs and other animals of the chase.

'I have come here with this little army,' he tells Teczynski, 'hoping to provoke the King of the Persians into battle. If he learns that I have many troops or that His Majesty the Sultan will take part personally, he will never dare come forward, so I am doing what is necessary to push him to fight. And if he does not dare attack me, but flees from combat, with the help of Almighty God I will endeavour to subjugate his towns and fortresses, which I hope to take hold of easily. Many of his nobles and men of high and low status are already fleeing to our side, putting themselves under the protection of His Majesty the Sultan and recognising him as their lord. And they do this partly out of fear and terror of my power and to obtain security for their lives and possessions, and partly because of the cruelty of the Shah of Iran.'

What Ibrahim tells Teczynski about the red-headed ones makes them out to be as bad as the Lutherans. 'They eat human flesh and live without law or norm . . . those among them who are in power do whatever they want, soiling virgins and young boys while banqueting and having sexual intercourse in public with other men's wives.'

While Ibrahim is in Aleppo, his informants at the Porte tell him that the Sultan has taken a shine to a stablemaster called Rustem, young and full of virtues, whom he permits certain liberties and whose talents he lauds as he would laud the talents of Ibrahim when they were setting out. It is a straightforward matter for Ibrahim to appoint Rustem to be Governor of a distant province. And when Rustem complains to Suleyman about the transfer, the King of the World can only reply than when he next sees his Grand Vizier – whenever *that* will be – he will do his best to have it reversed.

The thaw of 1534 brings news. Instead of getting ready to defend Baghdad, Shah Tahmasp has set off across Iran to defend Khorasan, his north-eastern border province, from Uzbek attack. Poor Iran: a country of exposed flanks. The Shah has not only left Baghdad undefended, but also his capital, Tabriz, in the far north-west of the country.

Iskender Celebi paints a picture for Ibrahim. Take advantage of the Shah's absence, he urges. Occupy Tabriz and bring Iran to heel. To subdue the plateau would be an achievement worthy of history's greatest generals, an achievement that eluded even Sultan Selim.

Ibrahim likes the advice. A man of his vast self-regard is bound to. But he hates the adviser. Throughout this winter of effortless mastery and power, Ibrahim hasn't forgotten the Treasurer's insolence in denying him the soldiers he asked for. It's not the number that matters, but the precedent. What if it became widely known that the Grand Vizier who made the Ottoman Empire what it is today can be insulted with impunity? One can easily imagine how this might give ideas to an ambitious young man like Rustem.

~

Aleppo in the spring; the time, the poets tell us, when arid knolls take on the lush and joyful aspect of a rose garden. The Ottomans break camp and the Treasury camels are on the point of moving off, husbanded by Iskender's men. Suddenly, shouts of 'thief!' ring out. With a promptness that suggests they are acting on a prearranged signal, Ibrahim's men come running and arrest dozens of Treasury servants. Under torture they confess to trying to steal the Sultan's gold and are punished according to the law.

For Iskender the execution of his men on trumped-up charges is more than an insult. It is a glimpse of his own perdition.

In May the army reaches Diyarbakir, the basalt city commanding the headwaters of the Tigris, and more levies are brought into the ranks. Although Ibrahim's eastward progress has so far been unopposed, and more Kurdish redoubts surrender their keys, it is well known that the feudal rulers in these parts are like poplar trees, bending with the wind and straightening after it passes.

The army is marching to war under a Commander-in-Chief and a Quartermaster who wish each other's destruction. The length of Anatolia divides the men from their talisman and protector, the Sultan, who is only just setting out from Istanbul to join them. And while Suleyman may never have lost a campaign, the Iranian Shah, heretic or not, is reputed to have divine powers. So there is unease in the ranks.

Much of Ibrahim's force is made up of regional levies. Yahya Bey commands one of them. Yahya is a veteran of Chaldiran. He is also a poet who wrote an elegy to the murdered poet Figani and enjoys the patronage of Iskender Celebi. And now Figani's executioner is driving Yahya and his men deep into the Persian plateau, which has a habit of swallowing armies. After defeating Shah Ismail at Chaldiran, Selim retreated to Istanbul rather than hazard an occupation. And that was with 100,000 men. What chance does the Frank stand with half that number?

Soon it becomes less than half, in fact, thanks to some Iranian defectors and an error of judgement. In the mountains of Kurdistan the defectors convince Ibrahim to act against some notorious brigands, but the operation ends with the death of thousands of Turkish troops in the gorges and defiles, from ambushes and hunger.

Still, the Grand Vizier is in high spirits. From the village of Khoy, deep into Iran, he writes to Muhsine to tell her how clever he is. 'No one knows we have come this way! Even the Sultan is unaware and thinks we are in Diyarbakir. But with the help and favour of God . . . we have taken many castles from the accursed red-headed ones. Not content with that, and risking our

231

lives for the Sultan, and in the name of the Prophet, we have now approached Tabriz.'

~

Marching a long way behind his Grand Vizier, progressing eastwards in easy, unhurried stages, Suleyman is seeing parts of his Anatolian homeland that he has only heard about. Long absences are the price that he pays for his pursuit of the Golden Apple.

At Konya he settles himself beneath the conical dome, liquid with turquoise faience, which marks the resting place of Our Master, the bard of Balkh. And here, to the accelerating rhythms of the drum and the reed flute of which Our Master tells – the reed that has been ripped from its divine bed and yearns to return – the dome is lifted and hovers, liberated from its pillars by the spinning of the dervishes and the miraculous truths contained in the poem.

> Schemes for gaining the things of this world are worthless,
> Those for renouncing the world are praiseworthy.
> This world is the prison and we are the prisoners,
> Dig a hole in the prison and let yourself out.
> What is this world but ignorance of God?
> It is not merchandise and silver and weighing scales and women!
> As for the riches you carry for the sake of religion,
> As the Prophet said, 'How good is the wealth of the righteous.'
> Water in the boat is the ruin of the boat,
> Water under the boat is its support.
> Since he cast out all desire for wealth and possessions,
> Solomon did not call himself by any name but 'poor'.

Nothing in this world is permanent. Ahmet, Ferhat and Gritti were taught this lesson the hard way. Hafsa his mother knew it the day she was born, which is why she returned to her Maker with a smile on her face.

~

After arriving at Erzurum, in eastern Anatolia, the Sultan gets a message from Ibrahim. Its tone and content are unusual. It's not like the Grand Vizier to panic.

The Shah has confounded all expectations, Ibrahim informs the Sultan. Upon reaching Khorasan, he promptly turned around and is hurrying back to meet the invader. Yes, Tabriz is ours. But perhaps not for long. And he begs his master to hurry. 'Servants,' he writes, feeling less than impregnable, less than a lion-keeper, 'cannot withstand the full might of kings.'

~

It takes Shah Tahmasp a mere 21 days to cover 1,000 miles and come within striking distance of the Ottomans. In the process he loses too many horses to the crippling effects of the forced marches, too many men to the attractions of hearth and home. After these depletions the Shah has just 7,000 fully equipped horsemen with which to take on an invasion force whose size, following the conjunction of the Sultan's army and that of Ibrahim, exceeds 150,000 men. The Grand Vizier's morale revives wonderfully.

In view of the disparity in numbers, the Sultan would be neglecting his religious duty if he did not press on to crush the head of the viper. The doctors of the law have issued a fatwa demanding the severest measures against the heresy. But what the clerics don't appreciate is that the lesson of Shah Ismail's suicidal decision to give battle at Chaldiran has been learned by his son. Tahmasp won't set his light cavalry against the Otto-man artillery and arquebuses. He won't condemn himself and his sect to ruin. He will tempt the enemy into the nooks of the plateau, which have been emptied of food and shelter, and let winter do the rest.

The Turkish soldiers are pursuing a foe that appears to have the gift of immateriality. They cruise through half-destroyed cities and over scorched earth while mysterious horsemen moni-tor them from afar. Arriving at Soltaniyeh, the Mongols' old summer capital, they pitch their tents near the giant mausoleum

of the Mongol Khan. Monument to a city that was abandoned because it was built in the wrong place. Monument to
folly and pride.

The snow falls, fine and dry, covering the high curving profile, the tiles and the minarets on each corner of the octagonal
drum. It does not stop. On and on, the snow comes down,
thicker and thicker, and inside the submerged tents of the soldiers there is nothing to do but embrace one's comrade and die
in the attitude of one telling a secret.

Much later, a poet – all Iranians are poets – passes this way.

> When I went to Soltaniyeh, that splendid pasturage,
> I saw two thousand corpses lying there without grave
>   or burial shroud.
> I said, 'who slew all these Ottomans?'
>
> The morning breeze replied, 'It was I.'

~

After the disaster the army surges southwards like a shoal
towards warmer waters. But the Iranians are only getting
started. As Suleyman's men stream across the frozen plain and
into the foothills of the Zagros, they are tormented by tribal
specialists in raiding baggage trains and mugging stragglers.
The Sultan's bodyguards have to be alert at all times for assas-
sins who streak on swift ponies towards the imperial tent.

Before Erzurum, Suleyman's campaign journal was a cheerful
record of saints honoured and bastions surrendered. Now it is
about death. One day there is panic; the red-headed ones have
infiltrated the army and are slaughtering good Muslims up the
line. In the confusion men are cut down until the lie is exposed,
the cries abate and the dead are buried ruefully under the ice.

Kasim Pasha loses eleven men to desertion. They are caught
and three are impaled. The rest are sawn in half.

A river in spate flips pack animals like corks and tosses
them downstream. Only those with the heaviest loads, and

consequently the most secure purchase, keep their footing and survive. Long nights are spent in the saddle, devilish cold. The chief bureaucrat of the Ottoman Empire, the Chancellor, Sidi Bey, succumbs. The Sultan hasn't seen a tree since Erzurum.

Accustomed to grassy highways and June campaigns, the supply train falters. Where is the barley, the flour, the firewood? There follows a long march along a narrow pass. Too narrow for the camels, heavy guns and the imperial litter, which have to be abandoned. On it crawls, over the spine of the Zagros, this cripple of an army. Yahya Bey keeps the blood flowing in his fingers by writing poems that describe the soldiers' agony.

Do calamities happen for no reason? Besides the will of God, that is, the turnings of fate? What about individual guilt? Ibrahim puts this question to his lord. He discourses on Iskender Celebi's attempt to steal from the Treasury, the lost artillery pieces and the lack of bread. The abortive pursuit of brigands in the mountains turns out to have been Iskender's idea. Tabriz was Iskender's idea.

Shall we consider the sources of Iskender's wealth? Is it likely that his palaces and gardens are paid for out of his salary? The Treasurer's job is to exact money and Iskender is too good at his job. His assessors are zealots who strip the rich of their last rug and tax dead trees the same as living ones. Those linens have to be paid for somehow.

In his conversations with the Sultan it is imperative that Ibrahim deflect attention from his own shortcomings. That the castles he captured are strategically unimportant; that Tabriz has been recovered by the Shah; that the magnificent Ottoman army, victor of Mohacs, victor of Constantinople and dozens of other battles down the centuries has run itself ragged and tens of thousands of the Sultan's sons have died . . .

Blame the Treasurer.

It is possible that Iskender gathers some loyal sentinels – Yahya Bey's men, perhaps – to make sure that no one enters his tent while he is sleeping. It is possible that the Sultan allows him to defend himself against Ibrahim's charges.

Whatever.

Suleyman's entry for 24 October 1534, reads, 'The Treasurer Iskender Celebi is removed from office.' His possessions – slaves, palaces, tassels – enter the Sultan's book. And yet Ibrahim will need to use all his powers of persuasion to bring the affair to a conclusion. Suleyman isn't Selim. He has pangs. And Iskender isn't Gritti. He has friends.

Not for a further four months and twenty days, not until Suleyman has occupied Baghdad, given out governorships, ordered cadastral reform and viewed the remains of Nizam al-Mulk's college on the banks of the Tigris; not until he has polished this dog turd of a campaign and his haunted, bedraggled men have taken on the form of an army again – not until the sixteenth day of the auspicious month of Ramadan, to be precise, is Iskender hanged in the city's horsemarket.

That night he comes to Suleyman. He comes close to the bed and reproaches him for doing nothing, for giving in to his favourite, who has so much power over him that he can make him order the death of an innocent man. He leans over the Sultan and winds his turban around the long swanlike neck, and pulls, tighter and tighter, and the Sultan is awoken by his own screams.

Taking the cup of water from his attendant, waiting for his breathing to regularise, Sulyeman makes a private vow.

~

Hurrem is delighted that, from this great distance, he has granted her request for enhanced bathing facilities. She says so in her letter, adding, 'only God knows how happy I was when I found out. May your every day be one thousand, may God be your helper. You see, my Sultan – don't take this the wrong way – but I only want the best. God knows I am not satisfied if you fall a single inch short of what you desire. As God is my witness I've spent 50,000 on food alone! Not that I put anything much towards my own needs. And now you have sent me word, my own soul, light of my eyes, my heart's joy, my Sultan. May God give you joy in this world and the next.'

How grateful he is for intimate and well-used formulas that

express love, and how he loves Hurrem for taking him away from thoughts of the Treasurer and the news from Tunis. Satisfied with his promise for a new hamam for her and her ladies, she has evidently decided to move on to winning his sympathy for her general state of poverty. A request for an increase in her stipend will no doubt follow.

'As for the boys,' Hurrem goes on, 'they press their faces against your blessed threshold and long to see your auspicious beauty. We cauterised Cihangir's shoulder and through God's grace the developed cyst was removed. It's quite well now. Don't forget him in your prayers. And speaking of the preceptor, he's virtually a corpse, neither dead nor alive. One minute he can breathe, the next he cannot, and only God really knows his condition.

'If you want to know about the city, the illness goes on, only not so bad as before. When my Sultan returns, with God's grace it will pass. An autumn leaf blows away the moment it falls. My King, I beg and implore you to send me letters often. By God, I'm not telling fibs, if a week or two goes by and the courier doesn't come, tongues start wagging. They say all kinds of things.

'As for this slave of yours, who is burning in the fires of separation, whose liver is seared meat, whose chest is a battlefield, whose eyes are full of tears, who doesn't know day from night, who is drowning helplessly in an ocean of longing, who is afflicted by love for you, worse than Farhad and Majnun; don't even ask about her! For each time I am separated from my Sultan, I cry and sigh like a nightingale and my condition is so pitiful that I wouldn't wish it on one of your infidel slaves.'

A letter from her brings the well-being of opium, the hilarity of wine, the warmth of a brazier on a cold day.

~

Baghdad is the resting place of Imam Abu Hanifa, founder of the Hanafi school of jurisprudence that is the basis for Ottoman law. The Imam's tomb is currently closed to pilgrims after being desecrated by the red-headed ones. They dug up his body and burned it. Or so runs the legend.

What really happened is that shortly before the red-headed ones took Baghdad, the Imam appeared to the guardian of the tomb and told him to move his headstone and put it over the grave of an infidel. And the red-headed ones, thinking that the body of the infidel was the body of the Imam, burned that one by mistake.

When he is informed of these events, Ibrahim Pasha orders a search for the Imam and in due course the workers unearth a vault from which emanates a powerful, musk-like odour. The fumes are so heady that one of the workers drops dead. The Grand Vizier hurries over and replaces the headstone over the vault with his own hands. It is as if the honour of discovering the Imam's remains was reserved, by God's wish, for him alone.

~

In Baghdad one is surrounded by reminders of the family that had it all. Jafar Market. Fadl Canal, Yahya Market. Khalid Market. All named after members of the Barmakid clan, who achieved the highest offices under four Abbasid Caliphs. The Barmakids were from Balkh, in Khorasan. In Baghdad they became so rich that their palaces were envied by the monarch himself. The most prominent of the Barmakids was Jafar. He presided over seventeen years of peace and prosperity in an empire at its zenith. He was perhaps too rich, perhaps too presumptuous, perhaps the Caliph, Harun al-Rashid, didn't appreciate his impregnation of his sister, despite the fact that he had encouraged the princess and the Vizier to wed. One day Harun admired his own glittering suite of slaves and servitors. Turning to a courtier, he asked, 'has there ever been so sumptuous a train?' The reply came, 'Nothing can compare with Jafar's.' One winter's day in 803, the people of Baghdad awoke to find the second most powerful man in the Abbasid Empire cut into three and each piece hanging from a gibbet on a bridge over the Tigris.

~

The evils of printing, without which the Lutheran heresy could not have expanded so quickly, have been successfully parried in the lands of Islam. Aside from the bans placed by the doctors of the law on religious grounds, the practical obstacles to putting each of the 900-plus elements of the Arabic font onto separate blocks for use on a Gutenberg press are all but insurmountable. It would take forever to print a single page. The upshot is that every Quran is a showcase for the skills of the copyist who inscribes it and the illuminator who fills its margins with scrolls, scallops and other geometric delights.

Over the years, Ibrahim has been given so many copies of the Quran, his feelings towards the holy book have soured into active dislike. When the city's best calligraphers present him with an example of their handiwork, he won't look at it. Rather than murmur the bismillah and drag the tips of his fingers over the soft leather, the creamy paper and the vigorous, manly Kufic letters, he flies into a fury and bawls the astonished donors out of the room, shouting that he doesn't want another Quran, he has more than enough already.

~

Baghdad is where it should be, in the Ottoman inventory. Suleyman has come into his Abbasid heritage and can contemplate a push south towards Basra and the Gulf at his leisure. With the exception of this happy acquisition, however, the substance of the eastern campaign has been disappointing and the optics disastrous. As far away as Rome they are chuckling at the thought of the Sultan stuck fast in the ice and the Shah's men dancing around him on their ponies. It is lucky for Ibrahim that Suleyman's definition of military success is more accommodating than that of his father. While they are in Baghdad, the Sultan rewards his Commander-in-Chief with a 20,000-ducat raise and one-off gifts of 20,000 ducats, a kaftan and a sword encrusted with precious stones.

The Pasha is perhaps allowed to feel a little complacent. Iskender has been neutralised. The Treasurer's father-in-law, who was also on the campaign, and might have harboured vengeful thoughts, was also executed. Impudent Rustem is far from the capital.

That winter Ibrahim catches up with his correspondence. In his letter to Ferdinand there is no nonsense about servants and the might of kings. 'With this army of mine,' he brags, 'which heaven and earth are unable to contain . . . I conquered the fortresses of Van, Vastan, Astwar and some thirteen other fortresses. After that, leading my army to the other side and pushing into the city of Tabriz, the ancient seat of the King of Persia, with the favour of Almighty God I conquered Tabriz together with its entire territory.' The aforementioned King, 'simply at the sight of one or our banners, shook in his heart and not daring to confront the Conqueror of the Whole World . . . turned tail, left all his treasures, defensive and offensive weapons and all his goods, and ran away.'

The Grand Vizier has learned that 'those traitors who had killed the son of the Lord of the Venetians came over to you in order to cause discord, and entered the Kingdom of Hungary in order to plunder it.' The Archduke, Ibrahim goes on, would be well advised to avoid helping the murderers of poor Alvise. 'Beware of these thieves who cause this discord which will make it easy for us to descend to those regions.'

From the Iranian defectors who came over during the campaign, he has learned that some of the Shah's key ministers have the word 'Sultan' in their names. Tahmasp was a boy when he inherited the throne from Ismail, and the country was run by regents, among them Div Sultan, Chuha Sultan and Kopek Sultan. That the 'Sultan' denoted a position of leadership in their respective tribes is immaterial to Ibrahim. If Ottoman usage and practice cannot be stretched for him, then for whom?

Ibrahim's instinct is to keep cutting footholds in the rock above him. He broaches the subject of his title during the long, dispiriting march back to Istanbul, which involves diversions to subdue a lot of the places that were subdued last year, including Tabriz, and which will doubtless be lost again next year. And during this march the Sultan obliges his Commander-in-Chief by starting to refer to him as Commander-in-Chief-Sultan. The Commander-in-Chief-Sultan convenes a council. The Commander-in-Chief-Sultan camps at such-and-such a place. And the Commander-in-Chief-Sultan begins signing letters using his new title.

He assures the master that his intention is not to overstep the bounds as Ahmet the Traitor did when proclaiming himself Sultan in Cairo. It is not his intention to supplant his dearly beloved lord, God forbid, but rather appropriate for his office a little of the charisma, the *farr*, that inheres in the Sultan's title. But the word Sultan comes from the Arabic S-L-T, from which many words that pertain to power and mastery derive. No, ambiguity is not among the properties of this sibillant little root.

~

Whether it is because he values their counsel, or because he fears that his absence for a long period might give encouragement to another Ahmet the Traitor, the Sultan has brought his whole government to the East. Cabinet meetings in Baghdad are attended by the Empire's top Pashas and officials while hundreds of miles away the capital goes to pot.

Around two thousand Janissaries have been left behind in Istanbul where they are supposed to keep order, which raises the question that Juvenal originally asked in relation to the Praetorian Guard: 'Who will guard the Guard themselves?' With the Sultan away and their pay in arrears, the Janissaries run riot. They want to cross the Horn into Pera but the authorities give the Christians exceptional leave to take up arms in their own defence and the Janissaries look around for softer targets. They board some ships of the fleet and seize weapons before coming ashore, sacking the houses of some Jews and pillaging armouries. They corner one of their own officers but he kills two of them with his sword before riding off. They sprint after him, drag him from his horse and cut off his head. Four days later the Janissaries receive their back pay and some other officers are cashiered.

In the absence of the government, Ottoman diplomacy passes into the hands of amateurs. In the summer of 1535, Jehan de la Forest, gentleman of Auvergne and envoy of the Most Christian King, comes ashore in Istanbul where he only finds second-tier dignitaries who pepper him with questions about a prophecy which says that the Empire will be destroyed by people wearing yellow, and isn't the French King's escutcheon adorned with yellow fleurs-de-lys? La Forest has to explain that the prophecy refers to the slashed breeches worn by the Landsknechte. They are sickly mustard in colour. And the Landsknechte are as much the enemy of the Most Christian King as they are of the Sultan. The dignitaries are mollified but one's time could be better employed speaking to the Grand Vizier; so the Frenchman goes east to find him.

~

The fall of Tunis causes panic in the capital. Where is Hayreddin? Dead? Where is the Sultan with his army? One thousand miles away? Istanbul will surely be next. The yard at Gallipoli is turning out galleys as quickly as it can, but what use are galleys without leaders? There is great relief when news arrives that the King of Spain has sailed to Sicily and Pope Paul is getting ready to receive him.

Finally, on 8 January 1536, a year and a half after he left his people fatherless, the Sultan arrives home in the company of the four Pashas, Ibrahim, Ayas, Kasim and Hayreddin. Yes, the pirate King has crossed the sea to confer with his lord and explain himself after Tunis. He intercepted the Sultan during the army's return journey through Cilicia and they sat together, though what was said can only be surmised.

Back in the capital La Forest and Ibrahim put the finishing touches to an alliance between France and the Porte. The visible bits allow French merchants operating in the Ottoman Empire to pay the same tariffs as Ottoman merchants. French nationals who are suspected of committing crimes in the Sultan's lands will be tried by special judges and in the presence of a translator. Enslaving each other's subjects is out. Sea captains passing a vessel from the other country will hoist their colours and fire a salvo in greeting. While in theory many of the provisions apply reciprocally, in practice the treaty benefits France more than Turkey.

The Sultan can afford to be generous if the invisible bits of the alliance achieve his cherished wish of expelling Charles from Italy and taking chunks of the country for himself. Which is exactly what they are designed to do. Money. Arms. Fitting yards. Intelligence. These are the elements of a military partnership to scandalise Christendom. A proper coalition between proper allies and no Venetian-style prevarication.

Andrea Gritti, arch-prevaricator, is the loser from the alliance. The exclusion of his ships from the Franco-Turkish common market marks the end of Venice's commercial preponderance in the Mediterannean. It is as heavy a blow as the shifting of the major trade routes to the Atlantic was a generation ago, and reason enough for the sad old Doge to sigh again for his son, who for all his faults never stopped lobbying for Venice in the heart of the Ottoman Empire.

~

She already has the bathroom. Now she gets the wedding party, the mourning period for her mother-in-law Hafsa having expired. The houses of the city are festooned and swings have been set up in the Hippodrome so people can fling themselves high and see what the great and the good see from their marble balconies, and she and her ladies are perfectly placed, sitting on their tribune and enjoying their refreshments, hidden from the people by a gilt lattice while the jousting and knockabout go on below. The giraffes have necks so long, they appear to touch the sky.

Were Suleyman to die now, in his forty-third year, his death would be considered premature but not aberrantly so. Each time he goes off to fight, there is a chance that he will not return. His father was taken by the plague in the prime of life. God is Great.

And then what?

In an absolute monarchy the natural unit is the faction. But the factions are not quite clear yet. Mustafa, the eldest son, and Mahidevran, his mother. Hurrem and ... who? She has yet to decide which of her three able-bodied boys to support. A decision any mother would prefer to delay indefinitely. And the Grand Vizier whose eye she caught in the slave market all those years ago? Between the pairings Ibrahim sits uncomfortably.

Mustafa sends the Grand Vizier reports about the goings-on in Manisa. In his replies, Ibrahim refers to himself as Mustafa's 'sincere friend' and expresses his wish to see him soon, to 'take profit from and be gladdened by [his] noble and blessed grace'. And there is an undeniable bond of sympathy between his wife Muhsine and Mahidevran. In a letter, Mahidevran writes effusively of the 'sisterhood and brotherhood' that Muhsine and her husband have shown her, and thanks them for their 'truly sincere kind friendship and compassion'.

But it isn't straightforward to have warm relations with Mahidevran and Mustafa and at the same time have warm relations with Hurrem. That's not how families work.

~

No matter how wealthy and titled he has become, no matter how many archdukes he counts among his brothers, his legal status has not changed since he asked Mustafa all those years ago, 'do you not know that his slave is also yours?'

It would be ludicrous if Ibrahim were scheming for a greater role than he already has. This disliked demi-Christian. And yet it is easy to forget that great men see the world differently to the rest of us. What from sea-level appears to be a huge cliff is the shallowest of steps to someone already in the clouds. Ahmet the Traitor thought he could become Sultan. And Ibrahim is more formidable than Ahmet was.

Rumours suggest that while Hayreddin Barbarossa was sailing to Anatolia he seized a Venetian ship that turned out to be carrying incriminating letters from Ibrahim to the Christian powers, and that these letters formed the substance of his conversation with the Sultan in Cilicia. Again, rumour has it that before his appointment with the executioner in the Baghdad horsemarket, Iskender Celebi called for pen and paper and denounced Ibrahim for conspiring with the Persians.

There are other rumours. That he wishes to make Mahidevran's son Sultan. That he wishes to be Sultan himself. That Hurrem has plans for Rustem the stable-master and is briefing against the Grand Vizier.

And it cannot be denied that, following the reverses of Tunis and Persia and the apprehensions over a possible invasion of Istanbul, and the repeated visits of the plague, the Porte is in a jerky, febrile state.

~

This year, 1536, the lunar month of Ramadan starts on 23 February and is concurrent almost to the day with the solar month that leads up to the spring equinox. The bayram festivities to mark the end of the fast will coincide with the first day of spring.

But the bayram must be earned. It is meaningless without the fast. And the fast is nothing without the build-up.

The criers go out on horseback to remind people of the approach of Ramadan and commend the virtues of modesty, frugality and godliness. The kitchens are pumping out wood smoke, preparing for war. The enemies are plunging sugar levels, lassitude and ill-temper. The weapons are jams, pickles, halva doused in orange juice and sprinkled with cinnamon, nuts, sherbets, stewed fruits, sweet pastes, rice puddings, filo pastries, starch wafers flavoured with rose water, sweetened rice coloured with saffron, and grape juice.

When the auspicious month finally gets underway, the pious ones spend their days asleep or reading the holy book and the nights eating and going out to the shops, which enjoy a month-long exemption from curfew. After about a week the people get used to the feeling of hunger that crawls up them as the day progresses, slowing everything, their reactions, their thoughts, their movements. They begin to enjoy the intensity of focus that is the companion of retracted possibilities. They enjoy the four walls of the fast.

The poor want for nothing. Every day, as Iftar approaches, they simply choose which bazaar, mosque or hospital to go to. Ramadan is the time when it pleases God to level up the poor to the limited extent that this is desirable in our necessarily unequal world, in which God has chosen some people to be higher than others.

By week four the pious ones are counting the days before the doctors of law detect the new moon and declare the bayram. They are unkind to those who eat or drink on the sly, particularly the wine drinkers and those who spend the night with prostitutes. When the pious ones find a tipsy Jew, they put him on a horse with ox-tripe on his head and a tail in his hand and lead him around the city.

~

On the twenty-first day of Ramadan, which corresponds to 14 March, Guillaume Postel, who arrived in Constantinople with Jehan de la Forest, keeps his appointment at the palace on the Hippodrome. An otherworldly young man of a fixed, somewhat troubling gaze, who has learned Hebrew and Arabic and goodness knows what else.

It is clear from Postel's conversation that he has the ardour and curiosity of the more intense kind of traveller. He has been spending Francis's money on manuscripts for the royal library in Paris and he has also been looking around him. He says that he is touched by the honesty of the Turkish tribunals compared to their French equivalents. He marvels at the fact that the Sultan, that 'paragon of humanity and justice', is able to observe trials through a grilled aperture. 'May it please God,' he concludes amusingly, 'that a guardian angel could make the same thing happen at the court of the True Christian King.'

And so to business. Postel brings instructions from Francis to retrieve the treasure of a certain Crozillon. A man of enterprise from Tours, Crozillon made a spectacular career selling Indian gems to the Portuguese. After eight years on the Ganges he was going home with 300,000 gold ducats when he died in Ankara. In accordance with Crozillon's instructions, the treasure was confided to his friend Ibrahim Pasha for safe keeping. Be so good as to keep the money safe, ran his request, until an accredited courier arrives to bring it home for the surviving Crozillons, and you will receive 4,000 ducats for your pains.

That courier, Postel explains, is me.

Is it unreasonable for the Pasha to consider 4,000 ducats a very thin reward for the service he has performed? And the Grand Vizier betrays a decided reluctance to give up the 300,000. That said, the new Franco-Turkish treaty stipulates that subjects of the French King have the right to dispose of their property by testament anywhere in the Ottoman Empire, and in the event that they die intestate, their property is to be reserved for their heirs or committed to the charge of the French envoy or consul. Knowing his rights, Postel indicates that he is ready to take matters to the Sultan. It is with relief that Ibrahim at that moment receives a summons from the Sultan to attend him in the New Palace, following which they will break the fast together and he will stay the night.

～

At this point, as Ibrahim gives his horse to his groom at the Gate of Salutations and makes his way on foot through the Second Courtyard towards the Inner Palace where he will dine and sleep, it is worth remembering Mustafa Pasha. Not to be confused with the Sultan's son Mustafa. All they share is a name.

Mustafa Pasha spent eight months of the year laid up with gout. This and other factors meant that he should go. The

Sultan gave him the choice between being demoted while keeping his privileges, and principled oblivion. Mustafa surveyed the things he wouldn't like to lose, the 700 slaves, the income of 70,000 ducats, the jewel collection and the house overlooking the water, and opted for demotion.

How is this story instructive? Mustafa never allowed power, a means for him, to become an end. Nor did he ever deceive himself into thinking that the Sultan couldn't do without him. This is where he and Ibrahim of Parga differ. His superior as a statesman, Ibrahim has two fatal flaws that Mustafa did not. He is fixated on power and he believes himself to be indispensable.

And the Sultan hasn't forgotten his vow of revenge, taken that night in Baghdad.

~

The next morning Ibrahim's body is discovered with marks on it, in the bedroom next to the Sultan's, the torn clothes and bloodstains on the walls indicating that only after a fierce struggle were the mutes able to put the bowstring around his neck. From the jetty at the bottom of the Palace garden the body is put in a boat and rowed across the Horn for burial in an unmarked grave. His estate, his palaces, his slaves, horses, clothes – and Crozillon's gold – all devolve to the Sultan.

For the sycophants at court it suffices to replace one letter in Ibrahim's sobriquet, *Makbul*, the favourite, or loved one, to reflect his decisively altered circumstances. Now he is *Maktul*, the killed one, not that he will be mentioned in public at all, only in private spaces, where the people apply themselves to work over and over the homicide of the Ides of March, 1536, and discover its meaning.

Ask the man who knows, who was listening through the wall to the sound of his own liberation, the death of his keeper, the passing of his youth.

Who, apart from God, can say what will come next? Not the Sultan, not Hurrem, not any of the contenders, not Rustem, not Hayreddin, nor any of the other ambitious people, yet to show themselves, who will find in the absence of the Sultan's friend a gap to rise. He will let them rise, this new Sultan, but he will not let them rule. He will not let them insult and oppress him. Would his father have entertained such a thing?

And perhaps as the days pass and the shock of deliverance shades into guilt and nostalgia, he thinks of his father, Selim, who killed men many times, so many times, and died in his own bed. For isn't that the strongest desire of the greatest king: to die in bed?

That year the bayram and the New Year are celebrated at once. The first tulips are out, the plane trees are coming into leaf and squalls off the Black Sea are being put to flight by warm currents from the south. The city is suffused by the fumes of sheep fat while the people make merry with drums and arrack. After returning from the mosque the Sultan visits his Treasury, which the pages have decked with magnificent objects acquired by gift and conquest since the dynasty's foundation, and thanks God for making him the possessor of such riches.

Acknowledgements

Particular thanks to Cecilia Riva, Sheila de Bellaigue, Gianpiero Bellingeri, Fiona Brown, Charles Cumming, Filippo de Vivo, Eric de Bellaigue, the late John Flood, Roger Jupe, Suzanne Press, Ilber Ortayli, Elvin Otman, John Gurney, Patricia Daunt, Nagihan Gür, the staff of the London and British Libraries, Zeynep Atbas, Inigo Thomas, Alain Servantie, the late Maria Pia Pedani, Francis Russell, Kaya Genc, Rupert Smith, Jonathon Bond, Stephen Parker, Henry Howard, to my superb editors at The Bodley Head, Will Hammond and Stuart Williams, and to Peter Straus, a nonpareil among agents, and his colleagues at Rogers, Coleridge and White.

Bibliography

Achard, Paul, *La Vie extraordinaire des frères Barberousse, corsaires et rois d'Alger*, Editions de France, 1939

Afyoncu, Erhan, *Venedik Elçilerinin Raporlarına Göre Kanuni ve Pargalı İbrahim Paşa*, Yeditepe, 2018

Alberi, Eugenio, *Le relazioni degli ambasciatori veneti al Senato durante il secolo decimosesto*, Società editrice fiorentina, 1839–1863

And, Metin, 'Eski Osmanlı Şenlikleri Üzerine Üç İtalyan Kaynağı', *Forum* XIV, No. 184, December 1961

Anonymous, *Copia de una lettera de la partita del Turcho de Constantinopoli*, Florence, *c.*1533

Appold, Kenneth G., *The Reformation: A Brief History*, Wiley-Blackwell, 2011

Atasoy, Nurhan, *İbrahim Paşa Sarayı*, T.C. Kültür ve Turizm Bakanlığı Yayınları, 2017

Atıl, Esin, *Süleymanname: The Illustrated History of Süleyman the Magnificent*, National Gallery of Art, Washington, 1986

Atıl, Esin, *The Age of Sultan Süleyman the Magnificent*, National Gallery of Art, Washington, 1986

Babinger, Franz, *Mehmed the Conqueror and his Time*, ed. William C. Hickman, trans. Ralph Manheim, Princeton University Press, 1978

Bacqué-Grammont, Jean-Louis, *Les Ottomans, les Safavides et leurs voisins*, Nederlands Historisch-Archeologisch Instituut te Istanbul, 1987

Barbarigo, Niccolò, 'Vita di Andrea Gritti, doge de Venezia', in Girolamo Ascanio Molin, *Orazioni, elogie e vite, scritte da letterati Veneti patrizj*, Venice, 1795

Barbaro, Josafa, and Contarini, Ambrogio, *Travels to Tana and Persia*, ed. [Henry,] Lord Stanley of Alderley, trans. William Thomas and S.A. Roy, Hakluyt Society, 1873

Barta, Gábor, *La Route qui mène à Istanbul (1526–1528)*, Studia Historica Academiae Scientarum Hungaricae, no. 195, Akadémiai Kiadó, 1994

Bassano, Luigi, *Costumi et i modi particolari della vita de'Turchi*, Institut für Gesichte und Kultur des Nahen Orients an der Universität des Nahen Orients, Casa Editrice Max Hueber, 1963

Bel, Matthias, *Adparatus ad historiam Hungariae, sive collectio miscella*, Bratislava, 1735

Bouwsma, William J., *Concordia Mundi: The Career and Thought of Guillaume Postel (1510–1581)*, Harvard University Press, 1957

Bradford, Ernle, *The Sultan's Admiral: The Life of Barbarossa*, Hodder and Stoughton, 1969

Busbecq, Ogier Ghiselin de, *Les Lettres turques*, Champion Classiques, 2010

Busbecq, Ogier Ghiselin de, *Life and Letters*, C. Kegan Paul and Co., 1881

Carboni, Stefano, et al., *Venise et l'Orient*, Gallimard, 2006

Cardini, Franco, *Europe and Islam*, trans. Caroline Beamish, Blackwell, 2001

Celâl-zâde Mustafa, *Selim-nâme*, ed. Ahmet Uğur and Mustafa Çuhadar, Kültür Bakanlığı, Ankara, 1990; repr. Milli Eğitim Bakanlığı, 1997

Çelebi Celalzade, Mustafa *Kanuni'nin Tarihçisinden Muhteşem Çağ*, Kariyer Yayınları, 2011

Charrière, E., *Négociations de la France dans le Levant*, Imprimerie nationale, 1848

Chesneau, Jean, *Voyage de Paris en Constantinople*, Cahiers d'Humanisme et Renaissance, no. 159, Librarie Droz, 2019

Clot, André, *Soliman le magnifique*, Fayard, 1983

Curipeschitz, Benedict, 'Wegrayss Keyserlicher Maiestät Legation im 32. Jar zu dem Türcken Geschickt', Augsburg, 1533, in vol. 1, part 5 of Anton von Gévay, *Urkunden und Aktenstücke zur Geschichte der Verhältnisse zwischen Oesterreich, Ungarn und der Pforte*, Vienna, 1840

Davis, James Cushman, 'Shipping and Spying in the Early Career of a Venetian Doge, 1496–1502', *Studi Veneziani* XVI, 1974, pp. 97–108

Decei, Aurel, *Aloisio Gritti au service de Soliman le magnifique d'après les documents turcs inédits (1533–1534)*, Anatolia Moderna/Yeni Anadolu III, Bibliothèque de l'Institut français d'études anatoliennes d'Istanbul, 1992

Demir, Necati, and Erdem, Mehmet Dursun (eds), *Saltık-nâme*, Destan Yayınları, 2007

Falsafi, Nasrullah, *Chand Maghale-ye Tarikhi va Adabi*, Vahid, 1970

Feneşan, Cristina, and Bacqué-Grammont, Jean-Louis, *Notes sur Aloisio Gritti*, Anatolia Moderna no. 3, Bibliotheque de L'Institut français d'études anatoliennes d'Istanbul, 1992

Finkel, Caroline, *Osman's Dream: The Story of the Ottoman Empire (1300–1923)*, John Murray, 2005

Finlay, Robert, *Politics in Renaissance Venice*, Ernest Benn, 1980

Finlay, Robert, *Venice Besieged: Politics and Diplomacy in the Italian Wars, 1494–1534*, Ashgate Variorum, 2008

Franzio, Umberto, *The Doge's Palace in Venice*, Edizioni Storti, 1979

Garnier, Édith, *L'alliance impie; Francois Ier et Soliman le Magnifique contre Charles Quint*, Éditions du Felin, 2008

Gibb, E.J.W., *A History of Ottoman Poetry*, Luzac and Co., 1904

Giovio, Paolo, *Gli elogi vite brevemente scritte d'huomini illustri di guerra, antichi et moderni*, Florence, 1554

Giovio, Paolo, *Commentario de le Cose de Turchi*, ed. Lara Michelacci, Cooperativa Libraria Universitaria Editrice Bologna, 2005

Giovio, Paolo, *Elogi Degli Uomini Illustri*, trans. Andrea Guasparri and Franco Minonzio, G. Einaudi, *c*.2006

Godkin, Edwin Lawrence, *The History of Hungary and the Magyars*, W. Kent and Co., 1856

Gökbilgin, M. Tayyib, 'Ibrahim Pasha', in *Encylopaedia of Islam*, ed. P. Bearman, Th. Bianquis, C.E. Bosworth, E. Van Donzel and W.P. Heinrichs, Brill, 1960

Graviere, Jurien de la, *Doria et Barberousse*, Plon, Nourrit et Compagnie, 1886

Grey, Charles (ed.), *A Narrative of Italian Travels in Persia*, Hakluyt Society, 1873

Güngör Şahin, Hüseyin, *İspanyol ve Osmanlı Kaynaklarına Göre Barbaros Hayreddin Paşa*, Panama Yayıncılık, 2019

Gürkan, Emrah Safa, 'The Centre and the Frontier: Ottoman Cooperation with the North African Corsairs in the Sixteenth Century', *Turkish Historical Review*, vol. 1 (2010), pp. 125–163

Gürkan, Emrah Safa, *Sultanın Korsanları; Osmanlı Akdenizi'nde Gaza, Yağma ve Esaret, 1500–1700*, Kronik, 2018

Hammer-Purgstall, J. de [von], *Histoire de l'Empire Ottoman*, trans. J.J. Hellert, Bellizard, Barthès, Dufour et Lowell, 1836

Hare, Christopher, *A Princess of the Italian Reformation*, Harper and Bros, 1912

Ḥasan-i Rumlu, *A Chronicle of the Early Safawīs Being the Ahsanu't-Tawārīkh of Hasan-i Rūmlū*. vol. 2, trans. C.N. Seddon. Gaekwad's Oriental Series, no. LXIX, Oriental Institute, Baroda, 1934

Hasluck, F.W., *Christianity and Islam under the Sultans*, Oxford University Press, 1929

Howard, Deborah, *Jacopo Sansovino; Architecture and Patronage in Renaissance Venice*, Yale University Press, 1975

Hughes, Bettany, *Istanbul: A Tale of Three Cities*, Weidenfeld and Nicolson, 2017

İnalcık, Halil, *The Ottoman Empire: The Classical Age 1300–1600*, Phoenix, 1994

Jackson, Peter, and Lockhart, Laurence (eds), *Cambridge History of Iran*, vol. 6: *The Timurid and Safavid Periods*, Cambridge University Press, 1986

Jenkins, Hester Donaldson, 'Ibrahim Pasha, Grand Vizir of Suleiman the Magnificent', *Studies in History, Economics and Public Law*, vol. 46, no. 2, 1891

Kangal, Selmin (ed.), *The Sultan's Portrait: Picturing the House of Osman*, Türkiye İş Bankası, 2000

Kaya, İ. Güven, 'Figânî'nin Ölümü ve Taşlıcalı Yahya Bey'in Bir Şiiri', *Atatürk Üniversitesi Türkiyat Araştırmaları Enstitüsü Dergisi*, no. 34 (2007), pp. 47–61

Kellenbenz, Hermann, 'Jacob Rehlinger, ein Augsburger Kaufmann in Venedig', in Hermann Aubin (ed.), *Beiträge zur Wirtschafts- und Stadtgeschichte. Festschrift für Hektor Ammann*, Franz Steiner Verlag, 1965

Kellenbenz, Hermann, *Handelsverbindungen zwischen Mitteleuropa und Istanbul über Venedig in der ersten Halfte des 16. Jahrhunderts*, Studi Veneziani, Fondazione Giorgio Cini, 1968

Knolles, Richard, *The Generall Historie of the Turkes*, London, 1610

Kretschmayr, Heinrich, *Ludovico Gritti: Eine Monographie*, Archiv für österreichische Geschichte, Wien, 1895

Krstić, Tijana, *Contested Conversions to Islam: Narratives of Religious Change in the Early Modern Otttoman Empire*, Stanford University Press, 2011

Kumrular, Özlem, '"Mir-i Venedik oğlu" Alvise Gritti', in *Tarih ve Toplum: Yeni Yaklaşımlar*, no. 6, 2007/8

Kuntz, Marion, *Guillaume Postel, Prophet of the Restitution of All Things: His Life and Thought*, Nijhoff, 1981

Labalme, Patricia H., and Sanguineti White, Laura, *Venice, Città Excelentissima: Selections from the Renaissance Diaries of Marin Sanudo*, trans. Linda L. Carroll, Johns Hopkins University Press, 2008

Lamansky, *Secrets d'état de Venise*, Académie imperiale des sciences, St Petersburg, 1884

Lane, Frederic C., *Andrea Barbarigo, Merchant of Venice (1418–1449)*, Johns Hopkins Press, 1944

Lanz, Karl (ed.), *Correspondenz des Kaisers Karl V aus dem königlichen Archiv und der Bibliothèque de Bourgogne zu Brüssel (1513–1532)*, F.A. Brockhaus, 1844

Lellouch, Benjamin, *Les Ottomans en Égypte; historiens et conquérants au XVIe siècle*, Collection Turcica, vol. 11, Peeters, 2006

Lellouch, Benjamin, and Yerasimos, Stephane (eds), *Les traditions apoca-lyptiques au tournant de la chute de Constantinople*, Institut francais d'études anatoliennes Georges Dumézil d'Istanbul, 1999

Lewis, Bernard, *The Middle East: A Brief History of the Last 2,000 Years*, Scribner, 1995

Lucchetta, Francesca, 'L' "affare Zen" in Levante nel primo Cinquecento', in *Studi Veneziani*, vol. 10 (1968), Leo S. Olschki, 1969

MacCulloch, Diarmaid, *Reformation: Europe's House Divided (1490–1700)*, Penguin, 2004

Machiavelli, Niccolò, *The Prince*, trans. Tim Parks, Penguin, 2011

Malcolm, Noel, *Useful Enemies: Islam and the Ottoman Empire in Western Political Thought, 1450–1750*, Oxford University Press, 2019

Mansel, Philip, *Constantinople: City of the World's Desire, 1453–1924*, John Murray, 1995

Mantran, Robert, *La vie quotidienne a Istanbul au siècle de Soliman le Magnifique*, Hachette, 1990

Marozzi, Justin, *Baghdad: City of Peace, City of Blood*, Allen Lane, 2014

Melikoff, Irène, 'Le Problème kızılbaş', in *Turcica, revue d'Etudes Tur-ques*, vol. 6, Association pour le développement des études turques, 1975

Merriman, Roger B., *Suleiman the Magnificent (1520–1566)*, Harvard University Press, 1944

Mikhail, Alan, *God's Shadow: Sultan Selim, his Ottoman Empire, and the Making of the Ottoman World*, Liveright, 2020

Monshi, Eskandar Beg, *History of Shah 'Abbas the Great*, trans. Roger M. Savory, Westview, 2 vols, 1978

Mosto, Andrea da, *I dogi di Venezia, nella vita publica e privata*, Aldo Martello, 1960

Murad, Seyyid, *Gazavat-i Hayreddin Paşa*, eds. Abdullah Gündoğdu, Hüseyin Güngör Şahin and Dilek Altun, Panama, 2019

Murphey, Rhoads, *Ottoman Warfare, 1500–1700*, Rutgers University Press, 1999

Navagero, Bernardo, 'Orazione nell' esquie del Doge Andrea Gritti', in Girolamo Ascanio Molin, *Orazioni, elogi e vite, scritte da letterati Veneti patrizj*, Venice, 1793

Necipoğlu, Gülru, 'Suleyman the Magnificent and the Representation of Power in the Context of Ottoman–Hapsburg–Papal Rivalry', *The Art Bulletin*, vol. 71, no. 3 (Sept. 1989), pp. 401–27

Necipoğlu, Gülru, *Architecture, Ceremonial and Power: The Topkapı Palace in the Fifteenth and Sixteenth Centuries*, Architectural History Foundation, 1991

Nicolay, Nicolas de, *Dans l'empire de Soliman le Magnifique*, ed. Marie-Christine Gomez-Géraud and Stéphane Yérasimos, Presses du CNRS, 1989

Nogarola, Leonhard von, and Lamberg, Joseph von, 'Bericht Leonhards Gräfen von Nogarola und Joseph von Lamberg an König Ferdinand I, übberreicht in Linz, 11–21 September, 1532', in vol. 1, part 5 of Anton von Gévay, *Urkunden und Aktenstücke zur Geschichte der Verhältnisse zwischen Oesterreich, Ungarn und der Pforte*, Vienna, 1840

Norwich, John Julius, *Venice: The Greatness and the Fall*, Allen Lane, 1981

Norwich, John Julius, *A Short History of Byzantium*, Knopf, 1997

Papo, Gizella Nemeth, and Papo, Adriano, *Ludovico Gritti: un principe-mercante del Rinascimento tra Venezia, i Turchi e la corona d'Ungheria*, Edizioni della Laguna, 2002

Parker, Geoffrey, *Emperor: A New Life of Charles V*, Yale University Press, 2019

Peçevi, Ibrahim Efendi Tarihi, ed. Bekir Sıtkı Baykal, Kültür Bakanlığı, Yayınları, 1982

Pedani, Maria Pia, *In nome del gran signore; Inviati ottomani a Venezia dalla caduta di Constantinopoli alla guerra di Candia*, Deputazione editrice, 1994

Peirce, Leslie P., *The Imperial Harem: Women and Sovereignty in the Ottoman Empire*, Oxford University Press, 1993

Peirce, Leslie P., *Empress of the East: How a European Slave Girl became Queen of the Ottoman Empire*, Basic Books, 2017

Perjés, Géza, *The Fall of the Medieval Kingdom of Hungary: Mohács 1526–Buda 1541*, trans. Márió D. Fenyő, Social Science Monographs / Atlantic Research and Publications, 1989

Preto, Paolo, *Venezia e i turchi*, G.C. Sansoni, 1975

Preto, Paolo, *I servizi segreti di Venezia*, il Saggiatore, 1994

Postel, Guillaume, *De la République des turcs, et là ou l'occasion s'offrera, des moeurs et loy de tous Muhamedistes*, Poitiers, 1560

Ramberti, B., *Libre tre delli cose de Turchi*, Venice, 1541

Reston, James, *Defenders of the Faith: Charles V, Suleyman the Magnificent, and the Battle for Europe, 1520–1536*, Penguin, 2009

Rogers, J.M., and Ward, R.M., *Süleyman the Magnificent*, British Museum Publications, 1988

Rumi, Jalaluddin, *Mathnawi*, ed. Reynold A. Nicholson, So'ad, 2002

Şahin, Kaya, *Empire and Power in the Reign of Süleyman*, Cambridge University Press, 2013

Saint-Genois, Baron de, and Yssel de Schepper, G.-A., *Les Missions diplomatiques de Corneille Duplicius de Schepper*, M. Hayez, 1856

Sandoval, Prudencio de, *The History of Charles the Vth, Emperor and King of Spain*, trans. John Stevens, London, 1703

Sanuto, Marino, *Diarii*, Deputazione di Storia Patria per le Venezie, 1879–1902

Savaş, Saim, *XVI. Asirda Anadolu'da Alevilik*, Vadi Yayınları, 2002

Savory, Roger, *Iran under the Safavids*, Cambridge University Press, 1980

Schulz, Juergen, 'Jacopo de' Barbari's View of Venice: Map Making, City Views, and Moralised Geography Before the Year 1500', *The Art Bulletin*, September 1978

Secret, F. (ed.), *Le Thrésor des propheties de l'Univers, de G. Postel*, Nijhoff, 1969

Servantie, Alain, *Raisons à faire paix plutôt que guerre; Charles-quint et Soliman*, Editions Isis, Istanbul, 2020

Servantie, Alain, 'Gritti et ses conseils', unpublished, n. d.

Servantie, Alain, and Sicking, Louis, 'L'origine de la diplomatie impériale a la cour ottomane, les missions de Corneille de Schepper, ambassadeur Hapsbourgeois, à Constantinople, 1533–1534', in *Publication du centre Europeen d'etudes Bourguignonnes (XIVe–XVIe s.)*, no. 56, 2016

Setton, Kenneth M., *The Papacy and the Levant (1204–1571)*, The American Philosophical Society, 1984

Sho'ar, Jafar, and Ravanpur, Nargess, *Gozide'i az Siyasatnama va Ghabusname*, Dāneshgāh Payām-e Nūr, n.d.

Sumner-Boyd, Hilary, and Freely, John, *Strolling through Istanbul*, Sev Matbaacilik, 1997

Szakály, Ferenc, *Lodovico Gritti in Hungary, 1529–1534: A Historical Insight into the Beginnings of Turco-Hapsburgian Rivalry*, Akadémiai Kiadó, 1995

Tafuri, Manfredo, *Renovatio Urbis; Venezia nell età di Andrea Gritti (1523–1538)*, Rome, Officina edizioni, 1984

Tolan, John, Veinstein, Gilles, and Laurens, Henry, *Europe and the Islamic World*, Princeton University Press, 2013

Turan, Ebru, *The Sultan's Favorite: Ibrahim Pasha and the Making of the Ottoman Universal Sovereignty in the Reign of Sultan Suleyman (1516–1526)*, unpublished doctoral dissertation, University of Chicago, 2007

Uğur, Ahmet, *Yavuz Sultan Selim*, Erciyes Üniversitesi Sosyal Bilimler Enstitüsü Müdürlüğü, 1992

Uluçay, Çağatay, 'Yavuz Sultan Selim Nasıl Padişah Oldu?' in *Tarih Dergisi*, vols 6, 7, 8 (1954–56)

Uluçay, M. Çağatay, *Padişahların Kadınları ve Kızları*, Ötüken, 1980

Uluçay, M. Çağatay, *Osmanlı Sultanlarına Aşk Mektupları*, Ufuk Kitapları, 2001

Uzunçarşılı, Ismail Hakkı, *Osmanlı Tarihi*, Türk Tarih Kurumu, 1988

Valensi, Lucette, *The Birth of the Despot: Venice and the Sublime Porte*, trans. Arthur Denner, Cornell University Press, 1993

Valle, Francesco Della, *Una breve narracione della grandezza, virtù, valore, et della infelice morte dell'Illustrissimo Signor Conte Alouise Gritti . . .* , ed. Iván Nagy, in *Magyar Történelmi Tár*, vol. 3, Magyar Tudományos Akadémia, 1857, pp. 9–60

Vivo, Filippo de, 'Walking in Sixteenth-Century Venice: Mobilizing the Early Modern City', in Roisin Cossar, Filippo de Vivo and Christina

Neilson (eds), *Shared Spaces and Knowledge Transactions in the Italian Renaissance*, University of Chicago Press, 2016

Weill, Georges, *Vie et caractère de Guillaume Postel*, trans. François Secret, Les Belles Lettres, Milan, 1987

Yıldırım, Ali, '16. Yüzyılda Büyük bir Devlet Adamı ve Edebiyat Hamisi Defterdar İskender Çelebi', *Fırat University Journal of Social Science*, vol. 10, issue 1 (2000), pp. 217–232

Zadeh, Kemal Pacha, *Histoire de la Campagne de Mohacs*, trans. [Abel] Pavet de Courteille, Imprimerie imperiale, 1859

Notes

Chapter I

7   **ridden to death in the bringing of it:** Norwich (1981), 124

7   **after coming ashore at the Molo:** Sanuto (XXVIII), 25

7   **the Collegio has convened to hear:** For Minio's briefing see Alberi (III-3), 71–91.

12   **nine years old at the time of the Conquest:** For the details of Grimani's career, see 'Grimani, Antonio', in the *Dizionario biografico degli Italiani*, Istituto dell'Enciclopedia Italiana, 1925–2020

13   **stupefying jokes she is capable of:** Giovio (1554), 290

14   **Gritti family's engagement there is exceptional:** For the careers of Battista and Triadano, see the relevant entries in the *Dizionario biographico degli Italiani*.

14   **beauty of the surrounding countryside:** Alberi (III–3), 18

15   **vowed to bed her no more:** Many details of Gritti's life and career are drawn from the *Vita di Andrea Gritti*, by Niccolo Barbarigo, and the *Orazione di Bernardo Navagero, patrizio Veneto, nell'esequie del Doge Andrea Gritti*, both reproduced in Girolamo Ascanio Molin's *Orazioni, elogie vite, scritte da letterati Veneti patrizj*, 1793.

15   **that of grains by twenty soldi:** Labalme et al., 232

16   **the Turkish fleet would sail then:** Preto (1994), 269

17   **distraught at the suffering of their favourite:** Barbarigo, 200

17   **nights outside his bolted door:** Norwich (1981), 182

18   **in danger of having his head cut off':** Davis, 106

18   **poor quality of her hired commanders:** This is the view of, among others, Machiavelli. See *The Prince* in its excellent translation by Tim Parks, Penguin Classics, 2011.

19   **people wanting to shake his hand:** Finlay (2008), 1002

19   **besieged Vicenza in a basket:** Finlay (2008), IX, 1002–3

19   **Grimani has done the decent thing:** The account that follows of the ducal election is drawn primarily from Robert Finlay's article, 'Politics and the Family in

Renaissance Italy: The election of Doge Andrea Gritti', reproduced in Finlay (1980), and from Sanuto vol. XXXIV.

22   **patricians to take his hand :** Labalme et al., 65

Chapter II

23   **Selim was Governor:** A visionary and a psychopath who has been neglected by posterity in favour of his grandfather and his son, Sultan Selim I's life and career are accessible through, among other sources, the hagiographic *Selim-nâme*, written by the head of Suleyman's chancellery, Celalzade Mustafa; the relevant chapters in the Austrian scholar Joseph von Hammer-Purgstall's compendious history of the empire, *Geschichte des osmanischen Reiches*, also available in a good French translation; the modern Turkish historian Ahmet Uğur's biography *Yavuz Sultan Selim*, and Alan Mikhail's *God's Shadow: Sultan Selim, his Ottoman Empire, and the Making of the Modern World.*

23   **makes good his escape:** For the Sarı Saltık legend, see Demir et al.

24   **the emperor held a golden apple:** For the origins of the legend of the Golden Apple, see Lellouche and Yerasimos, 153–192.

25   **and protect the weak:** A selection of tales from the Ghabusnama of Kaykavus and the Siyasatnama of Nizam al-Mulk can be found in Sho'ar et al.

25   **thousands of the Shah's acolytes:** Bacqué-Grammont, 18

26   **impaled and roasted on a spit:** Finkel, 99. Caroline Finkel's *Osman's Dream: The Story of the Ottoman Empire (1300–1923),* is an admirable concise history of the empire.

26   **with just a few retainers:** Hammer-Purgstall (IV), 144

27   **operating on a higher plane:** Falsafi, 71. Useful Iranian sources for the Battle of Chaldiran are Hasan-i-Rumlu's *Ahsanu't Tawarikh* (pp. 68–71 in the translation of C.N. Seddon), and Nasrullah Falsafi's article, 'Jang-e Chaldiran', in *Chand Maghale-ye Tarikhi va Adabi,* by the same author.

28   **whatever is decreed by God will occur:** Savory, 41

29   **Imperial ambassador reported:** For the ambassador's report, see Setton, 172.

29   **Suleyman came before this man:** Celâl-zâde Mustafa (1990), 441

31   **to call what is happening a coronation:** A depiction of Suleyman's accession ceremony has been left to us in the *Süleymanname,* an illustrated account of the Sultan's career that is conserved today in the Topkapı Palace Museum in Istanbul. The illumination in question was executed by an unidentified miniaturist and is considered a masterpiece of the genre.

31   **immense shadow over the earth:** Hammer-Purgstall (IV), 138

32   **and the infant Murat:** Peirce (2017), 35

32   **six thousand aspers a month:** Peirce (2017), 34

32   **claustration for his women:** Sumner-Boyd and Freely, 161

33   **encourage people to behave:** For many interesting details about Istanbul in the early years of Suleyman's rule, see the memoir the Hapsburg diplomat Cornelius de Schepper, in de Saint-Genois and de Schepper.

34   **on 28 May 1453:** For an account of the building's last hours as a Christian place of worship, see Norwich (1997), 379–81.

35   **courtyards, cloisters and belvederes:** The fullest history and description of the New Palace, nowadays known as the Topkapi, is found in Gülru Necipoğlu's superb book on the subject (Necipoğlu 1991).

35   **might pass but on their knees:** Alberi (III-1), 7

36   by a French gentlewoman: de Saint-Genois and de Schepper, 168
36   Papa sold animal skins: de Saint-Genois and de Schepper, 180
38   one of the Sultan's ancestors: For the origins of this tradition, see Alberi (III-1), 11.
38   what the son will bring: Turan, 64.
39   has no prepared bed: This description is from Necipoğlu (1991), 150.
39   the slave without the lord: Alberi (III-3), 103

Chapter III

41   no longer support two suns: Parker, 189
42   the monarchy of the world: Norwich (1981), 182
43   a respected uncle: Peçevi, 16
45   an income of 2,000 a year: Peirce (2017), 156
45   personal staff, all on foot: Ibrahim's commute is the subject of a painting in the
      illustrated Talikzade Sehnamesi: Topkapı Sarayı Müzesi III A. 1592, s. 41b-41a,
      cit. Atasoy, 22–3.
46   may they live long and happily: Jenkins, 37
46   the selection of his ministers: This paragraph is taken from Tim Parks' transla-
      tion of Machiavelli's The Prince, 91–2.
47   It will be their secret: For these incidents, see Alberi (III-3), 102.
48   this basic division: Turan, 191–2
50   endeavoured to kill me: Turan, 198
51   the Sultan remains silent: Alberi (III-3), 107–108
51   subdued all the East: Malcolm, 63–4
53   his Majesty the Sovereign: Lellouch (2006), 63
53   great with figures: Yıldırım, 218–9
53   in Albania is a nun: Alberi (III-3), 104–5
54   numerous pearls and rubies: Necipoğlu (1989), 406
54   tutti, non con te: Alberi (III-3), 109
55   less than enthusiastic: Turan, 219
55   Let us celebrate it: The account of Ibrahim's wedding celebrations that follows is
      drawn mainly from Hammer-Purgstall (V-25), 52–5, and And, cited by Atasoy,
      52–3.

Chapter IV

58   spread as far as Corfu: Sanuto (XLI), 292
59   six Vlachs caught looting: Hammer-Purgstall (V), 434–6
59   insomnia and equestrianism: Lamansky, 776
60   the guts of our kingdom: Sanuto (XLII), 191–2
60   We continue towards Buda: Hammer-Purgstall (V), 437
61   thickness of his cuirass: Reston, 192
62   Satires of Juvenal and Persius: Rogers and Ward, 31
63   such good fortune in the world: Sanuto (XLIII), 117
64   keep him away from danger: Sanuto (XLIV), 65
64   Sultan's Chief Treasurer: Turan, 249–50
65   the seat of the Vizier: Kemal Pacha Zade, 7
67   hit by a great storm: Labalme et al., 325
67   abetters of the Turk: Calendar of State Papers (Spain-3), 793

Chapter V

Chapter VI

Chapter VII

101 to Doria just before dawn: Parker, 182
102 directed miraculously by God': Parker, 186
102 before Charles's troops sacked it: Parker, 190–93
103 Cervia to the Holy See: Norwich (1981), 188
103 with the greatest devotion: Sanuto (LII), 610-612
104 the Grand Vizier's words: Sanuto (LIII), 173
105 source of this information secret?: Calendar of State Papers (Spain-4), 502
105 secretly contribute some money: Calendar of State Papers (Spain-4), 268
105 when it opens its mouth: Finlay (2008), X, 19

Chapter VIII

110 the waning of this charming moon': Hammer-Purgstall (V), 412
111 across the Black Sea to Istanbul: Peirce (2017), 23
111 The Russian Girl: Bassano, 44. A Venetian citizen of Dalamatian origin, Luigi Bassano spent more than a year in the Ottoman Empire in the early years of Suleyman's reign, during which time he collected much information about Ottoman society and mores which he went on to arrange into a treatise on the subject, *Costumi e modi particolari della vita de' Turchi*, dedicated to his patron, Cardinal Niccolo Ridolfi.
112 the door of the Privy Chamber: Leslie Peirce's biography of Hurrem, *Empress of the East*, is indispensable to the student of this remarkable woman, while the same author's *The Imperial Harem* provides much useful information about the evolution of one of the least understood and most misrepresented of Ottoman institutions.
113 recognise here as her senior: Alberi (III-1), 75
114 one of the girls stays at his side: Sanuto (XLI), 534–5
114 turn aside cannonballs: Rogers and Ward, 175
115 what else is to be expected?: Uluçay (2001), 57
115 hasta vu nalan deyesun: Uluçay (2001), 26. I am grateful to Nagihan Gür for her help in translating this poem.
115 send you many greetings: Peirce (2017), 74
116 You bring me joy: Peirce (2017), 143–4
116 the great and the good: The following account is drawn from Sanuto (LIII), 443–59, and Hammer-Purgstall (V), 138–45, 461.
117 both converts, both mediocre: de Saint-Genois and de Schepper, 169
123 they enter a room and are undressed: This description of the princes' circumcisions is extrapolated from Bassano, 38.
123 reminding me of this fact.': Hammer-Purgstall (V), 145

Chapter IX

125 Marino Sanuto is an abundantist: Sanuto's diaries are one of the unsung achievements of early modern journalism. I am grateful to Cecilia Riva for her invaluable help in deciphering his Venetian dialect.
125 Every day he comes out: For the life and habits of Marino Sanuto I have relied on Labalme et al. and Finlay (2008).

127 discretion isn't what this is about, is it?: Sanuto's descriptions of the crown and its mode of transport are in Sanuto (LV), 634–5 and Sanuto (LVI), 10–11
128 shipped directly to Italy: Finlay (2008), X, 16
129 Security is first class: İnalcıkI (1994), 147-8
129 mighty Emperor of the Turks: Szakály, 57
130 moves on to other business: R. Nino to Charles V, Venice, 30 November 1530, in Calendar of State Papers (England and Spain-4/1), 829–31, n. 519
130 identified as Janos Habardanecz: Hammer-Purgstall, 154
131 with the initials GR: Papo, 140
132 appropriate in this affair: Lanz, 411–12
132 render service to whomever seeks it: Alberi (III-1), 30
133 the city of Szeged: Papo, 149
133 session on Turkish affairs: Finlay (2008), X, 18
134 while he was in exile in Rome: Sanuto (LVI), 204
135 the bride-to-be has been disinherited: Papo, 57

Chapter X

137 Suleyman goes to Aya Sofia: Bassano provides a full description of the Sultan's manner of proceeding to Aya Sophia, 32–4.
137 perceptible tip of the head: Malcolm, 140–41
138 variety into his love life: Anonymous (c.1533)
138 an armada at Genoa: Sanuto (LVI), 363
139 the Sultan hands out punishments: Hammer-Purgstall, 476
140 the other is a step ahead: Anonymous (c.1533)
141 ... this minaret! Celalzade (2011), 173
142 being pulled through Nis: Suleyman's processions during this campaign are described in an anonymous letter, *Particolare de giornata in giornata insino a Belgrado*, and also in a letter from Ragusa reproduced in Sanuto (LVI), 828–30. The iconography is discussed by Gülru Necipoğlu in her article (1989).
143 a jade-green celadon vase: Sanuto (LVI), 828–30
144 his letters to European rulers: Necipoğlu (1989), 416
144 have their instructions: The Hapsburg embassy yielded two accounts by the diplomats in the question, both reproduced in Anton von Gévay's anthology of documents pertaining to relations between Hungary, the Hapsburgs and the Porte. I am grateful to Sheila de Bellaigue and John Flood for their help in deciphering these documents, from which I draw extensively for the pages that that follow.
146 having them tasted beforehand: Sanuto (LVI), 830–31
146 it is an extraordinary indecency: Hammer-Purgstall, 192
147 discharge their arquebuses into the air: Celalzade (2011), 176
148 left them for the inferno: Sanuto (LVI), 825
149 sap the mine with a countermine: Setton, 365
149 running out of bread: Reston, 330–32
150 collapsing from his wounds: Hammer-Purgstall, 162
151 on the great triumph: This report can be found in Charrière, vol. 1, 215–20.
151 400 defenders, would suggest: Curipeschitz, 14

Chapter XI

Chapter XII

229 with other men's wives: I am grateful to Alain Servantie for drawing my attention to Tecynski's report of this meeting, published in *Acta Tomiciana*, vol. 16, I, , 296–8. n. 147

229 Governor of a distant province: Alberi (III-1), 12

231 So there is unease in the ranks: Peçevi, 131

231 from ambushes and hunger: Peçevi, 132

232 we have now approached Tabriz: Uluçay (2001), 110–11

232 by any name but 'poor': Rumi (I), 201

233 And he begs his master to hurry: Peçevi, 132

234 mausoleum of the Mongol Khan: Eskandar Beg Monshi, 112

234 'It was I': Eskandar Beg Monshi, 112

234 tosses them downstream: Peçevi, 135

235 Sidi Bey, succumbs: Clot, 91

235 the same as living ones: Postel (III), 51

236 Celebi is removed from office: Hammer-Purgstall, 501

236 awoken by his own screams: Hammer-Purgstall, 252

237 one of your infidel slaves: Uluçay (2001), 54-8

238 the guardian of the tomb: Peçevi, 137

238 'nothing can compare with Jafar's': Marozzi, 59

239 astonished donors out of the room: Hammer-Purgstall, 513

240 descend to those regions': Gévay, II/3 (1536), 10–11 n. 7, cit. Papo, 285

241 Commander-in-Chief-Sultan: Hammer-Purgstall, 510

242 some other officers are cashiered: Charrière (I), 263-4

242 They are sickly mustard in colour: Secret, 102-3

243 fire a salvo in greeting: Charrière (I), 291

243 jousting and knockabout go on below: Peirce (2017), 146

244 noble and blessed grace: Peirce (1993), 78

244 friendship and compassion: Peirce (2017), 166

245 conspiring with the Persians: Jenkins, 92

246 lead him around the city: Bassano, 47

247 treasure of a certain Crozillon: Weill, 34-5

248 opted for demotion: Alberi (III-3), 104

249 with drums and arrack: Bassano, 47-8

249 the Sultan visits his treasury: Necipoğlu (1991), 140

Index

Austria – *cont.*
  Lamberg negotiations (1532), 141,
    144–8
  Ottoman invasion (1529), 92–6,
    104, 113, 124, 148
  Ottoman invasion (1532),
    148, 151
  Poland negotiations (1530), 129
  Treaty of Istanbul (1533), 161–3,
    166, 200, 202
Aya Sofya, *see* Hagia Sophia
Ayas Pasha, 53–4, 86, 109, 117, 139,
    142, 164, 183, 198, 226, 242
Ayat, 216, 218
Aydin Reis, 176
Azerbaijan, 181
al-Azhar University, 53

Badakhshan, 104
Baghdad, 25, 182, 230, 236, 237–41,
    245, 248
Balearic Islands, 176, 177, 179–80
Bali Bey, 64
Balkh, Khorasan, 232, 238
Banda Sea, 12
Bank of St George, 17, 198
de Barbari, Jacopo, 6
Barcelona, Catalonia, 102, 190
Barmakid clan, 238
Bathory, Istvan, 208
Batthyany, Orban, 207, 208, 209, 212,
    214, 217
Battle of Agnadello (1509), 18
Battle of Belgrade (1456), 62
Battle of Chaldiran (1514), 27–8, 55,
    154, 228, 231, 233
Battle of Guns (1532), 148–51, 161,
    165, 169, 215
Battle of Medias (1534), 212–21
Battle of Mohacs (1526), 61, 79, 94,
    96, 97, 119, 166
Battle of Pavia (1525), 66, 95, 102,
    103, 160, 181
Bayezit II, Ottoman Sultan, 13,
    14–17, 23, 25–6, 31, 33,
    75, 122
Bayezit Şehzade, 114
Bejaia, Algeria, 180

Belgrade
  caravans in, 128
  Mohacs campaign (1526), 58, 60,
    61, 62, 63, 64
  Suleyman's conquest (1521), 43, 44,
    48, 50, 110, 112, 165
  Vienna campaign (1532), 146, 149
Bellini, Gentile, 12, 14
Bergamo, 18
Berhan, 47, 50, 51
Bernardo, Francesco, 117
Besztercebanya, Hungary, 98
Beyoglu, *see* Gritti, Alvise
Bithynia, 170
Bohemia, 86, 105
Bologna, Papal States, 102–4, 124,
    142, 160, 185
Bosnia, 12, 64, 80, 106, 139, 147
Bostanci Pasha, 80
Bragadin, Pietro, 53–4, 58, 79
Brasov, Transylvania, 207, 208,
    209–10
Brescia, 18
Buda, Hungary, 57, 59, 77, 95, 96,
    129, 134–5, 203
  Hapsburg campaign (1527–8),
    83, 84
  Hapsburg campaign (1530), 127,
    129–32, 211, 215, 218
  Ottoman campaign (1526), 60,
    62, 84, 86–7, 113, 117, 133,
    138, 155
  Ottoman campaign (1529), 95,
    96–7
Bulgaria, 58, 106
Burgundy, 41, 105
Bursa, Anatolia, 184
Bustan, 53–4
Byzantine Empire, 12, 24, 32, 33

Cadiz, Spain, 177
Caesar, Julius, 210
Caffa, Crimea, 26, 32, 111
Cagliari, Sardinia, 190
Cairo, Egypt, 201
Caliph, 28
da Canal, Girolamo, 200
Candia, 7

Caorlini brothers, 126
caravansarays, 128, 205
Carthage, ancient, 19, 37
Carthage, Tunis, 187, 191, 192
Caspian Sea, 25
Cem Şehzade, 14–15, 110, 122
Cephalonia, 17
Cervia, Ravenna, 18, 103
Chalcis, 12
Chaldiran, Iran, 27–8, 55, 154, 228,
    231, 233
Chamber of Petitions, New Palace, 36,
    54, 76, 80–81
Charles V, Holy Roman Emperor,
    9–10, 41–3, 55, 77, 78, 82, 92,
    124, 243
  Battle of Pavia (1525), 66, 95, 102,
    103
  coronation (1530), 102–4, 142, 176
  Corone annexation (1532), 169–70,
    178
  Dalmatia annexations (1532), 133
  Doria, hiring of (1528), 101
  Gritti's defection (1534), 203–4
  horsemanship, 118
  Hungarian campaign (1530), 127,
    129–32
  Lamberg negotiations (1532), 141,
    144–8
  League of Cognac War (1526–30),
    59, 65–8, 101–3, 104
  Ottoman invasion (1532), 151
  Rome, sack of (1527), 66–7, 89,
    102, 104
  Siege of Naples (1528), 101
  Titian's portrait, 189
  Treaty of Bologna (1529), 103, 105,
    127, 160, 185
  Treaty of Cambrai (1529), 94, 102
  Treaty of Istanbul (1533), 161–3,
    166, 200, 202
  Tunis, capture of (1535), 189–96
Charles VIII, King of France, 6
Cherchell, Algeria, 177
Cicek Khatun, 110
Cicero of Arpino, 196
Cicogna, Vincenzo, 82
Cihangir Şehzade, 114, 197, 237

Cilicia, Anatolia, 63, 242, 245
circumcision festival (1530), 116–24
Clement VII, Pope, 60, 66–7, 72,
    102–3, 105, 143, 160, 161, 177,
    182, 187
Clissa, Dalmatia, 97, 129, 133
concubines, 32, 109–10, 111
Constantine I, Roman Emperor, 34,
    103
Constantine XI, Byzantine Emperor,
    34
Constantine the Greek, 78
Constantinople, see Istanbul
Corfu, 36, 57
Corner family, 91
Corner, Giacomo, 79
Corone, Morea, 169–70
Corsica, 173
Corvinus, Matthias, 59, 62, 86, 131
Crema, 18
Cremona, 18
Crimea, 26, 32, 41, 106, 111
Crown of Lombardy, 103, 143
Crown of St Stephen, 61, 97, 144
crown, 125–7, 138–9, 147, 227
Crozillon, 247
Crusades, 8, 11, 42, 105, 181, 189,
    229
Cunctator, 19, 89
Cyprus, 66
Czibak, Imre, 131, 134, 207–13, 219,
    220

Dalmatia, 13, 16, 97, 129, 133
Danube river, 58, 60, 83, 95, 97, 206,
    211
Dardanelles, 41, 183
David, King of Israel and Judah, 55
Della Valle, Francesco, 203, 217, 218,
    220
Diet of Medias (1534), 207–12
Diet of Worms (1521), 42–3
Diyarbakir, Anatolia, 181, 230, 231
Doby, Ferenc, 221
Doczy, Janos, 135, 207, 208, 213–14,
    220, 221
Doria, Andrea, 101, 138, 169–70,
    176–8, 182, 185, 190, 195

277